day trips® series

day trips®
hudson valley

W9-AEQ-412

first edition

 getaway ideas for the local traveler

randi minetor

Guilford, Connecticut

An imprint of Rowman & Littlefield

Distributed by NATIONAL BOOK NETWORK

Copyright © 2015 by Rowman & Littlefield

Text Design: Linda R. Loiewski
Maps: Alena Pearce © Rowman & Littlefield
Spot photography throughout courtesy of Nic Minetor

Day Trips is a registered trademark of Rowman & Littlefield.

British Library Cataloguing-in-Publication Information Available

Library of Congress Cataloging-in-Publication Data

Minetor, Randi.
  Day trips from Hudson Valley : getaway ideas for the local traveler / Randi Minetor. — First edition.
    pages cm. — (Day trips series)
  Includes index.
  ISBN 978-1-4930-0789-9 (paperback)
  1. Hudson River Valley (N.Y. and N.J.)—Guidebooks. I. Title.
  F127.H8M577 2015
  917.47'304—dc23
                                                    2014037962

∞™ The paper used in this publication meets the minimum requirements of American National Standard for Information Sciences—Permanence of Paper for Printed Library Materials, ANSI/NISO Z39.48-1992.

All the information in this guidebook is subject to change. We recommend that you call ahead to obtain current information before traveling.

contents

about the author

Randi Minetor has just traversed the beautiful routes and byways of New York State while writing *Hiking Waterfalls in New York* (FalconGuides) and *Scenic Routes & Byways New York* (Globe Pequot). Now she brings you this Day Trips guide to the Hudson Valley. She has written more than twenty other books for Globe Pequot, including five books on New York hiking in the *Best Easy Day Hikes* series, and she is the author of *Backyard Birding: A Guide to Attracting and Identifying Birds*.

acknowledgments

If there's one thing I love about writing books, it's the collaborative process with the crack team at Globe Pequot. We owe many thanks to the production team at GPP, including our editor, Tracee Williams, and all the people who work so hard to produce beautiful books about amazing places. Our agent, Regina Ryan, always provides the wise counsel and solid direction that keeps our publishing career on track.

To the friends and family who follow our travels on Facebook and share their energy and enthusiasm with Nic and me, we can't say enough about the value of your support. To Ken Horowitz, Rose-Anne Moore, Martha and Peter Schermerhorn, Kristen Kessler, Martin Winer, Paul and Debbie Trivino, and all the other people who look forward to our books and encourage us to keep going . . . we thank you so much for being there for us, and for being who you are.

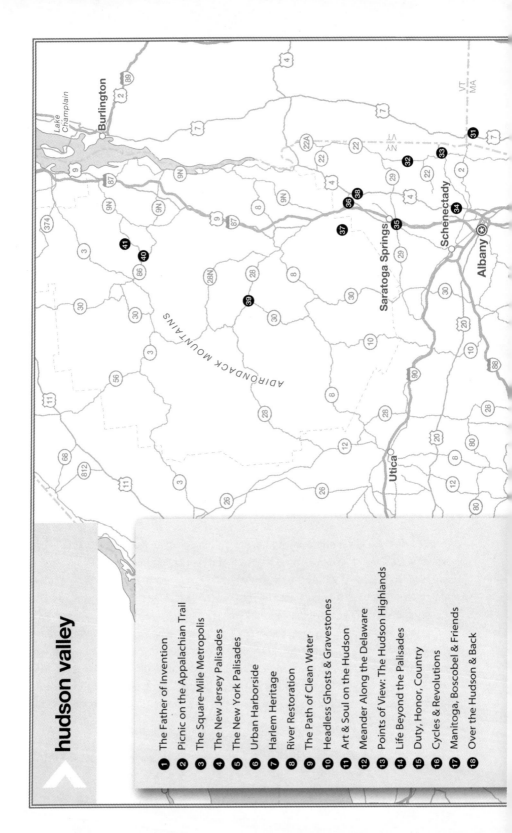

hudson valley

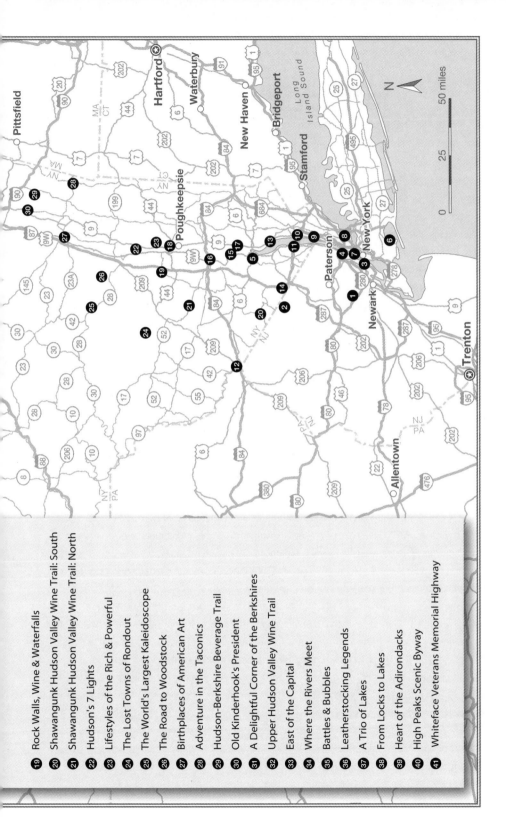

introduction

There's nothing like an all-day getaway to recharge your personal engines and rejuvenate your spirit, especially if you have the opportunity to explore somewhere you've never been. If you live in the eastern portion of New York State, you're in luck: The sheer quantity of places to go for a new experience, a great meal, and some retail therapy are virtually limitless, especially along the banks of the mighty Hudson River.

Looking for a measure of local history? You'll find plenty of that along the Hudson, a key waterway for transporting supplies during the Revolutionary War—and the center of some fairly innovative 18th-century strategy as the Continental Army constructed a 500-link iron chain and strung it across the mile-wide river. If you're fascinated by the Industrial Revolution, the river played a pivotal role there as well, supplying waterpower to hundreds of manufacturing operations and providing a route for transporting goods from the wharves of New York City to the beginning of the Erie Canal in Albany.

Are you curious about New York State's role in the lumber industry? You can discover which of today's small towns were boomtowns in the 1800s, transporting logs out of the Adirondack, Catskill, and Hudson Valley forests. If you're interested in the mysteries below ground, you can explore the remains of mining operations along the Taconic Mountains, deep in the Catskills or farther up at the source of the Hudson River, where iron ore found its way to the surface and traveled by water and rail to foundries.

If you'd like to learn about the people behind the processes, New York's big cities and small towns are particularly adept at preserving the stories of individuals and the challenges they faced as they worked to make a historic difference. Not only can you visit the spectacular homes of John D. Rockefeller, Franklin Delano Roosevelt, Cornelius Vanderbilt, and Thomas Jefferson, but you can discover people like Catheryna Rombout Brett, who raised her sons alone in a wilderness home, ran several businesses, and forced the men around her to respect her as a property-owning equal—and did all this in the years before the Revolutionary War. Stories like these are tucked into small towns throughout the Hudson Valley, many of them in places you may never have known existed.

If you live in one of New York's large cities, you may not have the pleasure of meeting cows, goats, and llamas on a regular basis or strolling through a vineyard filled with fragrant, fruit-laden plants—so it's high time you got out and enjoyed the extraordinary bounty that your state produces. Taste cheeses made using the milk of local cows, sample wines made with grapes grown within a few feet of the winery's door, enjoy scones spread with jam made from berries collected on hillsides covered with shrubs, or savor sausages made by artisans who source sustainably raised cattle and hogs. You'll find no end of delicious treats as you encounter the farms, dairies, orchards, distilleries, and wineries that make New York State one of the largest producers of a range of food products—especially milk, cheese, apples, and wine—in the entire country.

Day Trips Hudson Valley shows you where to find all kinds of one-day adventures along the river, from outdoor treks to museums, galleries, and shops. This book is not meant to be exhaustive—chances are you will find restaurants and shops that are not described here. Instead, this book introduces you to places you have not yet visited and may not even know are there, to help you find new experiences when you've just got to get away.

There's so much to see and do right here in the Hudson Valley, so start planning your next daylong getaway today.

using this guide

This guide is organized into five segments of the Hudson River Valley, from the mouth of the river in New York and New Jersey all the way up to the river's source in the Adirondack Mountains. Each destination focuses on attractions and activities, dining, and shopping, with lodging choices when there's something really special that may make you want to plan an overnight stay. The five segments include:

Lower Valley: New Jersey Skylands
Lower Valley: New York City
Mid-Hudson Valley
Upper Hudson Valley
Upper Hudson: To the River's Source

Day trips, along with directions, distances, and a map, are then suggested for each area. Day trips range from excursions to towns and villages clustered in one area to drives or train trips farther afield. For most of these trips, you can be back in your home or hotel in time for dinner. You can follow the itineraries described here or mix things up, including the elements that interest you most and fit into your schedule.

I've also included itineraries that allow you to explore segments of New York State's wine country, now considered one of the finest areas for wine tourism in the world. Combining scenery, artisan cheeses, other goodies from farmers' fields, visits with dairy and wool-bearing animals, and the bounty of New York State wines—or microbrews, or even distilled spirits—can make a day in the country an even more delicious and satisfying experience.

hours of operation, prices, and credit cards

Since hours of operation, attraction prices, and other facts are always subject to change, remember to confirm your plans by calling ahead or checking websites for updates before making your final travel plans. You can assume that all establishments listed accept major credit cards unless otherwise noted (i.e., "cash only"). If you have questions, call ahead for specifics.

pricing key

accommodations

The price codes are for a double room per night during the peak-price period. Peak periods are generally June through October throughout the entire region, and from Christmas through President's Week in the ski mountains. Room prices do not include state or local sales taxes or any other lodging fees that may be included in your final bill.

$	less than $125
$$	$125 to $250
$$$	$251 to $400
$$$$	more than $400

restaurants

The price code reflects an estimate of the average price of dinner entrees for two (excluding drinks, appetizers, tax, and tip) and is a benchmark only. Lunch and breakfast are usually 25 to 30 percent less.

$	less than $25
$$	$25 to $50
$$$	$51 to $100
$$$$	more than $100

driving tips

No matter where you travel, it's always wise to plan your route in advance. The itinerary map in this guide is representative of the Hudson Valley area; all distances are approximate. To get the most out of your travels, use GPS along with a conventional map so you can stay on your intended track.

In remote areas, rotaries (traffic circles) have replaced traffic lights at many intersections, allowing traffic to keep moving smoothly. If you're not used to these, here are the basic rules: Vehicles already in the rotary have the right of way; those entering must yield. If you miss your exit, go around again. You won't be the only one.

Once you get outside of New York City, your car is your best bet for day tripping. You can take trains from New York to the north as far as Poughkeepsie, but most towns described in this book are not on train routes, so you will need a vehicle once you arrive. If you do follow the day trips in upper Manhattan or Hoboken, having a car will be more of a nuisance (and an expensive one, what with the price of parking) than a help, so use mass transportation and expect to do some walking.

Finally, a word about New York's legendary winters: Driving in snow is no joke. It can be treacherous to use roads that have not been cleared by professionals, and there's no benefit to taking a scenic drive when you can't see the scenery because of a storm in progress. New York State residents know when it's a good day to curl up with a good book, so postpone your day trip for another day if a storm is heading into your intended area.

highway designations

Interstates—prefaced by "I"—are multilane, limited-access highways. US routes can be a mix of limited-access and two-lane blacktop, and state routes—prefaced by "NY"—are almost always two-lane or four-lane roads at best.

where to go for more information

Many of the larger cities mentioned in this book have tourism bureaus, and New York State has a tourism office of its own to connect visitors with the information they need to enjoy a vacation or day trip. If you'd like to learn more before you travel, here are some resources that may help:

I Love NY
New York State Division of Tourism
PO Box 2603
Albany, NY 12220-0603
(800) CALL-NYS
iloveny.com

Hudson River Valley National Heritage Area
625 Broadway, 4th Floor
Albany, NY 12207
(518) 473-3835
hudsonrivervalley.com

Erie Canalway National Heritage Corridor
PO Box 2019
Waterford, NY 12188
(518) 237-7000
eriecanalway.org

Albany County Convention and Visitors Bureau
25 Quackenbush Square
Albany, NY 12207
(800) 258-3582
albany.org

New York City Tourism
NYC & Company
810 Seventh Ave., 3rd Floor
New York, NY 10019
(212) 484-1200
nycgo.com

New Jersey Division of Travel and Tourism
PO Box 460
Trenton, NY 08625
(800) VISIT-NJ
visitnj.org

lower valley: new jersey skylands

day trip 01

lower valley: new jersey skylands

the father of invention
west orange, nj

west orange, nj

It may surprise you to discover that the world's exit from the "dark ages"—in this case, the period before every home had electricity—began in West Orange, New Jersey. Here a young, home-schooled, hearing-impaired inventor named Thomas Edison created an empire that would change daily life forever, eventually bringing power and light to every home and business in America. Beyond its history of innovation, West Orange features an assortment of neighborhoods that offer their individual charm to tourists as well as residents. While there's no town center here, your exploration can take you to the Victorian mansions of Llewellyn Park, quieter Upper Gregory and St. Cloud neighborhoods, or the more traditional Pleasantdale area.

getting there

There are no trains to West Orange from New York City. From the north, take I-95 south to exit 15W, and follow I-280 west to exit 10 in West Orange. From the south, take the Garden State Parkway to exit 145 for East Orange, and continue west on I-280 to exit 10 in West Orange.

where to go

Eagle Rock Reservation. Winding Way and Prospect Avenue; (973) 268-3500; eaglerock reservation.org. If you want to gain an overview of the local topography and get a sense of what New Jersey may have been like before urbanization took hold, Eagle Rock provides the hills, valleys, streams, and forested land you seek. Located in "the middle of the most densely populated county in the most densely populated state in the country," according to the reservation's own materials, this wonder of green-space preservation supplies 408 acres of respite from the crush of city traffic. Visit Lookout Point and see one of the area's most impressive views of the Manhattan skyline. Always open; free admission.

Glenmont Estate. 37 Honeysuckle Ave. in Llewellyn Park (get tickets at the Thomas Edison National Historical Park laboratory complex, below). The home of Thomas and Mina Edison, Thomas's three children from his first marriage, and three more children he and Mina would have together, the sprawling Glenmont contains 29.5 rooms, including 8.5 bathrooms. Edison purchased the home fully furnished—minus 6 of the bathrooms, which were added later—in 1886 and sold it to Mina in 1889 for $1, to be certain that his family would never lose the home in a lawsuit over one of his inventions. The tour of this impressive estate includes Edison's "thought laboratory," a library-like room on the second floor where he would withdraw after dinner and spend hours conceiving new inventions for his staff to build. Fri through Sun, 11:30 a.m. to 4 p.m., tours offered from noon to 3 p.m. Get tickets for tours at the Laboratory Visitor Center; $7 adults, good for 7 days, includes admission to Laboratory Complex.

South Mountain Reservation. South Orange Avenue and Cherry Lane; (973) 268-3500; essex-countynj.org/p/index.php?section=parks/sites/so. Turtle Back Zoo lies within this 2,047-acre natural area, where you can take a break from the pressingly urban atmosphere of West Orange and wander through hardwood and hemlock woodlands along the west branch of the Rahway River. View the cities of New York, Staten Island, Union, and Elizabeth from the 550-foot eastern ridge, or hike into the woods to see Hemlock Falls, a 25-foot waterfall. The Civilian Conservation Corps built many of the trails and footbridges here back in the 1930s, with the oversight of the famed Olmsted brothers, designers of New York's Central Park and Boston's Emerald Necklace of city parks. Open dawn to 10 p.m. daily; free admission.

Thomas Edison National Historical Park. 211 Main St.; (973) 736-0550, ext. 11; nps .gov/edis. Thomas Alva Edison found his way from his parents' home in Michigan to the extraordinary research and development center he built in West Orange by way of Boston, New York City, and Menlo Park. A well-established and successful inventor by the time he turned 40, Edison put this complex—the world's first official research center—to good use, creating more than 500 inventions including the phonograph, the first commercially practical motion-picture camera, and the first viable incandescent electric lightbulb. He followed this by introducing the world's first system of central electricity generation and distribution, founding the company that would become General Electric Corporation. Today his laboratory is preserved by the National Park Service, and a major renovation in the late 2000s opened an additional 20,000 square feet—including the second floor of Edison's production facility—for self-guided tours. Spend an hour or all afternoon, and don't miss the Black Maria, Edison's movie production studio, where the first movies in America were created in 1893. Open Wed through Sun 10 a.m. to 4 p.m.; $7 adults, good for 7 days, includes Glenmont tour.

Turtle Back Zoo. 560 Northfield Ave.; (973) 731-5801; turtlebackzoo.com. This charming little zoo features more than 100 different animal species from five continents, with a healthy sampling of creatures from the United States—including North American bison, porcupine, wolf, groundhog, fox, black bear, prairie dogs, and other large, easy-to-see animals. A petting zoo of farm animals, pony rides, a rope course and zip lines, a brightly colored and well-maintained carousel, and a picnic area and cafe make it easy to spend a day here, especially if you're visiting with young children. Open 10 a.m. to 3:30 p.m. daily, closed Thanksgiving, Christmas, and New Year's Day; $11 adults, $8 children and seniors 62 and over, free for children 23 months and under. Prices are lower in winter.

where to eat

Due Amici. 450 Main St.; (973) 669-0027; dueamicirestaurant.com. Just down the road from the Edison factory, this little Italian restaurant draws rave reviews from locals who frequent it. The substantial menu features a wide range of reasonably priced, homemade entrees from gnocchi in a sauce of prosciutto, onions, basil, and plum tomatoes to the ample seafood *marechiara*, loaded with shrimp, scallops, clams, and mussels in a white wine sauce over linguini. Bring your own wine—perhaps a Long Island or Hudson Valley vintage. Open Tues through Thurs 11 a.m. to 9:30 p.m., Fri 11 a.m. to 11 p.m., Sat 4 to 11 p.m., Sun 3 to 9 p.m., closed Mon. $$.

Highlawn Pavilion. Eagle Rock Reservation, 1 Crest Dr.; (973) 731-3463; highlawn.com. An excellent menu and a great view of New York make this pricey but popular restaurant a favorite with families and lovebirds throughout the northern New Jersey area. The menu features fresh, local ingredients served in highly original New American style, matched by sophisticated service in an appealingly festive atmosphere. Choose Highlawn for a special day out or a celebratory lunch. Lunch Mon through Fri 12 to 3 p.m., dinner Mon through Thurs and Sun 5:30 to 9 p.m., Fri 5:30 to 10 p.m., Sat 5 to 10 p.m. $$$.

day trip 02

lower valley: new jersey skylands

picnic on the appalachian trail
wawayanda state park, nj

If you've dreamed of hiking part or all of the 2,184-mile Appalachian National Scenic Trail, you can begin with a 20-mile segment here in Wawayanda State Park in northern New Jersey, just a few miles southwest of the New York state border. For non-hikers or more casual walkers, this park provides scenic vistas, 40 miles of easier trails, lakes, ponds, picnic areas, and lots of natural areas for birding and exploring.

getting there

From the north, take NY 17 to Chester (exit 126), and travel south/west on NY 94. Just before the New Jersey border, turn left on Barret Road. Continue into the park on this road and to the parking area near Wawayanda Lake. From the south, take I-287 to exit 52, and follow NJ 23 north to Union Valley Road. Turn right and follow Union Valley Road 6 miles to a stop sign. Continue to the second traffic light and turn left. Continue 2 miles to a fork in the road and bear left; go 0.5 mile to Warwick Turnpike. Turn left, and continue 4 miles to the park entrance.

where to go

Appalachian Trail (AT). Within Wawayanda State Park on the park's western border; (304) 535-6278; nps.gov/appa. Beginning six states away on Spring Mountain, Georgia, and extending all the way to Mount Katahdin in Maine, the Appalachian Trail is the grandfather of all the long-distance trails in the United States, and the only one listed among the 401 sites of the National Park System. By definition, the trail travels up and down just about every major peak in its path, including the 1,470-foot Wawayanda Mountain ridgeline here in the park, to offer you the opportunity to enjoy some of the most spectacular countryside views in the eastern United States. In Wawayanda, it also skirts the Hemlock Ravine Natural Area before disappearing into the Abram S. Hewitt State Forest and continuing into New York State. If you'd like to hike the AT but you're pretty sure you can't manage a five- to seven-month through-hike of the trail from end to end, take it one segment at a time—and this is as good a place to start as any. Follow the distinctive AT logo markers and the white blazes that you'll see no matter what little piece of the trail you choose to traverse.

Wawayanda State Park. 885 Warwick Turnpike; (973) 853-4462; state.nj.us/dep/parksand forests/parks/wawayanda. At 35,524 acres, this sizable park includes a wide range of habitat types, from hardwood and chestnut/oak forests to 300-foot rises from well-shaded creeks. An Atlantic white cedar swamp in the middle of the park provides a glimpse of the sort of ecosystem found closer to the ocean coast, while providing critically important habitat for the red-shouldered hawk, a majestic and locally endangered species. Hike a segment of the Appalachian Trail along the park's western border while enjoying a hemlock and mixed hardwood forest (more on this above), or chose one of the other (mostly easier) trails to explore natural areas throughout the park. Swimming, fishing, boating, or just enjoying the great outdoors are all encouraged in this widely varied park. Picnic near the bathhouse on Wawayanda Lake, or anywhere along the trails if you're willing to pack in and pack out your food and supplies.

where to eat

Just to the west of the park, Vernon Township offers services including gas, shopping for food and supplies, and restaurants for those who prefer sit-down meals to grab-and-go picnics.

Mixing Bowl Restaurant. 4 Church St., Vernon; (973) 764-7511. Look for the painted lady–style building with the crowd waiting for tables just inside the door, and you'll know you've found this place and its dollhouse appeal. Inside, regulars come for the excellent better-than-a-diner breakfast/brunch menu or drift in later in the day for lunch, all of it served up with grandmotherly charm and homestyle goodness. This is one of those places that know what "crispy bacon" and "eggs over easy" actually mean. Open daily 6 a.m. to 3 p.m. $.

Vernon Inn. 340 New Jersey 94, Vernon Township; (973) 764-9888; thevernoninn.com. Locals frequent this casual restaurant and bar for its down-home atmosphere, good food, and outdoor dining in summer. Burgers, sandwiches, steaks, ribs, chicken, and seafood selections are among the generous entrees, with pasta choices that feature pesto, vodka sauce, and scampi as well as the expected marinara. This may be just the kind of meal you crave at the end of the day in the park. Sun and Mon 11:30 a.m. to 9:30 p.m., Tues through Thurs 11:30 a.m. to 10 p.m., Fri and Sat 11:30 a.m. to 10:30 p.m. $$.

day trip 03

lower valley: new jersey skylands

>>> **the square-mile metropolis**
hoboken, nj

hoboken, nj

Need a break from New York, New York? The town may be tiny, but Hoboken's location on the Hudson River makes it an alternative hotspot for the young residents of the gentrified, hipster-rich West Village and Lower Manhattan on the other side of the Holland Tunnel—and for lots of families with children as well. Here on the less congested side of the river, you'll find a landscaped riverwalk along a drive named for the legendary Frank Sinatra, who was born here at 415 Monroe St. The sparkling views of the Hudson and the Manhattan skyline may remind you of another major event that happened here: Hoboken was the location of the Oscar-winning movie *On the Waterfront*, the tour-de-force that turned Marlon Brando into one of Hollywood's most celebrated stars. For visitors with 21st century sensibilities, there's plenty to please the palate and the pocketbook: The town's main artery, Washington Street, is loaded with family-run restaurants and nightspots, whether you're looking for a quick meal or a leisurely, romantic dinner—and you'll find plenty of specialty shops tucked in between the eateries.

getting there

Mass transit is your best option for reaching Hoboken, as traffic congestion can be an issue and parking is at a premium. Take the PATH subway from lower Manhattan, Jersey City, or Newark, or one of a number of New Jersey Transit commuter rail lines. The Hudson-Bergen

Light Rail lines all stop in Hoboken: the West Side Avenue line stops at Second and Eighth Streets in Hoboken, and the other two lines end at Hoboken Terminal. You can take the NY Waterway ferry from Manhattan (from the World Financial Center and Wall Street, Pier 11). If you do drive, your best bet for parking is in one of the municipal garages—while there is limited on-street parking, you can only park on the street for a total of 4 hours a day. Visit hobokennj.org/departments/transportation-parking/parking for up-to-date parking information. To reach Hoboken by car from Manhattan, take the Holland Tunnel (I-78) and bear right on NJ 139; take the right at Route 637 and continue to Newark Street in Hoboken. From the south and west, take I-95 north to I-78 east, cross Newark Bay on I-78, and continue to Hoboken. From the north, take the Palisades Parkway to Fort Lee and follow US 1 (Tonnelle Avenue) south to County Route 681. Bear right on 681 and continue until 681 becomes Newark Street in Hoboken.

where to go

Barsky Art Gallery. 49 Harrison St.; (888) 465-4949; barskygallery.com. Exhibiting contemporary art created by European artists you may not see in other galleries across the country, the Barsky Gallery also selects local and national artists whose work indicates the direction of the next generation of American art. You'll find paintings, sculpture, and works in many media, and you may discover your new favorite artist among the many fascinating pieces here. Open Wed through Sun 11 a.m. to 6 p.m., closed Mon and Tues; no admission fee.

Elysian Fields. 11th and Washington Streets; nj.gov/nj/about/baseball.html. On June 19, 1846, the Knickerbocker Club of New York City challenged the New York Nine to a competitive game of baseball on these grounds. This does not sound particularly significant to the modern ear, but this challenge is believed to have been the first organized baseball game ever to take place between two competing clubs. This field became recognized as one of the few in the New York metropolitan area that was suitable for baseball competition, and it soon attracted a number of clubs from Manhattan, leading them to form the National Association of Base Ball Players. A professional game of baseball hasn't taken place here since 1873, and the field eventually got subdivided for home construction, but you can still visit a bronze plaque on the 11th Street median at the intersection with Washington Street, noting the field's significance to the national pastime. Third base stood at the front door of Maxwell's music club, just down the street from the plaque. Always open (watch for oncoming traffic); free admission.

Hoboken Historical Museum. 1301 Hudson St.; (201) 656-2240; hobokenmuseum.org. While many museums showcase standing exhibits that will still be there if you visit twice in a decade, the Hoboken Museum creates a new exhibition every eight months or so, highlighting an interesting and often little-known aspect of the city's rich history. Recent exhibitions told the story of the area's response to Hurricane Sandy and its residents' ability to recover and move on in the wake of the superstorm's power, and about Hoboken's relationship to the Hudson River, the waterway that passes directly through the city. The upper gallery presents the work of six local artists each year. Whenever you visit, chances are good that you'll see something new and learn a few facts you didn't know about this mile-square city. Open Tues through Thurs 2 to 7 p.m., Fri 1 to 5 p.m., Sat and Sun noon to 5 p.m.; $2, free for children and museum members.

Mile Square Theatre. 1400 Clinton St.; (201) 683-7014; milesquaretheatre.org. Recently merged with Hoboken Children's Theatre and moved to the Artisan in North Hoboken in 2014, this professional regional theater presents a mix of classic and contemporary theater for adults, as well as productions for children in its MSTKids! program. Check the website for the current production before your day trip, and get your tickets in advance.

Monroe Center for the Arts. 720 Monroe St.; (201) 795-4130; monroecenter.com. Once a factory for Levelor Blinds, this building became a multidisciplinary arts center in 1990 and now houses artists' studios, fashion and jewelry designers, film companies, photographers, and many others in a newly renovated studio complex. You can visit the galleries and retail shops year-round, though it's anyone's guess which venues will be open to the public on the day of your visit. Check the website for more information.

where to shop

Air Studios Boutique. 92 Hudson St.; (201) 239-1511; fiftyfivegroup.com. Stop here to check out the up-and-coming new designer brands—this boutique launched names like 3.1 Phillip Lim and Catherine Malandrino. If you're looking for women's and men's fashion-forward looks, this is the place to try. Open Mon through Fri 12 to 8 p.m., Sat 11 a.m. to 6 p.m., Sun noon to 6 p.m.

Mackey Blue. 1200 Washington St., Store #E; (201) 469-6947; mackeyblue.com. For home goods, personal sundries, textiles, and prints and such on paper, explore this vintage store and its inventory of one-of-a-kind, found items. Open Wed 6 to 9 p.m., Fri noon to 8 p.m., Sat 10 a.m. to 7 p.m., Sun noon to 5 p.m.

Zin Home. 257 First St.; (201) 795-3448; zinhome.com. Newly renovated in 2014, this remarkable furniture store features items you won't find in your local big-box home store— from tables made from reclaimed wood to ottomans inspired by the construction of World War II aircraft. The rapid expansion of this establishment speaks to its ability to showcase the work of artisans and small businesses, giving you access to items that make your home one of a kind. Open Mon through Sun noon to 8 p.m.

where to eat

Amanda's. 908 Washington St.; (201) 798-0101; amandasrestaurant.com. Hoboken's streets are lined with Victorian brownstones, so why not have dinner in one? This upscale New American restaurant can be the perfect place for a romantic interlude or a special night out with the family. The menu only hints at the gentility of the experience—whether you warm up to homemade porcini pappardelle with a confetti of fresh local vegetables, or sea scallops with roasted fennel and a luscious herb risotto. Locals have voted Amanda's one of the most popular restaurants in New Jersey. Open Mon through Thurs 5 to 10 p.m., Fri 5 to 11 p.m., Sat 11 a.m. to 11 p.m., Sun 11 a.m. to 9 p.m. $$$.

Benny Tudino's. 622 Washington St.; (201) 792-4132; bennytudinos.com. The wide-ranging Italian menu you expected to find in New Jersey is here at this family-friendly restaurant, from baked manicotti to ziti matruttana—but the number-one draw is the giant pizza slice large and tasty enough to serve as a meal. Go for the slice, but come back for the bountiful menu of satisfying dishes—at very reasonable prices. Bonus: Benny's delivers. Open Mon through Sat 11 a.m. to 1 a.m., Sun 11 a.m. to midnight; slice $, meal $$.

Carlo's Bakery. 95 Washington St.; (201) 659-3671; carlosbakery.com. If you're a fan of the television series *Cake Boss*, you must stop at Buddy Valastro's bakery to see the Cake Boss's operation in action. Not only can you pick up a box of utterly irresistible pastries—cannolis, butter cookies, crumb cake, and much more—but you can also take a class in piping, making fondant layer cakes, or making flowers out of icing. Pick up decorating tools, bakeware, and other gadgets right at the bakery to make your own luscious creations. Open Mon through Thurs 7 a.m. to 8 p.m., Fri and Sat 7 a.m. to 9 p.m., Sun 7 a.m. to 7 p.m. $$.

Cucharamama. 233 Clinton St.; (201) 420-1700; cucharamama.com. Elevating South American cuisine to an art form, this unusual restaurant is the brainchild of Chef Maricel Presilla, a culinary historian (with a doctoral degree) whose research explored Latin American agriculture. Bringing this sensibility to the menu, she has collected recipes from her travels in the southern hemisphere and brings a mix of Peruvian, Ecuadorian, and Brazilian flavors to Cucharamama's tables. She also cooks for Zafra in Hoboken, and she owns Ultramarinos, the gourmet Latin American market and bakery nearby. Mon 5 to 6 p.m. (early dinner special only), Tues through Thurs 5 to 10 p.m., Fri and Sat 5 to 11 p.m., Sun brunch 11 a.m. to 3 p.m., dinner 3 to 9 p.m. $$$.

Elysian Cafe. 1001 Washington St.; (201) 798-5898; elysiancafe.com. If your tastes lean more toward bistro fare than elegant New American, try a taste of Provence for lunch or dinner at this French-themed eatery. The lunch menu has some specialties you might find on the continent, but the pastrami Reuben and BLT offer familiar favorites. For dinner, you'll find a number of continental staples like a rosemary-brined pork chop and rigatoni with Sunday sauce, as well as chicken breast cut in the French style and steak au poivre. The weekend brunch shows the most creativity of the entire menu—check out the cinnamon-amaretto French toast or the *croque-madame,* a Benedict for the upper crust. Open Mon through Thurs noon to 11 p.m., Fri noon to midnight, Sat 10 a.m. to midnight, Sun 10 a.m. to 10 p.m. $$.

Maxwell's Tavern. 1039 Washington St.; (201) 798-0406; maxwellsnj.com. You're here for the ambiance, not the food (although the menu is solid, featuring burgers, quesadillas, salads, and a chicken pot pie that the menu calls "famous"), because this is where Bruce Springsteen's "Glory Days" video was filmed back in 1985. A number of bands recorded live albums here, and just about every band worth its salt in the 1980s and 1990s played a gig here at least once, from REM to the Red Hot Chili Peppers. The legendary music club has since wound down into a bar and restaurant—at least for now; as of this writing, the owners are looking for a buyer. Check out the club's website to see what's up before your visit. Open Tues through Sat at 5 p.m., Sun at 1 p.m., closed Mon. $$.

Piccolos. 92 Clinton St.; (201) 653-0564; facebook.com/piccolos.hoboken. Ask the locals and Jerseyites from miles around, and they'll all tell you the same thing: When in Hoboken, you've got to go to Piccolos for the cheesesteak sandwich. Get yourself a mouthwatering pile of steak on a crusty roll, smothered in cheese and sautéed onions, and you'll understand why this restaurant has been around for more than half a century, serving lunches daily to "the cops and the criminals." Open Mon through Wed 8 a.m. to 4:30 p.m., Thurs through Sat 8 a.m. to 4:30 p.m. $.

day trip 04

lower valley: new jersey skylands

the new jersey palisades
fort lee, alpine, nj

Steep cliffs along a river's edge may not be the first icons that come to mind when you think of New Jersey, but that's just what make the New Jersey Palisades such a fascinating area. Here along the banks of the Hudson River, the cliffs form an almost perfectly vertical wall that rises as much as 540 feet above water level. By the time drivers reach the George Washington Bridge in Fort Lee, these high walls have formed a canyon—perhaps not with the majesty of the Grand Canyon, but enough to make this the most dramatic and interesting natural feature in the vicinity of New York City. The drive through this National Natural Landmark provides striking scenery, easily accessible towns, and a little bit of scandal to spice up your day in the Palisades.

getting there

From the George Washington Bridge in Fort Lee, New Jersey, follow the signs along US 9 to Palisades Parkway, or take exit 73 on I-95 as you come off of the bridge. From New Jersey, take US 9W in Fort Lee to the interchange with the Palisades Parkway.

fort lee, nj

The original home of the Barrymore family, one of the most famous and celebrated dynasties of stage and screen actors, Fort Lee has a storied history of seminal moments in the movie industry—including the earliest work of filmmaking giant D. W. Griffith, and the lesser-known work of Alice Guy Blache, the first woman filmmaker and an originator of movies as a story-telling art. Here in "Hollywood on the Hudson," pioneering filmmakers shot myriad silent movies—beginning as early as 1907, when Thomas Edison used the Palisades cliffs as a location for his film *Rescued from an Eagle's Nest,* featuring turn-of-the-20th-century stars like Mary Pickford, Dorothy and Lillian Gish, and Lionel Barrymore. Pick up a Film Industry Historical Sites map of Fort Lee at the Chamber of Commerce building or at a number of places in town, and watch for the buildings around town that once provided services to this industry in its infancy. (You can also download the map at fortleefilm.org/history.html.)

where to go

Fort Lee Museum. 1589 Parker Ave.; (201) 592-3580; thefortleehistoricalsociety.org. The hours here are tricky, but if you're a Revolutionary War buff or you just love museums of local history, this one is worth the planning it requires. The Fort Lee Historical Society put considerable effort into determining the location of the long-vanished Fort Lee—a guard encampment to protect the Hudson River from invasion by the British during the American Revolution—and once they determined the right spot, they commissioned this museum and nearby Monument Park. Open Wed 7 to 9 p.m., Sat and Sun noon to 4 p.m.

Fort Lee Historic Park. Hudson Terrace just south of the George Washington Bridge; (201) 461-1776. The park provides scenic overlooks from the top of a Palisades cliff, as well as a reconstruction of the Revolutionary War encampment that fell to the British during the campaign to control New York City in late 1776. In a series of losses that prompted patriot Thomas Paine to observe, "These are the times that try men's souls," General George Washington was forced to lead his men in a retreat from this area as General Cornwallis ferried some 5,000 British Regulars across the Hudson River toward Fort Lee. The visitor center here provides interpretive information about this dark time in the American Revolution, as well as modern conveniences including beverage vending machines, restrooms, and a gift shop. The park is open daily dawn to dusk; visitor center is open Wed through Sun, 10 a.m. to 4:45 p.m.

George Washington Bridge interchange. If you want to see the area where the September 2013 traffic jam took place when the Port Authority of New York closed two lanes of the George Washington Bridge on the New Jersey side, drive across the bridge from New York to New Jersey and look to your left (take care not to get distracted from the heavy traffic here) as you reach the New Jersey side. Allegations suggested that the bridge lanes were closed in retribution against Mayor Mark Sokolich of Fort Lee, who did not support New Jersey Governor Chris Christie in his 2013 reelection bid. We may never know what really happened, but several people lost their jobs in 2014 for their involvement in the lanes closure.

Henry Hudson Drive. Through Palisades Interstate Park from the Edgewater park entrance in Fort Lee (take Hudson Terrace south from the George Washington Bridge to the park entrance) to Alpine Approach Road in Alpine, where it joins the Palisades Parkway. This 7-mile scenic byway through Palisades Interstate Park travels along the Hudson River to the east with the impressive Palisades cliffs to the west, bringing you to one sweeping view of the river after another. Picnic areas at Ross Dock, Englewood, Undercliff, and Alpine provide places to stop and admire the view. On high-traffic days along the parkway, this can be a delightful alternative route at a more leisurely pace, especially if you don't need to get to your next destination in a New York minute. Open year-round, though it's a good idea to check the Parkway Police's Twitter feed at @ParkwayPolice before planning to take Henry Hudson Drive in winter or after major weather events.

Kearney House. At the north end of the Alpine Picnic Area at exit 2 on the Palisades Parkway; (201) 768-1360; njpalisades.org/kearney.html. Recently reopened after taking heavy damage during Hurricane Sandy, this former homestead and tavern became a landmark on the Closter Dock Road as far back as 1761, when colonists passed it on their way to the Hudson River to ship goods to the markets in New York City. It may have started its life as a dock master's house, but it eventually became the home of James and Rachel Kearney, who moved into it in 1817 and raised eight children there together. After James's death in 1831, Rachel turned the house into a tavern. New rooms added in the mid-1800s stand in sharp contrast to the older parts of the house. Open on weekends and holidays from May through Oct, noon to 5 p.m., closed Nov through Apr; free admission.

Rockefeller Lookout. A pull-off overlook about a mile north of exit 1 on the Palisades Parkway, no phone or website. From 400 feet above the Hudson River, you can enjoy a remarkable view of the river, the state of New York on the other side, and the Palisades cliffs. This viewpoint is only accessible from the northbound lanes. Always open, no fee.

where to eat

Franco's Metro. 1475 Bergen Blvd.; (201) 461-6651; francosmetro.com. For casual dining and made-fresh-to-order Italian dishes, this northern New Jersey restaurant tops the locals' lists—especially for seafood fresh from the nearby ocean. The extensive menu provides all of your pasta and entree favorites, as well as a daily special based on the availability of fresh ingredients. *Mangia!* Mon through Thurs 11 a.m. to 11 p.m., Fri and Sat 11 a.m. to midnight, Sun 10 a.m. to 10 p.m. $$.

Gammeeok. 485 Main St.; (201) 232-1333; gammeeok.com. Featured on PBS and noted with distinction in several New York City newspapers, this Korean restaurant started as a Manhattan hot spot and has expanded with locations in Fort Lee and Queens. Its hearty ox-bone soup has become a classic, while the bibimbap—authentic down to the raw egg—offers a variety of traditional meat and vegetable toppings. Open 24 hours. $$.

Hiram's Roadstand. 1345 Palisades Ave.; (201) 592-9602. Voted one of the best burgers in New Jersey by *Zagat's* and lauded with praise by fans of the meaty, deep-fried hot dogs and crispy French fries, this roadside joint makes for a quick, hearty meal before you hit the parkway. There's nothing fancy about this stand, but it's always crowded with locals enjoying dogs and burgers smothered in chili sauce and cheese at lower than average prices. Don't be surprised if the people next to you are downing bottles of Yoo-Hoo with their lunch—the cult classic drink was invented in the area, right around the time that Hiram's opened back in 1928. Not a Yoo-Hoo fan? Have a birch beer, or a real beer from the bar. Open daily 11:30 a.m. to 9:30 p.m. $.

alpine, nj

Alpine turned up at the top of *Business Insider*'s list of the wealthiest zip codes in the United States back in 2011, and we can assume that the number of mega-mansions in evidence here means that this borough of 2,400 has retained its tony status. You won't find much of a town center—or, for that matter, any interesting shopping or restaurants—in this fairly small town, but a drive along the roads of these 6 square miles will turn up glimpses of the homes of Sean "P. Diddy" Combs, Wesley Snipes, Stevie Wonder, Lil' Kim, and Chris Rock. Homes here average $4.5 million, with some going for as high as $53 million.

where to go

State Line Lookout. At the unnumbered exit just south of the New York state border on the Palisades Parkway; (201) 750-0465; njpalisades.org/stateline.html. The highest point on the New Jersey Palisades Cliffs—527 feet above the Hudson River—affords you a splendid opportunity to take in the spectacle of the opposite bank from a platform right off the parking area. Stop at the Lookout Inn for lunch, a snack, and a browse through the bookstore and gift shop. The Works Progress Administration built this inn in the 1930s during the Great Depression, making it an open-air facility originally—but the realities of New Jersey winters set in, so an enclosure with many windows soon surrounded the snack stand. Grounds are open in daylight hours year-round; the Lookout Inn is open daily 9:30 a.m. to 5 p.m.; free admission.

lower valley: new york city

>>>

day trip 05

lower valley: new york city

the new york palisades
tappan, mount ivy, stony point, harriman & bear mountain state parks, ny

Named for the line of ridges and cliffs skirted by this winding road in New Jersey, the Palisades Parkway traveled a rocky route to its opening over the course of more than 20 years. Developer William A. Welch first conceived of a scenic road that would follow the Hudson River from the New Jersey border to the state parks along the river in New York, and he inspired industrialist John D. Rockefeller to donate 700 acres of his land along the river to the project as far back as 1934. Everything came to a halt, however, when the New Jersey Highway Commission determined that it did not wish to see such a road built at that time. When Rockefeller picked up the ball again in the 1940s, he chose Robert Moses, the extraordinarily powerful urban and suburban planner who developed New York City's system of highways and parkways. By the time Moses championed the Palisades Parkway, he had already completed the Long Island parkway system, a network of roadways designed to be more picturesque and pleasant to drive than the urban highways. With Moses at the helm, the project moved forward quickly, with a groundbreaking for the New York segment on April 1, 1947. The last segment saw completion in 1958. In 1965, the National Park Service named Palisades Interstate Parkway a National Historic Landmark.

tappan, ny

Just 12 miles north of New York City, the hamlet of Tappan lies west of the Hudson River and preserves a particularly interesting nugget of Revolutionary War history. Not only did

George Washington eat, sleep, and work here in his headquarters at the DeWint House, but he confronted the man whose name will forever stand for the traitorous double-cross: Benedict Arnold.

Here the Lenape tribe handed the new settlers—a group of 16 families, including three free black men—a land patent that allowed these Dutch colonists to create a home in the New World. Homes built in the early 1700s still remain among the more modern structures, giving the entire town of Tappan a sense of enduring history. A walk through the historic area reveals Dutch Colonial, Federal, and Greek Revival architecture, styles that give us glimpses into the hamlet's storied past.

getting there

From the south, take NY 9A north to exit 14 for I-95 and the George Washington Bridge. Cross the bridge and take exit 74 to the Palisades Parkway. Merge onto the Palisades going north, and continue about 13 miles to exit 5S to NY-303 south. At the end of the ramp, turn right onto Kings Highway. Follow Kings Highway into Tappan.

where to go

DeClark-DeWint House. Corner of Oak Tree Road and Livingston Street; (845) 359-1359; dewinthouse.com. One of the oldest surviving structures in Rockland County, this home of Johannes and Antje DeWint served as General Washington's temporary headquarters on four separate occasions throughout the Revolutionary War in 1780 and 1783. Washington stayed here during the trial and execution of Major John André, a British spy who had conspired with American General Benedict Arnold to betray the fort at West Point. The Grand Lodge of New York Masons purchased the house to save it from commercial use in 1932, and restored it in the 1990s to its condition when Washington established his headquarters here. Open Tues through Sun 10 a.m. to 4 p.m., closed Mon, Thanksgiving, and Christmas; free admission.

Tappan Historic District. Main Street, Greenbush and Old Tappan Roads, Oak Tree Road, and Livingston Street; tappantown.org. A walk through this historic district brings you to 15 different sites that provide a look back as far as the arrival of the Dutch colonists in the late 17th century. From the site of the first courthouse in the county at the Village Church Green to the monument that stands where Major John André met his end at the gallows, this neighborhood provides a glimpse of New York State history that had an effect on the birth of the United States. Public streets are always open; free admission.

where to eat

Giulio's Restaurant. 154 Washington St.; (845) 359-3657; giulios.biz. Extend the sense of history with dinner in a romantic, 1880 Queen Anne Victorian home, complete with fireplaces, polished wood walls and trim, sweeping staircases, and beveled glass windows. The Italian-style menu brings contemporary flair to traditional dishes, with a complete menu of gluten-free offerings as well as the regular dinner menu. Reserve your table in advance of your visit. Open Mon through Sat, dinner from 5 p.m.; Sun from 3 p.m. $$$.

La Fontanella Ristorante. 52–54 NY 303; (845) 398-3400; lafontanellatappan.com. Whether you're looking for a quick, economical lunch (all Express Lunch choices are $8.95) or a leisurely dinner with multiple courses, this Tappan favorite provides hearty and flavorful solutions. The extensive dinner menu features all the usual Italian favorites along with some house creations to satisfy any craving. Whole-wheat and gluten-free pastas are available. Open Tues through Fri 11:30 a.m. to 10 p.m., Sat 4 to 10 p.m., closed Sun and Mon. $$.

Old '76 House. 110 Main St.; (845) 359-5476; 76house.com. Built in 1668 in the old Dutch style, this house stands as one of the nation's oldest taverns. Beyond its use as a safe meeting place for Patriots during the Revolutionary War, it also did duty as the jail in which Major John André was held through his trial in 1780, until his execution by hanging in October of that year. Today you can enjoy this National Historic Landmark as a restaurant with a menu of international and continental dishes—including venison, Hudson Valley duckling, and wild boar sausage. (You'll find roast Amish chicken and lobster macaroni and cheese as well, for the more domestic appetite.) Sun brunch 11 a.m. to 3 p.m., dinner 4 to 9 p.m.; Mon through Thurs, lunch 11:30 a.m. to 3 p.m., dinner 5 to 9 p.m.; Fri lunch 11:30 a.m. to 3 p.m., dinner 5 to 9:30 p.m.; Sat lunch 11:30 a.m. to 3 p.m., dinner 5 to 10 p.m. $$.

Stateline Family Restaurant. 96 NY 303; (845) 359-8764; facebook.com/pages/State -Line-Family-Restaurant. For a casual breakfast, lunch, or dinner with generous portions, this local favorite provides the friendly atmosphere, fast service, and wide variety you seek. Sandwiches, salads, a substantial breakfast menu, and an assortment of entrees all provide the choices we expect from family restaurants, with a little more style and lots of smiles. Open daily 7 a.m. to 11 p.m. $$.

where to shop

The Old & Weary Car Shop. 33 NY 303; (845) 680-0405; oldandwearycarshop.com. With a staggering stock of N, HO, S, O, and large-scale model trains and access to "just about everything produced," as owner Allan Seebach Jr., says on his website, this store is a trainaholic's dream destination—and a famous spot among model train enthusiasts across the country. Open Mon through Fri 3 to 7 p.m., Sat noon to 6 p.m., closed Sun.

mount ivy, ny

The primarily residential hamlet of Mount Ivy appears at exit 13 on the Palisades Parkway. If you're looking for a place for a picnic, this exit provides access to High Tor State Park, a day-use park with capacious views of the Hudson Valley. This is also the exit for Hook Mountain State Park, an undeveloped park that features a brisk walk to the 730-foot summit. The

National Audubon Society designated this prime hawk-watching destination as an Important Bird Area back in 1997; you may catch glimpses of Cooper's, sharp-shinned, broad-winged, red-shouldered, and red-tailed hawks from the summit during spring and fall migration.

getting there

From Kings Highway in Tappan, take NY 303 north to the Palisades Parkway. Drive 12 miles on the parkway to exit 13 (US 202/Haverstraw/Suffern). Take exit 13 and merge onto Thiells Mount Ivy Road. Turn left onto US 202 east and arrive in Mount Ivy.

where to eat

Mt. Ivy Cafe. 14 Thiells Mt. Ivy Rd., Pomona; (845) 354-4746; mtivycafe.com. Good food and plenty of it—that's what you will find at this long-established restaurant, where a 4-course prix-fixe meal costs less than $25 and the chef regularly adds unusual items to the menu. You'll find a wide range of fresh seafood choices, as well as innovative twists on rack of lamb, chicken, and pasta dishes. Creative presentation and reasonable prices make this spot a favorite with area residents. Open Mon 11:30 a.m. to 9 p.m., Tues through Thurs 11:30 a.m. to 9:30 p.m., Fri 11:30 a.m. to 10 p.m., Sat 3 to 10 p.m., Sun 3 to 9 p.m. $$.

stony point, ny

Stony Point, a town of roughly 15,000 residents, supplies a dipperful of American colonial history among its clusters of communities and neighborhoods. Here on the cliffs above the Hudson River's west bank, you'll find pleasantly busy streets with necessities of daily living and a scattering of interesting restaurants, and more historical markers than you might expect in a town of this size. A stroll around Stony Point can reveal the lookout where Generals George Washington and Anthony Wayne plotted a surprise attack on the British; a mansion built before the Civil War; and a barn from the 1880s that now houses a professional theater—not to mention the stunning views of the river and the surrounding valley.

getting there

From exit 15 on the Palisades Parkway, take Gate Hill Road east. Gate Hill Road becomes Central Drive; continue on Central Drive east to West Main Street. Turn left on West Main Street and continue to Wayne Avenue; bear left on Wayne and follow this to US 202. Turn right on US 202 and continue to Battlefield Road. Turn left on Battlefield Road and take this to the state historic site.

what to do

Nyack Beach State Park. 698 N. Broadway, Upper Nyack; (845) 358-1316; nysparks .com/parks/156/details.aspx. Here the state of New York preserves 61 acres of riverfront along the Hudson, where you can enjoy a hike in the woodlands on a park trail, a leisurely walk along the river, or a picnic. Open year-round for day use, fees are charged on summer weekends from 8 a.m. to 6 p.m. The park may close due to weather from Nov 1 to Apr 1.

Stony Point Battlefield State Historic Site. 44 Battlefield Rd.; (845) 786-2521; nysparks .com/historic-sites/8/details.aspx. This historic site provides a slice of Revolutionary War history that's not at the forefront of the common narrative. Here in July 1779, General Anthony Wayne led the American Corps of Light Infantry in a surprise midnight attack on the British Regulars, capturing the point in about 33 minutes. Today this artfully landscaped site features walking paths to the Stony Point Lighthouse (see below) and around the battleground, a military museum, and pleasant trails through trees, wildflowers, and a small wetland. Winter hours: Mon through Fri 10 a.m. to 4 p.m., weather permitting. Closed Sat and Sun in winter. Spring through fall: Open mid-Apr through Oct. Grounds are open Mon through Fri 9 a.m. to 5 p.m., Sat 10 a.m. to 5 p.m., Sun noon to 5 p.m. Museum open Wed through Sat 10 a.m. to 4:30 p.m., Sun noon to 4:30 p.m., closed Mon and Tues, but open on Memorial Day and Labor Day. Free admission.

Stony Point Lighthouse. 44 Battlefield Rd.; (845) 786-2521; nysparks.com/historic-sites/ 8/details.aspx. The lighthouse, built in 1826, is the oldest one on the Hudson River, and it offers long views of the Hudson from its post above the river. It marked the water entrance to the Hudson Highlands for boats and barges heading upriver to the Erie Canal and points west, acting as an important navigational aid as traffic increased dramatically with the canal's opening. Winter hours: Mon through Fri 10 a.m. to 4 p.m., weather permitting. Closed Sat and Sun in winter. Spring through fall: Open mid-Apr through Oct. Grounds are open Mon through Fri 9 a.m. to 5 p.m., Sat 10 a.m. to 5 p.m., Sun noon to 5 p.m. Free admission.

harriman & bear mountain state parks

One of the delights of driving the Palisades Parkway is the access the route provides to more than 89,000 acres of contiguous protected land, in remarkable proximity to the nation's largest metropolis. Harriman State Park borders Bear Mountain State Park and the United States Military Academy's forest reserve to the north—mixed hardwood forest that will remain forever wild. To the south, you can find Sterling Forest State Park, a fairly new park established in 1998, protected to ensure habitat for animals including black bear, fox, many songbirds and hawks, and even the timber rattlesnake, a fairly scarce species and the only poisonous snake in New York State.

Iron mining once dominated these landscapes, but the mines closed in the 1920s and local residents fought hard to keep the land from becoming more fodder for rampant development. Today the New York–New Jersey Trail Conference maintains many trails that cross the parks and wander through the Hudson Highlands and the Ramapo Mountains. You can see a great deal of wonderful scenery from your car, but the real magic of these parks is only accessible on foot or with a boat and a paddle.

getting there

From the Palisades Interstate Parkway in New York State, take exit 18 to Harriman State Park, or exit 19 to reach Bear Mountain State Park.

what to do

Palisades Interstate Park Commission Visitor Center. When you return to the parkway after visiting Stony Point, watch for this visitor center and bookstore on the median after exit 16. This is the bookstore and gift shop for Bear Mountain State Park, as well as for other historic and natural areas en route to the park. You'll find information on all the area's parks, lots of gift items, and helpful rangers who can direct you to specific points of interest in the park. Second Sun in Mar to first Sat in Nov: open daily 8 a.m. to 6 p.m.; first Sat in Nov through second Sun in March: open daily 8 a.m. to 5 p.m. Free admission.

Anthony Wayne Recreation Area. Just off exit 17 on the Palisades Interstate Parkway; (845) 942-2560; nysparks.com/parks/26/details.aspx. Named for the American general who scored such a great success at Stony Point, this unit of Harriman State Park provides picnic grounds, ball fields, and hiking trails in a pretty valley surrounded by the local mountains, making it a nice stop if you're looking for a place to enjoy your lunch. Park hours are subject to change; check with the park before you travel. Free admission.

Appalachian Trail. Bear Mountain State Park, 3006 Seven Lakes Dr.; (845) 786-2701; nysparks.com/parks/13/details.aspx. Eighty-eight miles of the Appalachian Trail are in New York State, passing through Sterling Forest, Bear Mountain, and Harriman State Parks, all of which are along the parkway. The 2,180-mile footpath and national park begins at Springer Mountain, Georgia, and ends atop Mount Katahdin in Maine. Always open (though impassable in bad weather); free admission.

Bear Mountain State Park. 3006 Seven Lakes Dr. (exit 19 on the Palisades Interstate Parkway); (845) 786-2701; nysparks.com/parks/13/details.aspx. If scrambling over boulders and traversing natural areas on foot does not appeal to you the way it does to me, you can still enjoy the best of the Palisades by driving to the top of Bear Mountain. Take exit 19 (Seven Lakes Drive) and follow the signs to Perkins Memorial Drive, the road to the summit. In about 10 minutes—perhaps longer on a high-traffic day—the winding road ends at a large parking area at the mountaintop. You'll find plenty of vantage points from which to enjoy the expansive view of the Hudson Highlands and Harriman State Park. If you like, climb the Perkins Memorial Tower for even more spectacular vistas.

Once you've seen the main attraction, take time to make a satisfying exploration of the rest of Bear Mountain State Park. An easy, winding nature trail leads you to four Trail-side Museums, where you can learn about the Palisades region's natural features through exhibits on the area's geology, ancient and colonial human history, warm-blooded animals, reptiles, and amphibians. Between these museums, you'll pass a black bear den and exhibits that contain a live bobcat, porcupine, coyote, fox, beaver, otter, and white-tailed deer, as well as a number of birds of prey. Open daily 8 a.m. to sunset; $8 per vehicle.

Fort Montgomery State Historic Site. 690 NY 9W, Fort Montgomery; (845) 446-2134; nysparks.com/historic-sites/28/details.aspx. The American Patriots took a beating and suffered a colossal defeat at this fort on October 6, 1777, when British, Loyalist, and sympathetic Hessian troops attacked Fort Montgomery and Fort Clinton, just down the road. The Americans had only about a third of the forces of their enemies, but they fought valiantly until the British and their allies drove them out at bayonet point. In the end, more than half of the Patriots died in the battle. The site provides the remains of the 14-acre fort, a museum filled with original artifacts of Revolutionary War times, a 15-minute movie depicting the battle, and an expansive view of the Hudson River. Open mid-Apr through Oct 31, Wed through Sun 9 a.m. to 5 p.m. Closed Mon, Tues, and Nov through mid-Apr; tour $3 per person.

Harriman State Park. Off exit 18 on the Palisades Interstate Parkway; (845) 786-2701; nysparks.com/parks/145/details.aspx. If you prefer a more secluded setting, exit 18 gives you the easiest access to Harriman State Park, which at roughly 44,000 acres is the second largest park in the New York State Parks system. Thirty-one bodies of water grace this park, from pristine lakes surrounded by dense foliage to reservoirs that supply water to New York City. Rocky streams, trails through fascinating geologic formations, challenging but manageable hikes, and views of the Hudson Highlands from atop many hills make this park a more than agreeable place to spend a day or a weekend.

where to stay

Bear Mountain Inn. 55 Hessian Dr., Bear Mountain; (845) 786-2731; visitbearmountain .com. Newly renovated in a rustic contemporary style, the Bear Mountain Inn, Overlook Lodge, and Stone Cottages offer sweeping views of the Hudson Highlands and valley, quick access to the Appalachian Trail, and comfortable accommodations with a number of dining options. The Bear Mountain Inn offers 15 deluxe guest rooms, while the Overlook Lodge provides fairly traditional hotel rooms with views of the mountain. The Stone Cottages are the kinds of cabins you expect to find in America's national parks. Whichever you choose, you'll have access to the Spa at Bear Mountain (for additional fees), another way to treat yourself on a weekend away from the city. Inn and Lodge $$$, Cottages $$.

day trip 06

lower valley: new york city

>>> **urban harborside**
gateway national recreation area,
new york harbor, ny

Tens of thousands of commuters pass New York Harbor on the Belt Parkway, I-78, I-278, and I-478 every day, but a comparatively small number return in their leisure time to explore the areas that line the mouth of the Hudson River. Here the National Park Service has had the foresight to gather together a number of disparate sites and extend to them the protection they require to survive. You can visit these sites—from the first airfield in the New York metropolitan area to the forts that guarded this strategically important waterway through two World Wars and beyond—at any time of the year. This area also provides access to two of the most visited points in the National Park system: the Statue of Liberty and Ellis Island National Monuments.

gateway national recreation area

What's unusual about Gateway is not its geological or natural significance, but the fact that it exists at all in the most developed urban area in the country. As one of the nation's few urban national parks, Gateway National Recreation Area offers visitors a natural getaway complete with pristine beaches and wildlife refuges, as well as historic military sites, music and other cultural events, sailing, surfing, and organized sports. Visitors can see New York's first municipal airport at Floyd Bennett Field, the military fortifications at Fort Tilden, Miller

Field, Fort Wadsworth, and Fort Hancock, and the thriving ecosystem that survives despite encroaching development around Jamaica Bay and New York Harbor. These 26,000 acres provide a haven from city life for more than 7 million people every year.

getting there

- To reach Floyd Bennett Field, follow the Belt Parkway to exit 11S. Take Flatbush Avenue south to the main entrance.

- To reach Jamaica Bay Wildlife Refuge, follow the Belt Parkway to exit 17/Cross Bay Boulevard. Proceed south on Cross Bay Boulevard across the north Channel Bridge. The refuge visitor center is about 1 mile past the bridge, at the traffic light.

- To reach Jacob Riis Park/Fort Tilden, follow the Belt Parkway to exit 11S, and take Flatbush Avenue south across the Marine Parkway Bridge to the park. Alternately, take Woodhaven Boulevard to Cross Bay Boulevard, then go west on Beach Channel Drive to the park.

- To reach Fort Wadsworth from Brooklyn, take the lower level of the Verrazano Narrows Bridge/I-278. Beyond the toll, take the Bay Street exit. Turn left at the light, and proceed to Bay Street and the park entrance.

- To reach Miller Field from Fort Wadsworth, return to the Staten Island Expressway (I-278), and take the Hylan Boulevard exit. Proceed south on Hylan Boulevard and turn east on New Dorp Lane to Miller Field.

- To reach Great Kills Park from Miller Field, go south on Hylan Boulevard to the Great Kills Park entrance.

what to do

Breezy Point Tip. At the end of Rockaway Point Boulevard, Brooklyn; (718) 318-4340; nyharborparks.org/visit/brpo.html. It's not easy to find unspoiled beach in New York City, but if you need a walk along the sand while the tide ebbs and flows to the west, make the trip out to the end of the Rockaway Peninsula. Here you might spot a piping plover sitting on an egg in the middle of the sand, demonstrating exactly why this species is facing extinction. Watch for roseate tern, common tern, least tern, black skimmer, and American oystercatcher, all of which rest and feed here in summer in the marshes and coastal grasslands. Open daily dawn to dusk; admission is free, though you may need to pay to park your car.

Floyd Bennett Field. 509 Aviation Rd., Brooklyn; (718) 338-3799; nyharborparks.org/visit/flbe.html. Start at the Ryan Visitor Center and find out what's happening on the day of your visit to this former New York City airport. Floyd Bennett was the first aviator to fly over the North Pole, and this airport named in his honor became the takeoff point for Amelia Earhart's record-breaking flights, as well as those of Howard Hughes. Today the field's Hangar B hosts the Historic Aircraft Restoration Project, restoring and maintaining a number of historically significant planes and other flying craft—and you are welcome to stroll around inside the hangar for close looks. Ecology walks, gardening events, ranger-led walks through wild areas on the grounds, and sports activities in the Aviator Sports & Events Center are all open to the public. The visitor center (or ranger station during extended renovations) is open daily, 9 a.m. to 5 p.m. Free admission.

Fort Tilden. 169 State Rd.; (718) 338-3799; nps.gov/gate/historyculture/fort-tilden.htm. This U.S. Army Coast Artillery Post began guarding the entrance to New York Harbor in 1917, first watching for naval attacks during World War I and World War II, and then for air-strikes during the Cold War with Nike anti-aircraft missiles at the ready. The fort was deac-tivated in 1974, and now its buildings provide a home to the Rockaway Artist Alliance and the Rockaway Theatre Company. Check their websites for exhibitions and performances scheduled during your visit: rockawayartistsalliance.org and rockawaytheatrecompany.org.

Fort Wadsworth. 1598 Bay St., Staten Island; (718) 354-4500; nps.gov/gate/historyculture/fort-wadsworth.htm. Since 1779, some form of fortification has stood in this strategic posi-tion at the Verrazano Narrows, just under the modern bridge by that name. The British built the first defensive structure here and held it until their surrender in 1781, and New York State built a masonry fort here during the War of 1812. A new fort, named Fort Richmond, was constructed from 1847 to 1862, and the state replaced this one with a granite and brick structure that was renamed Fort Tompkins. After the Civil War, the government renamed the fort again—this time to honor Brevet Major General James Wadsworth, who died in the Battle of the Wilderness. Grounds open daily year-round, Apr 1 to Oct 31, 5 a.m. to 10 p.m.; Nov 1 to Mar 31, 5 a.m. to 8 p.m. Free admission.

Great Kills Park. Hylan Boulevard and Buffalo Street, Staten Island; (718) 987-6790; nyharborparks.org/visit/grki.html. These 580 acres of open space provide lifeguard-protected beach, trails for walking or running, and some of the only habitat on Staten Island for seabirds. Preserved through the foresight of a businessman named John J. Crooke back in the 1860s, this patch of land and oceanfront never succumbed to development or military use—and while no area this close to New York City can be completely pristine, Great Kills Park has had the luxury of remaining open and natural. Grounds open daily year-round, Apr 1 to Oct 31, 5 a.m. to 10 p.m.; Nov 1 to Mar 31, 5 a.m. to 8 p.m. Ranger Station open Fri through Mon, 9 a.m. to 4:30 p.m. Free admission.

Jacob Riis Park. 157 Rockaway Beach Blvd.; (718) 354-4606; nyharborparks.org/visit/jari.html. The pristine beach you see at this park was the creation of Park Commissioner Robert Moses back in 1936, a recreation area that Moses imagined would be used by poor immigrants who would access it using public transportation. Indeed, with the park becom-ing part of Gateway National Recreation Area in 1972, Moses's vision has become a reality, with people from every background coming to this seashore to enjoy time out of the crush of city noise and traffic. Don't miss the vintage art deco bathhouse, restored to its 1932 condition and the home of exhibits about the area's history. Open daily 9 a.m. to 5 p.m.; parking fee $10 from Memorial Day weekend to Labor Day.

Jamaica Bay Wildlife Refuge. Broad Channel, Queens; (718) 318-4340; nps.gov/gate. The Jamaica Bay Wildlife Refuge is one of the most important urban wildlife refuges in the United States, with more than 330 bird species found here over the years. If you have never seen hundreds of tiny shorebirds (those little "peeps" that run back and forth along the beach) in one place, or heard the sheer decibel power of tens of thousands of ducks and geese as they flock during their annual migration, Jamaica Bay is one of the few places in the country where you can witness these *National Geographic*–style moments. This refuge has become a stopping point for monarch butterfly migration as well, one of the most astonishing natural phenomena on our planet. Thousands of these delicate creatures rest on milkweed and other familiar plants in the park while they store up the strength to move onward. Open daily 9 a.m. to 5 p.m.; trails are open sunrise to sunset. Admission to the park is free.

Miller Field. 600 New Dorp Lane, Staten Island; (718) 351-6970; nps.gov/gate/historyculture/ millerarmyfield.htm. This former US Army airfield sprang from a farm field owned by Cornelius Vanderbilt in the 1800s, passed down through generations until the family sold it to the US government in 1919. Almost immediately, it was pressed into service as the only Air Coast Defense Station on the east coast of the United States, manned by Coast Artillery soldiers during World War II. The Army kept a number of its military helicopters here during the Cold War. There's not much to see here now, but the staff can provide plenty of knowledge about the field's military history. Grounds open daily year-round, Apr 1 to Oct 31, 5 a.m. to 10 p.m.; Nov 1 to Mar 31, 5 a.m. to 8 p.m. Ranger Station open Tues through Thurs, 9 a.m. to 4:30 p.m. Free admission.

where to eat

There are literally thousands of restaurants in New York City, and a startling number of places to eat along the Brooklyn/Staten Island route defined by your trip to Gateway—so we've chosen a few that rate the highest with locals and tourists alike.

Bayou. 1072 Bay St., Staten Island; (718) 273-4383; bayounyc.com. If the name doesn't quite say New Orleans to you, the Cajun/Creole menu and the intimate atmosphere will put you in the French Quarter frame of mind. You can choose a traditional remoulade or étouffée dish here, but it's the creative use of the uniquely Louisiana spice palate and cooking techniques that make Bayou a real standout: Try the truffle chicken, the N'awlins chicken, the summer lamb (drizzled with sweet pecan vinaigrette), or the seafood gone wild—in a cilantro-garlic white wine broth, rather than a heavier tomato or cream-based sauce—and you will wish they offered seconds. Luckily, there's banana chocolate bread pudding for dessert. Mon through Thurs 11:30 a.m. to 11 p.m., Fri and Sat 11:30 a.m. to midnight, Sun noon to 10 p.m. $$$.

Hokkaido. 3295 Amboy Rd., Staten Island; (718) 980-0880; hokkaidostatenisland.com. Great sushi is all about the freshest fish and the most artistic presentation, and this Japanese restaurant stands out on both counts. All of your Pacific Rim favorites are here, plus some varieties you may not see on every sushi bar's menu. You'll find a handful of entrees that do not involve raw fish as well, for the sushi-timid in your group. Mon through Thurs 11:30 a.m. to 10:30 p.m., Fri and Sat 11:30 a.m. to 11:30 p.m., Sun 1 to 10:30 p.m. $$$.

Lakruwana. 668 Bay St., Staten Island; (347) 857-6619; lakruwana.com. The transporting atmosphere of this Sri Lankan restaurant may make you feel as if you've traveled far away from the bustle of Staten Island and into a world of visual textures, tantalizing spices, and unhurried but efficient service. If you're a fan of Indian food, you will recognize many of the items on the menu—but the presentation and the variety will surprise and delight you. Open daily noon to 3 p.m. and 5:30 to 10:30 p.m. $$.

Nurnberger Bierhaus. 817 Castleton Ave., Staten Island; (718) 816-7461; nurnberger bierhaus.com. If you're enthusiastic about beer, this is the place to go for an impressive assortment of draft beers and another 30 or so in bottles. (In spring and summer, the Biergarten next door may be just the place for you.) The menu is packed with Bavarian delights, from a game sausage sampler platter featuring lamb, wild boar, duck, and rabbit, to thick, soft pretzels served with two kinds of mustard. Schnitzel, spaetzle, pickled herring, smoked trout, and all the wursts you can imagine appear on the lunch and dinner menus, along with a wide variety of potato-based side dishes. You're sure to find your inner German here. Mon through Sat 11 a.m. to 11 p.m., Sun noon to 9 p.m. $$ ($$$ if you add several beers).

Pizzeria Giove. 278 New Dorp Ln., Staten Island; (347) 286-0635. If you have to wait for a table, take it as a sign that this place serves some of the best pizza you'll find in the New York metropolitan area—and that's really saying something. Thin, crispy crust, cheeses and sauces made on site, and culinary skill that led chef Giorgio Giove to a *Throwdown* win over Bobby Flay—all of this will make you want to try a variety of pies before you leave. Try the Variopinta (stracciatella, pancetta, zucchini, and cheese with garlic and herbs) and/or the Gustosa (San Marzano tomatoes, stracciatella, hot sopressata, sweet Italian sausage, and garlic-and-herb cheese). Mon through Thurs 10:30 a.m. to 10:30 p.m., Fri and Sat 10:30 a.m. to 11:30 p.m., Sun noon to 10:30 p.m. $$.

new york harbor, ny

Don't wait for distant relatives to visit you—be a tourist in your own hometown, and explore some of the most visited national parks in the United States here in New York Harbor. A day trip on the ferry—departing from Castle Clinton in Battery Park to Liberty Island and Ellis Island—not only provides some of the most classic views of Manhattan from the water, but it also allows you to experience that view much the way that 12 million immigrants did when they traveled across the Atlantic Ocean and arrived here in the United States from 1892 to 1954—and earlier, when Castle Clinton served as the nation's immigration center. This day trip is about as quintessentially American as it gets.

getting there

Liberty and Ellis Islands are only accessible by ferry service. Statue Cruises, LLC, operates ferries from New York and New Jersey. One round-trip ferry ticket includes visits to both islands. For current ferry schedule information and advance ticket purchases, call (212) 269-5755 (for New York) or (201) 435-9499 (for New Jersey), or go to statuecruises.com. The Statue Cruises ferry terminal in Manhattan is in Battery Park. From the east, take any bridge or tunnel to Manhattan. Take FDR Drive south to exit 1. Take Broad Street to Water Street. Turn left on Water Street to Battery Park. By bus, take the M1, M6, or M15 bus to Battery Park. By subway, take the 1 train to South Ferry, 4 or 5 to Bowling Green, R or W train to Whitehall Street.

Governors Island National Monument is only accessible from May to Sept by ferry from the Battery Maritime Building at 10 South St. in Manhattan, from Brooklyn Bridge Park's Pier 6 at the foot of Atlantic Avenue, and on the East River Ferry summer ferries. In Manhattan, take FDR Drive south to exit 1—South Ferry, and stay in the left lane. Take the U-turn to the left at the end of the street in front of the Staten Island Ferry terminal. The Battery Maritime Building is the historic ferry terminal northeast of the Staten Island Ferry terminal. The Governors Island ferry leaves from the northernmost slip of the Battery Maritime Building. Brooklyn Bridge Park in Brooklyn is at the intersection of Atlantic Avenue and Columbia Street; park in the lot at Pier 6 on Columbia Street for a fee.

what to do

American Family Immigration History Center at Ellis Island. Accessible only by ferry service (see "getting there," above); (212) 363-3200; ellisisland.org. This exciting interactive program at the museum helps descendants of families who arrived at Ellis Island to find information about their ancestors. Bring whatever information you have when you visit Ellis Island, and access passenger records of the ships that carried some 22 million immigrants, crewmembers, and other passengers to the Port of New York and Ellis Island. More than 100 million Americans may find records of their families' beginnings here. Highly skilled, well-informed experts on American genealogy are ready to help you find your ancestor's name in a ship's manifest using the center's powerful search engines, and to track other information that may be useful in learning more about your heritage. Open daily 9:30 a.m. to 5 p.m., closed Christmas. Free admission.

Ellis Island. Accessible only by ferry service; (212) 363-3200; nps.gov/elis. This extraordinary museum chronicles its history as the largest American gateway to the nation of freedom and opportunity from 1892 to 1954. When the entire museum reopens (the force of Hurricane Sandy in October 2012 caused extensive damage to the building's water, sewer, electrical, and ventilation systems), you will need at least 3 hours to truly understand the magnitude of the massive period of immigration of which it was an integral part, and its significance in changing the American way of life through the work of these newcomers' hands and the vitality of their cultural backgrounds. Tour Ellis Island's 3 floors on your own, take a ranger-guided tour, or rent the audio tour—my personal favorite—and listen to the music, stories, and the voices of people who passed through the island's screening and examination procedures. A first visit to Ellis Island can be overwhelming, but the tours bring home the most important messages simply and with great entertainment value. Open daily 9:30 a.m. to 5 p.m., closed Christmas. Free admission.

Governors Island National Monument. Accessible only in summer via ferries; (212) 825-3045; nps.gov/gois. If you're not looking in the right direction as you take the ferry from Battery Park to the Statue of Liberty, you'll probably miss Governors Island, but this unassuming little spot played a major role in the American Revolution, the War of 1812, the Civil War, and in peacetime military maneuvers. Originally the home of the Lenape Indian tribe, the island came to General George Washington's attention as an important defensive point against the encroaching British. During the Battle of Brooklyn, the largest battle of the Revolution, the island's strategic position gave it strength as its artillery did its best to beat back the opposing force. Despite their best efforts, the American forces lost the battle and suffered an eight-year occupation of New York City by the British—but the island remained a useful place for the US military, serving as a prisoner-of-war camp, a military prison, an Army headquarters, and a Coast Guard station. Today it's a national monument within the National Park Service, and you can visit Castle Williams and Fort Jay, stroll its paved trails, and enjoy waterfront views of New York Harbor. Open on weekends from early June through early Sept; call the park for this year's schedule and hours. Free admission.

Statue of Liberty National Monument. Liberty Island; (212) 363-3200; nps.gov/stli. Arguably the most recognized symbol of freedom and democracy in the world, the Statue of Liberty came to the United States in 1885 as a gift of friendship from France, and continues to be hailed as a marvel of engineering and artistic expression. Three hundred and five feet high, the monument was designed by sculptor Frederic Auguste Bartholdi and recently underwent an extensive renovation to improve security and safe passage to Lady Liberty's crown from the inside. Alternately, visitors can enter the monument and look up through a glass ceiling to see the internal structure of the statue, and then continue to the pedestal observation deck to view the New York City skyline. Plan to spend at least an hour or more at Liberty to stand in the shadow of this magnificent work of art, and consider how many people traveled thousands of miles at great personal peril to glimpse this statue and know that they would live, work, and raise their children in a free country. Open daily 9:30 a.m. to 5 p.m., closed Christmas. Free admission.

day trip 07

lower valley: new york city

>>> **harlem heritage**
upper west side, manhattan, ny

Along the banks of the Hudson River, and throughout the streets of the Upper East Side, Upper Manhattan presents a fascinating cross-section of New York immigration and national history that makes this area one of the most interesting parts of the city. You may not be able to take in all of the sights—especially the museums—in a single day trip, so plan to return here once you've gotten your bearings and found your way around.

getting there

Take public transportation to avoid the high parking fees in Upper Manhattan's parking garages. By subway, the 1 train follows the west side, while the 2 and 3 trains run through the center of Upper Manhattan above Central Park, and the 4, 5, and 6 trains follow Lexington Avenue on the east side. The A train goes north to Inwood Hill Park, while the B train goes north to 155th Street before turning east for the Bronx. Download the subway map at web.mta.info/nyct/maps/subwaymap.pdf, or choose from more than a dozen NYC mass transit apps at web.mta.info/apps.

upper west side, manhattan, ny

The treasures of Upper Manhattan begin with a national park site and include the only museum that provides a complete history of New York City, natural and cultural evidence of New York's beginnings hundreds and thousands of years ago, and ethnic cultural institutions that enlighten visitors about the continued immigration that takes place here on a daily basis.

where to go

Apollo Theater. 253 W. 125th St.; (212) 531-5300; apollotheater.org. The day that the 125th Street Apollo Theater opened in 1934, it welcomed the African-American community to a showplace of its uniquely American sound—and in almost no time at all it became the premier stage in Harlem for live theatrical entertainment. Its Amateur Nights—still hosted by the Apollo every Wednesday to this day—introduced performers including Ella Fitzgerald and Pearl Bailey, and acts that debuted at the Apollo included Lena Horne, Billie Holiday, and the Count Basie Orchestra. Even its backstage policies made history as the Apollo became the largest employer of black theatrical workers in the country, and the only one in New York City to hire black stagehands. Today the theater functions as a nonprofit organization presenting concerts, special events, and its legendary Amateur Nights. Ticket prices and start times vary with the production; visit apollotheater.org for more information.

The Cloisters. 99 Margaret Corbin Dr., Fort Tryon Park; (212) 923-3700; metmuseum.org/visit/visit-the-cloisters. This branch of the Metropolitan Museum of Art is devoted exclusively to the art and architecture of medieval Europe, and was assembled from architectural elements that actually date from the 12th through the 15th centuries. Inside you'll find roughly 2,000 works of art, most notably a wide range of stained-glass windows that make a trip to the Cloisters a breathtaking experience. Open daily, Mar through Oct, 10 a.m. to 5:15 p.m.; Nov through Feb, 10 a.m. to 4:45 p.m.; closed Thanksgiving, Christmas, and New Year's Day; adults $25, seniors 65 and older $17, students $12, children under 12 free.

El Museo del Barrio. 1230 Fifth Ave. at 104th St.; (212) 831-7272; elmuseo.org. New York's premier Caribbean and Latin American cultural institution, El Museo presents a solid representation of the diversity of art and culture in the Caribbean and Latin America. Founded in 1969 by artist and educator Raphael Montanez Ortiz and a group of community activists, educators, artists, and parents, it has since evolved into one of the leading Latino and Latin American museums in the nation. Wed through Sun 11 a.m. to 5 p.m., closed Mon and Tues; adults $6, students and seniors $4, children under 12 free.

General Grant National Memorial. W. 122nd Street and Riverside Drive; (212) 666-1640; nps.gov/gegr. Who's buried in Grant's Tomb? The 18th president of the United States, General Ulysses S. Grant, and his wife, Julia Dent Grant, are entombed here. The venerable general led the Union to victory in the Civil War, and went on to succeed Andrew Johnson as president. During his two terms in office, Grant signed into law the Civil Rights Act of 1875, which gave African Americans the right to equal treatment with whites in public places. He also named Yellowstone as the first national park on March 1, 1872. While Grant was laid to rest in New York City in August 1885, overwhelmingly positive public opinion demanded that this much-loved president be honored with the largest and most permanent monument money could buy—and to this end, more than 90,000 people contributed cash for its construction. Grant was entombed in April 1897, with more than one million people attending to honor his memory.

You don't need much time to enjoy the memorial, so take a few minutes to examine the mosaics around the inside. You'll see Grant at his most glorious, battling armies at Vicksburg and Chattanooga, and accepting Robert E. Lee's surrender at Appomattox. Open daily 9 a.m. to 5 p.m.; closed Thanksgiving, Christmas, and New Year's Day. Admission is free.

Hispanic Society of America. 613 W. 155th St. (Audubon Terrace) at Broadway; (212) 926-2234; hispanicsociety.org. Perhaps the most comprehensive survey in the United States of the arts and culture of Spain, Portugal, and Latin America, this museum features more than 800 paintings and 6,000 watercolors and drawings from the Middle Ages to present day. In addition, nearly a thousand works of sculpture and thousands of art objects—jewelry, furniture, textiles, and glass—round out the extraordinary collection. Tues through Sat 10 a.m. to 4:30 p.m., Sun 1 to 4 p.m., closed Mon. Free admission.

Inwood Hill Park. At the end of W. 218th St., bounded by Dyckman Street, Hudson River, Harlem River South; call 311 in NYC or (212) NEW-YORK; nycgovparks.org/parks/inwood-hill-park. Where did Dutchman Peter Minuit make his famous purchase of the island of Manhattan from the Lenape Indians back in 1626? Somewhere within these 196 acres of undeveloped land, you'll find Shorakapok Rock, where this transaction may have taken place—not for $24 worth of trinkets, but for tools and dry goods worth about $1,000 in today's U.S. currency. Now partially developed with ball fields, a marina that provides access to the Hudson River Greenway Water Trail, and New York City's last remaining salt marsh, this park preserves a landscape that has existed for thousands of years. You may find the forests, caves, and views of the Hudson River worth a brisk clamber. Open daily dawn to dusk; no admission fee.

Morris-Jumel Mansion. 65 Jumel Terrace; (212) 923-8008; morrisjumel.org. The oldest house in Manhattan, the Morris-Jumel Mansion was built in 1765 by Colonel Roger Morris of the British army. Morris and his American wife used this Palladian-style house as a summer home until they were forced to return to England as the Revolutionary War began. Most likely, they were infuriated when General George Washington used their mansion as his headquarters during the Battle of Harlem Heights in 1776. Wed through Sun, 10 a.m. to 4 p.m., closed Mon and Tues and major holidays; adults $5, seniors and students $4, free to children under 12.

Museum of the City of New York. 1120 Fifth Ave. at 103rd St.; (212) 534-1672; mcny .org. Just across the street from El Museo, this museum is a treat—the one place in town where you'll find the narrative of the Dutch conquest of New Netherland in the 1600s. Permanent exhibitions provide one of the city's only lingering looks at the upscale homes and furnishings of New York's well-to-do. Tues through Sun 10 a.m. to 5 p.m., closed Mon; adults $10, seniors and students $6, children under 12 free.

National Jazz Museum. 104 E. 126th St.; (212) 348-8300; jazzmuseuminharlem.org. Whether jazz speaks to your soul, sets your feet in motion, or simply sparks your curiosity, this remarkable museum will bring you closer to the musicians—many of them legends—who created and shaped this uniquely American art form. The museum houses the Savory Collection of jazz recordings from the late 1930s, as well as changing exhibitions and an enormous library of CDs and DVDs for your listening pleasure. Mon through Fri 10 a.m. to 4 p.m., free admission (donations encouraged).

Riverbank State Park. 679 Riverside Dr.; (212) 694-3600; nysparks.com/parks/93/details .aspx.This 28-acre park sits high atop the North River Wastewater Treatment Plant on the Hudson River, and it features an 800-seat theater and a 2,500-seat athletic complex, as well as an Olympic-size pool and a skating rink. The Hudson River Greenway passes on its west side at water level, providing a bicycling route to the park (though bikes are not permitted in the park).

Sakura Park. Riverside Drive and Claremont Avenue to W. 122nd Street; call 311 in NYC or (212) NEW-YORK; nycgovparks.org/parks/sakurapark. Just east of General Grant Memorial and across from Riverside Park, Sakura Park contains hundreds of cherry trees given to New York City by the Committee of Japanese Residents of New York. While the cherry trees arrived from Japan in 1912 and were planted here and in Riverside Park, the park underwent a major renovation in 1932 and 1933 when John D. Rockefeller hired the Olmsted Brothers—the most famous and celebrated landscape architectural firm in the United States—to reimagine the park. The cherry blossom season here easily rivals that of Washington, D.C., so why travel to the capital when you can drive down the road? Open daily dawn to dusk, no admission fee.

Sugar Hill Historic District. Bounded by W. 145th and 155th Streets, Edgecombe Avenue, and Amsterdam Avenue; en.wikipedia.org/wiki/Sugar_Hill,_Manhattan. Designated a historic district on the National Register of Historic Places in 2002, this neighborhood filled with genteel homes and elegant row houses became the place for wealthy African Americans to live in the 1920s at the height of the Harlem Renaissance. You'll find a number of these homes on St. Nicholas Place and Edgecombe Avenue. Notable residents included W. E. B. DuBois, Thurgood Marshall, Duke Ellington, Adam Clayton Powell, Walter Franic White, Cab Calloway, and Roy Wilkins. Always open, no admission fee.

where to eat

There are literally hundreds of restaurants, cafes, coffee shops, and other eateries in Upper Manhattan, so you won't go hungry no matter where you decide to stop in for a bite. For a really special experience, however, you might want to choose one of these highly touted restaurants near the sights on your day trip.

Community Food & Juice. 2893 Broadway between 112th and 113th Streets; (212) 665-2800; communityrestaurant.com. One of the toughest things to find in this part of Manhattan is fresh, organically farmed food made with seasonal local ingredients, so Community Food brings a breath of fresh air to the Manhattan streets. Open for breakfast, lunch, and dinner, this restaurant's one-of-a-kind menu includes choices like ravioli with truffled spring-pea filling, edamame dumplings with soy vinaigrette, and marinated lamb skewered and grilled with zucchini, red onions, and mint-yogurt sauce. Mon through Thurs 8 a.m. to 9 p.m., Fri 8 a.m. to 10 p.m., Sat 9 a.m. to 10 p.m., Sun 9 a.m. to 9:30 p.m. $$$.

Dinosaur Bar-B-Que. 700 W. 125th St.; (212) 694-1777; dinosaurbbq.com/locations/harlem. One of the top barbecue restaurants north of the Mason-Dixon Line, Dinosaur originated in Syracuse, New York, and has become the favorite rib joint for upstaters of all stripes. The ribs are the stars here, though you'll find all your barbecue favorites from brisket to sausage, as well as a fine selection of tasty sandwiches and a lengthy menu of sides. The restaurant is easy to find under the Riverside Drive Viaduct in Harlem. Mon through Thurs 11:30 a.m. to 11 p.m., Fri and Sat 11:30 a.m. to midnight, Sun noon to 10 p.m. $$.

La Fonda Boricua. 169 E. 106th St. between 3rd and Lexington Avenues; (212) 410-7292; fondaboricua.com. Head uptown to Spanish Harlem for homestyle Puerto Rican cooking in a restaurant with no printed menus—the chef uses the day's freshest ingredients to plan lunch and dinner. Stews, steaks, and roasted pork may be on the board, along with mofongo, a concoction of fried green plantains or yucca mashed with garlic and pork cracklings. Best of all is chef Jorge Ayala's *arroz con pollo* (chicken with rice), which beat a challenge on the Food Network show *Throwdown* from celebrity chef Bobby Flay, who thought he could make it better. He couldn't. Open daily 11 a.m. to 9 p.m. $$.

Sylvia's Harlem Restaurant. 328 Malcolm X Blvd.; (212) 996-0660; sylviasrestaurant.com. There's a very good reason that Sylvia Woods has been designated the Queen of Soul Food, and you'll know why as soon as your meal is served at this world-famous restaurant. Choose the Carolina-style catfish—fried or grilled—or fill up on fried chicken or short ribs of beef. There is absolutely no chance that you will leave this restaurant without a full belly and a deep sense of satisfaction. Mon through Sat 8 a.m. to 10:30 p.m., Sun 11 a.m. to 8 p.m. $$.

day trip 08

lower valley: new york city

>>> river restoration
hartsdale, tuckahoe, bronx park,
yonkers, ny

Back in 1639, a Swedish businessman named Jonas Bronck bought some land along a pretty river in what would become downstate New York, from the local Native Americans of the Weckquaesgeek and Siwanoy tribes. These tribes used the Aquehung, or River of High Bluffs, for drinking water, fishing, and annual ritual baths—and with this limited use, the river ran clear and sparkling through a densely wooded landscape. In the early 17th century, Dutch trappers arrived to hunt and gather pelts from beavers, mink, otters, and other animals, and when they could not keep up with the demand from European merchants for these pelts, the Dutch settlers turned to milling and other more industrial pursuits. By the mid-18th century, more than a dozen mills got their power from Bronck's river, and the character of the river began a dramatic change. The river that poet Joseph Rodman Drake had called "a ravishing spot formed for a poet's dwelling" in 1817 now had a more apt descriptor: In 1906, the newspapers called it an "open sewer."

It took until 1974 for a group of concerned citizens to create an organization called the Bronx River Restoration, partnering with governmental agencies, other nonprofit organizations, and hundreds of like-minded volunteers to clean the river and keep it as pristine as its urban location will allow. Today you can drive along this meandering waterway and see trees, mowed lawns, flowers, and birds where mills once belched pollutants into the current.

This day trip gives you lots of choices along the 23-mile length of the parkway, from colonial history in Hartsdale to exotic plants and animals in Bronx Park.

getting there

The southern terminus of the Taconic State Parkway is in Kensico Dam Plaza County Park, at the northern end of the Bronx River Parkway. Take the last exit on the Taconic to the Bronx River Parkway, and follow the roundabout into Kensico Park. From here, take the Bronx River Parkway to the stops detailed below.

what to do

Kensico Dam Plaza County Park. 1 Bronx River Parkway, Valhalla; (914) 328-1542; parks.westchestergov.com/kensico-dam-plaza. The 300-foot-high dam on the south end of Kensico Reservoir stands as one of the area's most impressive construction projects, mainly because of the feat of engineering and material movement required to create it. Using turn-of-the-20th-century transportation and technology, the largely Italian immigrant workforce moved stone from the quarry at nearby Cranberry Lake Park, and hauled away construction debris to landfills on a railroad built exclusively for this project. Here in this Westchester park, you can also visit The Rising, the county's September 11 memorial. It's easy to find in the park—an open structure with a tall spire that becomes unmistakable as you move toward it. The memorial contains the names of all the Westchester residents who perished in the terrorist attack and the collapse of the World Trade Center towers, as well as a quote about each of the victims, supplied by their families. It can be approached from any direction, and its structure allows visitors to move in, through, and around it to view all of the names and quotes. Open daily year-round 8 a.m. to dusk; free admission.

hartsdale, ny

A quiet farm village until 1865, Hartsdale nonetheless played a role in the Revolutionary War, becoming the scene of a battle along the Bronx River on October 28, 1776. Later Comte de Rochambeau would make Hartsdale his headquarters for six weeks in 1781 as he readied his French troops to aid General George Washington in securing the surrender of the British army at Yorktown. This would be enough to put most small towns on the historical map, but Hartsdale has another peculiar trademark: its cemeteries, one a resting place for an unusual number of famous people, and the other for an unusual number of pets.

what to do

Ferncliff Cemetery. 280 Secor Rd.; (914) 693-4700; ferncliffcemetery.com. This local cemetery serves as the final resting place for a long list of celebrities including Ed Sullivan, Basil Rathbone, Judy Garland, Jerome Kern, Joan Crawford, Jam-Master Jay, Heavy D, Aaliyah, Oscar Hammerstein, Thelonious Monk, Paul Robeson, and Malcolm X. John Lennon and Jim Henson both were cremated here, as was former New York State governor

Nelson Rockefeller. Captain of industry Tom Carvel (born Carvelas) is buried here, not far from the site of his very first Carvel Ice Cream store on Ridge Road in Hartsdale. (The 1936-built store closed in 2008 and was torn down when developers bought the land for other purposes.) Open daily 9 a.m. to 4 p.m.; the cemetery closes at 1:30 p.m. on Martin Luther King Jr. Day, Lincoln's Birthday, Presidents' Day, Columbus Day, Election Day, and Veterans Day. Closed on New Year's Day, July 4, Labor Day, Thanksgiving, and Christmas. No admission fee.

Hartsdale Pet Cemetery and Crematory. 100 N. Washington Ave.; (800) 375-5234; pet cem.com. When a hamlet's claim to fame is America's first pet cemetery, you know this is a town with heart. Hartsdale was the home of Manhattan veterinarian Samuel Johnson, who played a key role in founding the American Society for the Prevention of Cruelty to Animals. He founded his cemetery for dogs purely by chance in 1896, when he allowed a grieving pet owner to bury her dog here in his apple orchard after she discovered that she could not legally bury her pet in a cemetery in Manhattan. Today the Hartsdale Pet Cemetery is the last resting place for more than 80,000 pets, including a lion cub, horses, and monkeys. Don't miss the War Dog Memorial, dedicated after World War I. Mon through Sat 8 a.m. to 4:30 p.m., Sun 9:30 a.m. to 4 p.m., holidays 9:30 a.m. to 3 p.m. Free admission.

Odell House. 425 Ridge Rd. If you have a passion for Revolutionary War history, you may want to stop and see the headquarters of Comte de Rochambeau, commander in chief of the French expeditionary forces in the summer of 1781. The 7,000 French troops Rochambeau added to the Patriot forces virtually doubled the size of General George Washington's army, making it possible for the Continental Army to seize Yorktown and win the Battle of the Chesapeake—and hence, the war for American independence. The Odell House—named later for John Odell, who purchased the house in 1785—is a stop on the Washington-Rochambeau Revolutionary Route, a new National Historic Trail that tells the story of the French statesmen, armies, and fleets that helped the United States win the Revolutionary War. This National Historic Landmark is open only by appointment.

tuckahoe, ny

The adorable village of Tuckahoe makes exit 3 on the parkway a worthwhile stop. If you're old enough to remember the television situation comedy *Maude,* one of Norman Lear's several *All in the Family* spinoffs, the Findlay family lived here in this tony Westchester County community. Tuckahoe became a center of commerce in the early 19th century when miners unearthed a vein of bright-white marble beneath the town. Builders and architects sought such a material for high-end municipal construction projects, so the marble quarry soon provided jobs to immigrants from Italy, Ireland, and Germany in the 1840s, and later to recently freed African Americans after the Civil War. Two train depots opened nearby, and for more than 60 years this little town thrived with carloads of its prized metamorphic rock leaving daily for New York City and Washington, D.C. By the early 20th century, however, the vein had been harvested beyond its capacity, and the marble industry shrank to a shadow of its heyday. Today the 0.5-square-mile town center features shops, restaurants, and services for the 6,000 or so residents.

getting there

From the Bronx River Parkway driving north or south, take exit 8/Tuckahoe.

what to do

Bronx River Parkway Reservation. Thompson Street, along the Bronx River; (914) 723-4058; parks.westchestergov.com/bronx-river-reservation. Westchester County's oldest park was one of the first linear parks in the country, stretching 13.2 miles along the western banks of the Bronx River. Tuckahoe provides on-street parking and some lots where you can leave your car and walk along the paved path that parallels the Bronx River. Joggers, skaters, cyclists, and dog-walkers all use this trail, so you are likely to be in good company, even in the middle of a weekday afternoon. Open daily year-round, 8 a.m. to dusk. Free admission.

where to eat

An American Bistro. 296 Columbus Ave.; (914) 793-0807; anamericanbistro.com. With dedication to its name, this restaurant offers a wide range of solid American favorites, from meatloaf—dressed up with shiitake mushrooms—to herb-roasted chicken. Substantive entrees, meaty sandwiches, plenty of salad choices, and a Sunday brunch with lots of choices round out the menu. Lunch: Tues through Fri 11:30 a.m. to 3 p.m. Sunday brunch: 11:30 a.m. to 2:30 p.m., Sept through June. Dinner: Mon through Thurs 5:30 to 9:30 p.m., Fri and Sat 5:30 to 10:30 p.m., Sun 5:30 to 9 p.m. $$.

Mambo 64. 64 Main St.; (914) 222-9964; mambo64.com. Latin fusion blending the flavors of more than a dozen countries in Central and South America and the Caribbean—if you can get your mind around that concept, you're ready to dine at Mambo 64. Take Colombian corn cakes and top them with mango chutney from an island recipe, or pair a Cuban-style sandwich with a salad with manchego and medjool dates . . . and you've got a great new twist on a cuisine you thought you knew. Then come back for brunch and try the coconut pancakes. Yum! Lunch: Tues through Fri 11:30 to 2:30. Dinner: Tues through Thurs 5 to 10 p.m., Fri and Sat 5 to 11 p.m.; closed Mon. $$.

Roma Restaurant. 29 Columbus Ave.; (914) 961-3175; romarestaurantinc.com. For more than 80 years, this community mainstay has served classic Italian food at moderate prices to Tuckahoe residents and visitors, using recipes perfected within the family many generations ago. Choose your favorite pasta shape and one of five sauces, or one of more than two dozen traditional Italian or American entrees—all served with spaghetti if you wish. Roma's brick oven pizzas bring customers back on a weekly basis to sample another variety. Save room for tiramisu or spumoni. Tues through Thurs, 11:30 a.m. to 10 p.m., Fri and Sat 11:30 a.m. to 10:30 p.m., Sun 3 to 10 p.m., closed Mon. $$.

bronx park, ny

Back on the parkway, it's only a 10-minute drive to the interchange for Bronx Park. Central Park gets all the attention, but Bronx Park rivals it in plant and animal diversity, bird populations, and scenic quality. Here the Bronx River creates a deep gorge, where a floodplain forest and a red maple swamp shelter the river along the gorge's floor. Walking along the river, fishing, bird-watching, and leaf-peeping all attract visitors from throughout the five boroughs of New York City, and chances are good that you will hear a number of different languages spoken here as you enjoy the natural surroundings in the heart of the Bronx.

getting there

Take exits 9W-E or 8W and follow the cloverleaf around to Dr. Theodore Kazamiroff Boulevard, which leads to the park entrance.

what to do

New York Botanical Garden. 2300 Southern Blvd.; (718) 817-8700; nybg.org. New York Botanical Garden occupies 250 acres of Bronx Park, with more than one million plants in 50 separate gardens and collections. Just about every season produces a different spectacle here, from the azalea garden that begins to bloom in April to the chrysanthemum beds in fall. In winter, the conservatories produce gorgeous flowers and exotic plants that you can tour in the cozy warmth of a well-tended greenhouse. The park also features a 50-acre forest, a tiny sample of the natural woods that covered this entire area when the Weckquaesgeek fished in the Aquehung. Open year-round, Tues through Sun 10 a.m. to 6 p.m.; winter hours (mid-Jan through Feb) 10 a.m. to 5 p.m. Closed Mon except for holidays. Prices vary by season; All-Garden Pass is $25 for adults in spring, $22 for students and seniors 65+, $10 for children 2 to 12 years. Check the website for the prices on the day and time you wish to visit.

Bronx Zoo. 2300 Southern Blvd.; (718) 367-1010; bronxzoo.com. If you've got an urge to see an aardvark, a collared lemur, or an Asian elephant before you leave Bronx Park, pay a visit to the Bronx Zoo, where 265 acres of habitats will provide you with enough animal entertainment to fill your entire afternoon. Choose the Total Experience Ticket to add the Butterfly Garden, Congo Gorilla Forest, Wild Asia Monorail, and other special attractions to your day, and plan to spend the time you need to enjoy as many exotic creatures as you can. Open early Apr through early Nov, Mon through Fri: 10 a.m. to 5 p.m.; Sat, Sun, and holidays 10 a.m. to 5:30 p.m. Adults $16.95, children 3 to 12 $12.95, seniors 65 and older $14.95, children 2 and under are free. Additional fees for special attractions and parking.

Edgar Allan Poe Cottage. 2640 Grand Concourse (Fordham—East Kingsbridge Road/ Grand Concourse); (718) 881-8900; bronxhistoricalsociety.org/poecottage.html. Edgar Allan Poe, one of America's most famous authors and poets, lived the last of his days here in the Bronx in this small wooden farmhouse, which has been restored to its 1846–49 condition. Here he wrote some of the poetry that has endured for generations: "Annabel Lee," "The Bells," and "Eureka." Poe's wife, Virginia, died of tuberculosis in this cottage in 1847, and Poe lived another two years here until his own death during a trip to Baltimore. Open Sat 10 a.m. to 4 p.m. and Sun 1 to 5 p.m.; closed weekdays; $5 adults, $3 students and children.

where to eat

When you get hungry at the zoo, head for Arthur Avenue—the Belmont section, also known as the Little Italy of the Bronx—and choose one of the many restaurants you'll find there. New eateries pop up regularly and some don't stay for very long, but here is a selection of the standouts that have made the Bronx their home for generations.

Ann and Tony's. 2407 Arthur Ave. near 187th Street; (718) 933-1469; annandtonysonline .com. Since 1927, this Napolitano family-owned, multigenerational establishment has served its homestyle Italian cooking to untold thousands of patrons. Congenial service, large portions, and authentic sauces that bubble with flavor will satisfy your craving for your favorite Old World dish—but don't miss the specials and the original selections on the extensive menu. Tues through Sat 11 a.m. to 9 p.m.; Sun 11 a.m. to 3 p.m.; closed Mon. $$.

Casa Della Mozzarella. 604 E. 187th St.; (718) 364-3867; nycgo.com/venues/casa-della -mozzarella. One of the most famous landmarks in Little Italy, this delicatessen hand-pulls its own mozzarella daily, and sells it in large balls of salted or unsalted cheese. You can get deli meats, other cheeses, pasta, cookies, and sandwiches here as well, but the lines form early in the day to get the mozzarella—and people come from all over the metropolitan area for their ball. Come early to avoid the crowds. Mon through Sat 7:30 a.m. to 6 p.m.; Sun 7:30 a.m. to 1 p.m. $.

Madonia Brothers Bakery. 2348 Arthur Ave.; (718) 295-5573. Locals and tourists alike call the Madonia brothers' canollis the best in New York—perhaps, in part, because the bakers fill them with sweet cream right in front of you when you order them. The breads bring people from all over the New York metro area, and the many varieties of fresh biscotti delight visitors enough that the bakery produces 400 to 500 pounds of the cookies every week. Mon through Sat, 6 a.m. to 7 p.m.; Sun 7 a.m. to 6 p.m. $.

Roberto's. 603 Crescent Ave.; (718) 733-9503; roberto089.com. Widely hailed as the most popular Italian restaurant in the Belmont area, Roberto's features an innovative menu that combines traditional flavors in elegant, nontraditional ways. Pasta made from scratch on premises, hand-pureed tomatoes, and the freshest ingredients make this restaurant an adventure in imaginative southern Italian cuisine. Chef Roberto Paciullo also owns **Zero Otto Nove** (2357 Arthur Ave.), famous for its Neapolitan pizza. Lunch Mon through Sat noon to 2:30 p.m., dinner Mon through Thurs 5 to 10 p.m., Fri and Sat 5 to 11 p.m.; closed Sun. $$$.

where to shop

Arthur Avenue Retail Market. 2344 Arthur Ave.; (718) 295-5033; nycedc.com/project/arthur-avenue-market. Whether you're looking for unusual gift items, fresh pastry and espresso, hand-rolled cigars, or crusty bread and handmade mozzarella, this market will never disappoint. You'll find the ready-to-eat and packaged wares of restaurants, pastry shops, butchers, pasta makers, bakeries, gourmet delicatessens, fish markets, coffee shops, housewares, gifts, and more. The brainchild of Mayor Fiorello LaGuardia back in the 1930s, this market brings together the best of the Belmont neighborhood and stands as a microcosm of the Bronx's Little Italy—now a more extensive Italian neighborhood than the traditional one on Mulberry Street in Lower Manhattan. Bring a big market bag—you'll fill it up. Mon through Sat 8 a.m. to 5 p.m., closed Sun.

Cerini Coffee & Gifts. 2334 Arthur Ave.; (718) 584-3449; cerinicoffee.com. More than 25 varieties of imported coffee beans, coffee makers, espresso machines, kitchen wares, specialty foods, flavored syrups, gift baskets, and more stock the shelves at Cerini, where you can sample any of the coffees offered and pick up a massive jar of Nutella to spread on your biscotti (which you bought at Madonia Brothers, no doubt). This old-school cafe and gift emporium will help you find just the right item for the coffee aficionado on your list. Mon through Sat 9 a.m. to 6:30 p.m.; Sun 11 a.m. to 5 p.m. $$.

yonkers, ny

Never thought to spend a day exploring Yonkers? You're going to be pleasantly surprised. The fourth most populated city in New York State and the largest in Westchester County, Yonkers became an industrial city back in the mid-1800s as new companies sprang up along its streets and on the Saw Mill River. Otis Elevator got its start here in Yonkers, and the Alexander Smith and Sons Carpet Company raised 45 buildings and employed more than 4,000 people. In the early 1900s, Bakelite—the material used to make 78-rpm-speed records, along with many other synthetic plastic items—was invented and manufactured here, and the Waring Hat Company dominated the nation's hat market from Yonkers. The first-ever FM radio broadcast came from the Yonkers home of C. R. Runyon, working with inventor Edwin Howard Armstrong; and a long list of celebrities were born here or lived here in the last century, from actor Jon Voight to jazz singer Ella Fitzgerald.

Today this city of nearly 200,000 people hosts communities of immigrants from Poland, Ukraine, the former Yugoslavia, Czechoslovakia, Russia, and Croatia, as well as a larger Arab population from Jordan, Palestine, and Lebanon—in addition to the Irish and Italian populations that settled here in the 19th century. Among the ethnic neighborhoods, visitors find a number of fascinating historic sites, a wealth of art and entertainment, the "daylighted" Saw Mill River at Van der Donck Park, and some mighty fine views of the Hudson River.

getting there

From the south, take the Henry Hudson Parkway (NY 9A) north to US 9. Take US 9 north to Yonkers. From the north, take I-87 to its junction with US 9 in White Plains; take US 9 south to Yonkers.

what to do

Beczak Environmental Education Center. 35 Alexander St.; (914) 377-1900; beczak .org. The Interpretive Center at this remarkable facility provides exhibits that explore the health, ecology, marine life, and functions of the Hudson River. Here on the banks of the river, you have the opportunity to learn about the marsh, tides, inhabitants, and detritus that populate the Hudson, including a cutaway view of the river through the center's 300-gallon tidal tank. Meet an American eel or a blue crab, find out what's turned up in the center's nets, and discover just how much trash washes up in the river every day—and what's in all that garbage. Mon through Fri 9 a.m. to 5 p.m., closed weekends. Free admission, but donations are encouraged.

Empire City Casino at Yonkers Raceway. 810 Yonkers Ave.; (914) 968-4200; empire citycasino.com. More than 5,000 slot machines with denominations ranging from 1 cent to $100, electronic versions of roulette, craps, sic-bo, and baccarat, and easy-to-use self-redemption units (for your winnings, not your soul), make this "racino" at the famous Yonkers Raceway a go-to spot for self-service gaming. The raceway, founded in 1899, still features standardbred harness racing 5 nights a week (no races on Wed or Sun). Open daily 9 a.m. to 4 a.m. The raceway's first post is at 7:10 p.m. on Mon, Tues, Thurs, Fri, and Sat nights. No admission fee, but expect to spend money on gaming.

Hudson River Museum. 511 Warburton Ave.; (914) 963-4550; hrm.org. American art from the Hudson River School, the first uniquely American style of landscape painting, represents the heart of this museum's collection, but its holdings extend beyond the work of artists Asher B. Durand, Jasper Cropsey, and Samuel Coleman to include contemporary artists, 20th-century artists Georgia O'Keeffe and Andy Warhol, and exhibitions of modern painting, sculpture, art created on computer, and other media. The museum also features Glenview, the 19th-century home of the John Bond Trevor family, with six rooms fully restored to their turn-of-the-century opulence. Open Wed through Sun, noon to 5 p.m.; closed Mon and Tues; $6 adults, $3 children 3 to 18, $4 seniors 62+ and students with ID.

Legoland Discovery Center. 39 Fitzgerald St.; (866) 243-0770; legolanddiscoverycenter .com/westchester. If you're traveling with children between 3 and 10 years old, you will have difficulty getting out of Yonkers without spending at least a couple of hours at this extraordinary attraction. Tour the Lego Factory and help make bricks, see New York's skyline made from nearly 1.5 million Lego bricks, see what it's like to be Merlin's apprentice, climb the jungle gym in the Fire Academy, learn the tricks of the masters—yes, the Lego masters—in building amazing structures, and play in another 10 attractions throughout this fantasy world. Finally, don't forget to stop in the Discovery Center Shop next door to Legoland, where you can find just about any set your children want. Open Sun through Thurs 10 a.m. to 7 p.m. (last admission at 5 p.m.), Fri and Sat 10 a.m. to 9 p.m. (last entry 7 p.m.). Tickets $18 to $22 for walk-up; discounts for prebooking online.

Philipse Manor Hall State Historic Site. 29 Warburton Ave.; (914) 965-4027; nysparks .com/historic-sites/37/details.aspx. This colonial manor house was constructed in 1682 as the home of Frederick Philipse and his wife, Margaret Hardenbroeck, wealthy Dutch colonists who eventually owned all the land currently covered by the city of Yonkers. During the American Revolution, Philipse's grandson, Frederick Philipse III, chose loyalty to the British and demonstrated his sympathies by signing a "Declaration of Dependence" on November 28, 1776, just a few months after the Declaration of Independence had been signed in Philadelphia. With such a public gesture of loyalty to King George III of Great Britain, Philipse had no choice but to abandon his property and flee to England once the British lost the Revolutionary War. The new government of New York State sold his land and eventually turned this impressive home into a museum, first using it as Yonkers City Hall from 1872 to 1908. Open Apr through Oct, Tues through Sat noon to 5 p.m.; Nov through Mar, Tues through Sat noon to 4 p.m.; closed Mon and holidays; $5 adults, $3 seniors and students, free to children under 12.

Saw Mill River Daylighting. Van der Donck Park, Dock Street; (914) 377-6450; daylight yonkers.com. In 1917, with cities growing at a fast pace, developers in Yonkers thought it would be a great idea to build Larkin Plaza directly over half a mile of the Saw Mill River. Trapping the river underground and constructing Getty Square and North Broadway over it, these developers then directed the Saw Mill River to dump out into the Hudson as if it were a sewer overflow—because essentially, that's exactly what the river had become. Luckily, 21st-century environmentalists have a more enlightened view of city waterways—literally, in this case—and they devised a plan to bring the river back into the daylight and make it the centerpiece of Van de Donck Park. The Saw Mill River park will replace the parking lot bordered by Dock and Nepperhan Streets, Larkin Plaza, and the Yonkers train station. The daylighted portion of the river to date recreates nearly 14,000 square feet of aquatic habitat including a tidal pool and a stepped weir, making it possible for fish and eels to migrate naturally. Always open, free admission.

Science Barge. 99 Dock St.; (914) 375-2151; groundworkhv.org/programs/science-barge. NY Sun Works developed this prototype sustainable urban farm, and Groundwork Hudson Valley acquired it in 2008 to operate it as an education center. This floating greenhouse grows fresh produce with zero net carbon emissions, no pesticides, and no runoff. Solar panels, wind turbines, and biofuels generate the power the barge requires. The hydroponic greenhouse uses nothing but collected rainwater and purified river water for irrigation—so the entire operation is off the grid. Open mid-Apr through Nov, Sat and Sun noon to 6 p.m. Weekdays are only open for educational programs and field trips for schools, camps, and other groups. $3 suggested donation on weekends.

Sherwood House. 340 Tuckahoe Rd.; (914) 961-8940; yonkershistory.org. Not many tenant farmhouses of the pre–Revolutionary War era remain in the United States, so this 1740 structure becomes especially precious. Its original owner, Thomas Sherwood, built this home on land he leased from Frederick Philipse. Dr. John Ingersoll, Yonkers' first physician, bought the house in 1801. Today the house is protected and maintained by the Yonkers Historical Society, and is open on occasional Sundays in spring and summer for tours. Call the historical society for more information.

Untermeyer Gardens. 945 N. Broadway; (914) 377-6427; untermeyergardens.org. Samuel Untermeyer, the first attorney in America to earn a $1 million fee on a single case, made his fortune as a trust-busting lawyer who played a key role in establishing the Federal Reserve System. He amassed a considerable fortune in his career, and used a portion of it to indulge his passion for horticulture here at Greystone—the former family estate of New York Governor Samuel Tilden. Untermeyer started the gardens you see here in 1912, hiring Beaux Arts landscape artist Welles Bosworth to design them. At one time, the gardens covered 150 acres; today 43 of those acres belong to the City of Yonkers, and only the core gardens are intact. Apr 1 through Dec 1: Open daily 7 a.m. to sunset. Dec 2 through Mar 31: Mon through Sat 7 a.m. to sunset; closed Sun. The Walled Garden is closed on some holidays. Free admission, but donations are encouraged.

where to eat

Dolphin. 1 Van der Donck St.; (914) 751-8170; dolphinrbl.com. On the waterfront near the Yonkers railroad station, this trendy restaurant lights up in neon at night, creating the kind of vibe you expect from uptown Manhattan. Specializing in seafood, Dolphin brings together dishes from around the world, providing a wealth of culinary styles and flavors from Italian (penne and salmon in a creamy tomato sauce) to Asian (wasabi tuna over ginger sesame slaw). The artistic presentation just makes you want to order more. Lunch daily 11:45 a.m.

to 3 p.m.; dinner Mon through Thurs, 4 to 10 p.m.; Fri and Sat, 4 to 11 p.m.; Sun brunch, noon to 3 p.m., dinner 4 to 9 p.m. $$.

Xaviar's X20 on the Hudson. 71 Water Grant St.; (914) 965-1111; xaviars.com/restaurants/ xaviars-x20-on-the-hudson. Stunning views of the George Washington and Tappan Zee Bridges are the finishing touch to the highly original cuisine you'll find here. Combining French technique with Asian, Italian, and Spanish influences, Xaviar's creates something new—and you'll want to sample your dining companions' entrees just to experience more of it. Whether you order the whole roast duckling (meant to be shared), the veal sweetbreads with roasted figs, or the grilled salmon with ssamjang glaze, you'll have the sense that you've found an unusually interesting place to dine. Lunch Tues through Fri noon to 2 p.m.; Sun brunch noon to 2 p.m.; dinner Tues through Fri 5:30 to 10 p.m., Sat 5 to 10 p.m., Sun 5 to 9 p.m. $$$.

Yard House. 237 Market St.; (914) 375-9273; yardhouse.com. This high-quality national chain has only two restaurants in New York State—the other is in West Nyack—so that makes it worth mentioning here. You could make a meal from the snack menu alone, perhaps choosing the shrimp ceviche and shiitake garlic noodles, or adding one of the flatbreads (perhaps pear and gorgonzola), or make the most of the menu of house favorites, with a high-end macaroni and cheese that involves truffle oil, or the spicy jambalaya. You won't be hungry when you leave. Open daily at 11 a.m.; last call for food Sun through Thurs at 11:30 p.m., Fri and Sat at 1 a.m. $$.

Yonkers Miasarnia. 39 Lockwood Ave.; (914) 965-1665. This is more of a meat shop than a restaurant, but if you're missing your grandmother's authentic pierogies and kielbasa, a stop here is an absolute must. Polish cooking and baking can be hard to find outside of lower Manhattan, so stock up on babkas, strudel, and smoked meats before you head home—and you'll have a feast when you arrive. Tues, Wed, and Sat 8 a.m. to 6 p.m.; Thurs and Fri 8 a.m. to 8 p.m.; closed Sun and Mon. $.

day trip 09

lower valley: new york city

>>> **the path of clean water**
hastings-on-hudson, dobbs ferry, ny

What did it take to bring enough clean water into a vast metropolis crowded with millions of new residents? As immigration swelled in the first half of the 19th century, New York City became overwhelmed with families and neighborhoods using the limited water system and inadequate sewage management methods, stretching resources and polluting all of the area water supplies. New York's elected officials knew they had to take action as quickly as possible. The solution: Croton Aqueduct, a complex water distribution system that began at the Croton River in Westchester County and stretched 41 miles, using nothing but the power of gravity to move clean water into Manhattan's reservoirs.

Now known as the Old Croton Aqueduct, this water system remained in service until 1955—and today we can enjoy its route as a green space and walking trail through some of Westchester's most pleasant residential towns.

getting there

From the south, take NY 9A (Henry Hudson Parkway) to the Saw Mill River Parkway, and continue 5.3 miles on the Saw Mill to the Farragut Parkway/Hastings-on-Hudson exit. Turn left onto Farragut Parkway and continue to Broadway; take a slight right and then a left onto Main Street in Hastings-on-Hudson. **From the north,** take I-84 east or west to exit 135 in Fishkill. From the exit, take US 9 south to Hastings-on-Hudson. **By train:** Take Metro North's Hudson Line to Hastings-on-Hudson, Dobbs Ferry, or Irvington.

hastings-on-hudson, ny

Look north at the stunning expanse of the Hudson River, and south to the George Washington Bridge and the classic view of the Manhattan skyline, and you will understand how Jasper F. Cropsey, one of the leading artists in the Hudson River School, chose Hastings-on-Hudson as the place to build his home and studio. Cropsey was far from the first to appreciate the sweeping views and subtler charms of this town—a self-guided walking tour known as the Museum in the Streets takes visitors to 32 historic sites in the town's cozy neighborhoods, including many former homes. Linger here to enjoy the Main Street that *Westchester Magazine* honored with its 2008 Best Main Street Award.

what to do

Ever Rest, the Jasper F. Cropsey Home and Studio. 49 Washington Ave.; (914) 478-1372; newingtoncropsey.com/EverRest.html. The carpenter gothic–style home you see today was built in the 1830s, and became the property of Hudson River School artist Jasper and Maria Cropsey toward the end of Jasper's career. The Cropseys purchased the home with their retirement in mind, added a studio where Jasper continued to paint, and lived here together until the end of their days. Today the Newington-Cropsey Foundation maintains the home in much the way it appeared in Jasper and Maria's time. Tours on weekdays by appointment only, 10 a.m. to 1 p.m. Closed Sat, Sun, Dec 15 to Feb 1, and the month of Aug. No admission fee; donations are encouraged.

MacEachron Waterfront Park and Kinnally Cove. On River Street on the shores of the Hudson River; (914) 478-2380; hastingsgov.org/pages/HastingsNY_Recreation/parks. Here is the best place to see the Hudson River, the Palisades, the George Washington and Tappan Zee bridges, and the iconic Manhattan skyline from the comfort of a 1.3-acre park. Bring a picnic lunch and linger here to enjoy the view, or launch a kayak from Kinnally Cove and take in the view from the middle of the river. Open daily dawn to dusk; no admission fee.

Museum in the Streets. Beginning in Boulanger Plaza on Main Street and including Farragut Avenue, Olinda Avenue, Broadway, Draper Park, and Washington Avenue; (914) 478-2249; hastingshistorical.org/museuminthestreets.shtml. This walking tour of Hastings-on-Hudson opened in 2005 and now takes visitors to 34 locations throughout the village, with large informational signs at each of the stops. The signs provide all the information you need to understand the links between historic sites, and to piece together a vivid picture of this village's colorful past, complete with dozens of photos. Always open; no admission fee to walk the tour route.

Newington Cropsey Foundation Gallery of Art. 25 Cropsey Lane; (914) 478-7990; newingtoncropsey.com/NCFGallery.html. This newly constructed gothic revival building houses the Newington-Cropsey Foundation's collection of paintings by Jasper Cropsey in an octagonal gallery with 30-foot-high ceilings and in the Cross Gallery. Sculpted works by Frederick Hart and George Kelly are also featured here. Tours on weekdays by appointment only, 1 to 4 p.m. Closed Sat, Sun, Dec 15 to Feb 1, and the month of Aug. No admission fee; donations are encouraged.

where to eat

Harvest On Hudson. 1 River St.; (914) 478-2800; harvesthudson.com. Using the freshest vegetables and herbs from the garden on the restaurant's grounds, Harvest On Hudson bases its menu on the traditional cuisine of Italy. You'll find ingenious twists on your favorite pasta, pizza, and antipasti, as well as entrees that make the most of the area's farm-raised beef and poultry and delicacies from the sea. Lunch: Mon through Fri 11:45 a.m. to 2:30 p.m. Dinner: Mon through Thurs 5:30 to 10 p.m., Fri 5:30 to 11 p.m., Sat 5 to 11 p.m., Sun 4 to 9 p.m. $$$.

Juniper. 575 Warburton Ave.; (914) 478-2542; juniperhastings.com. Cozily intimate, Juniper provides a highly acclaimed and very popular weekend brunch as well as its lunch and dinner menus, with French touches and a focus on "new American" techniques. The result is a menu filled with surprises: duck breast dressed with picked ramps, roasted carrots with almond butter and pickled raisins, or a brisket burger topped with gruyère cheese, vegetables, and mustard aioli. The hands-down winner, however, is the French toast on the brunch menu, laden with seasonal fruit, wildflower honey, toasted almonds, and—what else?—crème fraîche. Wed through Fri 11 a.m. to 3 p.m. and 5:30 to 9 p.m., Sat 10 a.m. to 3 p.m. and 5:30 to 9 p.m., and Sun brunch 10 a.m. to 3 p.m., closed Mon and Tues. $$.

Sakura Garden. 531 Warburton Ave.; (914) 478-1978; sakurahastings.com. It's not often that you come across a Japanese restaurant that receives comparable raves for its hot dishes as well as its sushi, but this one brings guests back again and again. Attractive presentation is a staple of Japanese cuisine, and Sakura Garden meets and exceeds expectations with its special rolls, even incorporating fresh flowers among the sliced rolls and drizzled sauces. Dinners from the kitchen include many favorites and some surprisingly light stews (nabe mono), as well as hibachi dinners for those who love them. Lunch: Mon through Fri 11 a.m. to 3 p.m., Sat noon to 3 p.m. Dinner: Mon through Thurs 4:30 to 10 p.m., Fri 4:30 to 11 p.m., Sat 3 to 11 p.m., Sun 1:30 to 10 p.m. $$.

dobbs ferry, ny

The starting point of the 400-mile march by General George Washington's Continental Army to victory in Yorktown, Virginia, in 1781, Dobbs Ferry takes its name from Captain William H. Dobbs, who ran a ferry service across the Hudson River from this town. The town's Waterfront Park provides panoramic views of the river, as do restaurants that offer riverfront dining.

what to do

Old Croton Aqueduct State Historic Park. 15 Walnut St.; (914) 693-5259; nysparks .com/parks/96/details.aspx. It took 5 years, $13 million, and upwards of 4,000 workers— mostly Irish immigrants—to build the 41-mile-long aqueduct and dam that brought desperately needed fresh water into New York City's reservoirs. When the aqueduct opened in 1842, thousands of people came out for the celebration and enjoyed Croton cocktails, a mix of Croton River water and lemonade, as they hailed a feat of engineering that designers believed would last for centuries. The population of New York City continued to spiral upward at alarming rates, however, so by the 1880s a new aqueduct joined this one, and the two worked together to bring water into Manhattan until 1955.

What remains today is one of the area's oldest and most established walking trails. The Old Croton Aqueduct Trail connects the Lower Hudson Valley with Yonkers and the Bronx, providing a comfortable trail atop the protective covering of the earth that shields the aqueduct from the elements. The surface level has served as an informal walkway for local and long-distance pedestrians ever since that day in 1842, so you can walk in the footsteps of those who constructed this lifeline for the most congested areas of Lower Manhattan. Open daily dawn to dusk, no admission fee.

day trip 10

lower valley: new york city

headless ghosts & gravestones
tarrytown, sleepy hollow, ny

What kind of landscape could make an author of fantastical stories imagine a man with a jack-o-lantern head riding a skeletal horse? Find out when you visit Tarrytown, the home of legendary American writer Washington Irving, and the wooded glades and spooky cemetery in neighboring Sleepy Hollow.

getting there

From the south: Take the Henry Hudson Parkway (NY 9A) north to its junction with US 9 in Riverdale. Continue on the combined NY 9A and US 9 north 13 miles to Tarrytown. **From the north:** Take I-84 east or west to exit 135 in Fishkill. From the exit, take US 9 south to Tarrytown. **By train:** Take Metro North's Hudson Line to Tarrytown.

tarrytown, ny

Whether you believe that Tarrytown's name comes from the mispronunciation of "Terve Town," using the Dutch word for wheat, or you prefer Washington Irving's claim that the name came from local men's habit of tarrying at the local tavern, you must agree that this lovely little town is one of Westchester County's most picturesque. Its rolling hills, green spaces, striking architecture, and emphasis on its agricultural heritage make Tarrytown a must-stop in any tour of the lower Hudson Valley. A walk through town reveals the Warner Library, an impressive example of Beaux Arts architectural style, as well as a number of historic churches and the Old Croton Aqueduct Trail (see day trip 9). A recently renovated section of the aqueduct trail from the Lyndhurst grounds (see below) to Gracemere Park reopened in June 2014, joining two sections of the trail with a link that had been dormant for some time.

what to do

Lyndhurst. 635 S. Broadway; (914) 631-4481; lyndhurst.org. This 1838 gothic revival mansion is one of the finest in America, according to *Forbes* magazine and the National Trust for Historic Preservation. The castle-like structure sits atop a rise and is surrounded by parklike landscaping, creating a feeling of old world luxury just minutes from downtown New York. The three families who lived here sequentially throughout the 19th century transformed the original house from a country villa to this extraordinary mansion. Tours Fri through Sun, 10 a.m. to 5 p.m. (last tour begins at 4); closed Mon through Thurs; $14 adults, $13 seniors 65+, $10 children 6 to 12, free for children 5 and under.

Stone Barns Center for Food and Agriculture. 630 Bedford Rd.; (914) 366-6200; stonebarnscenter.org. Open and farming year-round, this visitor-friendly farm uses organic, regenerative farming practices to make sustainable agriculture a modern reality. Your self-guided tour will help you and your family understand how food gets from the field to your refrigerator, by visiting the ingredients as they grow and witnessing their harvest. There's plenty of livestock as well, grazing in the fields from May through Nov. Open Wed through Sun 10 a.m. to 5 p.m. May through Nov; $10 per vehicle on Fri, Sat, and Sun; otherwise admission is free.

Sunnyside (Washington Irving Home Museum). 89 W. Sunnyside Lane; (914) 631-8200; visitsleepyhollow.com/historic-sites/sunnyside. If you want to see where Washington Irving sat when he wrote *The Legend of Sleepy Hollow,* you've come to the right place. Irving lived in this house—originally a Dutch farmer's house—and the cottage-like home still contains many of the author's own possessions. Costumed guides provide commentary and interesting facts about Irving as you tour the home. Open May 4 through Nov 11, Wed through Sun for tours at 10:30 a.m., noon, 1:30 p.m., and 3 p.m.; Sat and Sun, additional tour at 3:30 p.m.; $12 adults, $10 seniors 65+, $6 children 3 to 17, free for children under 3.

Tarrytown Music Hall. 13 Main St.; (914) 631-3390; tarrytownmusichall.org. The oldest theater in Westchester, Tarrytown Music Hall was built in 1885 and currently presents music, theater, dance, and film, including performances by its resident companies: Westchester Symphonic Winds, Random Farms Kids' Theater, and Ars Viva Chamber Orchestra. Visit the website to find out what's playing during your planned visit. Ticket prices and performance dates vary; visit tickets.tarrytownmusichall.org for specific information.

where to eat

Bistro 12. 12 Main St.; (914) 909-2770; bistro12.net. Conveniently located just across the street from Tarrytown Music Hall, Bistro 12 succeeds with more than its prime position. The Mediterranean-style menu pushes the boundaries of traditional Italian fare to include delicacies like grilled octopus and a distinctly Ibero-style steamed clam dish, as well as caldo verde—collard greens and Portuguese sausage. Locals are overwhelmingly positive about this fairly new restaurant. Tues through Thurs noon to 10 p.m.; Fri and Sat noon to 10:30 p.m.; Sun 1 to 9:30 p.m.; closed Mon. $$$.

Equus. 400 Benedict Ave.; (914) 631-3646; castlehotelandspa.com/equusrestaurant.aspx. Seasonal menus of Auberge-style French cuisine based on locally sourced ingredients would make any restaurant special, but this one is in a castle—so be prepared for an exciting dining experience. Once you've selected which of the 3 dining rooms you'd prefer—the Garden Room with views of the gardens and the Hudson River Valley, the richly paneled Oak Room, or the Library with its paneled ceiling and mahogany bookcases—you'll then choose from the prix-fixe tasting menu or a range of a la carte items. Business-casual attire is appropriate, and the restaurant recommends that you experience this without your children. Breakfast 8 to 10 a.m. daily; lunch Mon through Sat noon to 2 p.m.; Sun brunch 11:30 a.m. to 2:30 p.m.; and dinner daily 6 to 9:30 p.m. $$$.

Lefteris Gyro. 1 N. Broadway; (914) 524-9687; lefterisgyro.com. Rave reviews for this taverna's Greek food led to its 2014 Certificate of Excellence from TripAdvisor—which makes it a must-stop when you're in Tarrytown if you're a fan of gyros, hearty soups, spanakopita, saganaki, and all manner of Mediterranean favorites. The bargain here is the selection of platters, each with a variety of Greek delicacies to sample: the Aegean platter, for example, provides moussaka, pastitsio, spanakopita, and gyro, as well as a salad, pita bread, and rice. Fast service (once you get a table at this very popular place), excellent food, and reasonable prices keep customers coming back. Open daily 11 a.m. to 10 p.m. $$.

sleepy hollow, ny

If this is your first trip through Westchester County, it may come as a surprise that there really is a Sleepy Hollow. Author Washington Irving penned his classic tale of Ichabod Crane and the Headless Horseman about this little village, and the real Sleepy Hollow has made the most of its frightening reputation with a pull-out-the-stops annual Halloween celebration, complete with street fairs, scary hayrides, parades, and a professionally produced haunted house called Horseman's Hollow. Even in the middle of July, however, you can get a sense of the macabre by visiting Irving's remains in the Sleepy Hollow Cemetery (not far from those of legendary industrialist and philanthropist Andrew Carnegie). Alternately, you can enjoy this small town's real-life history as the home of the ultra-rich Rockefeller family, the site of a tenant farming operation in the 1750s, and the unlikely location of a church that showcases stained glass windows created by Henri Matisse and Marc Chagall.

what to do

Kykuit. 381 N. Broadway; (914) 631-8200; hudsonvalley.org/historic-sites/kykuit. Four generations of the Rockefeller family lived in this glorious estate, starting with Standard Oil founder John D. Rockefeller, at the time the richest man in America. The 6-story stone house is open for tours of its main rooms, terraced gardens, underground art galleries where New York Governor Nelson Rockefeller's priceless tapestries still hang, and the Coach Barn with its classic automobile collection. All tours leave from Philipsburg Manor (see more below). Admission by timed tours only; tour times vary by date. Open in May, Sat, Sun, and Memorial Day; June through Sept, Wed through Sun and Labor Day; Oct, Wed through Mon (closed Tues); Nov 1 through 9, Sat and Sun. Closed Nov 10 through May 1. Tour tickets range from $23 to $40, based on the tour you choose.

Philipsburg Manor. 381 N. Broadway; (914) 631-8200 weekdays, (914) 631-3992 weekends; visitsleepyhollow.com/historic-sites/philipsburg-manor. Long before Tarrytown and Sleepy Hollow became the villages they are now, this entire area was part of the 52,000-acre tenant farming operation at Philipsburg Manor. Owner Frederick Philipse, a Dutch carpenter with an extraordinary business sense, assembled this massive amount of land and held onto it even when the British arrived and evicted his Dutch countrymen. While the Americans won the land from Philipse's descendants in the Revolutionary War, the tenant farming story remains so compelling that today's Philipsburg Manor continues to tell it. Your visit takes you back in time to 1750, when two dozen African slaves and hundreds of farmers grew crops on this land and turned over most of their harvests to the wealthy landowners. The Old Dutch Church in *The Legend of Sleepy Hollow* is part of this estate. Open Apr through Oct, Wed through Mon (closed Tues) 10 a.m. to 5 p.m.; Nov and Dec, Sat and Sun only, 10 a.m. to 4 p.m. Call for this year's admission fee.

Rockefeller State Park Preserve. 125 Phelps Way, Pleasantville; (914) 631-1470; nysparks.com/parks/59/details.aspx. Renowned nationwide for their love of the outdoors and their efforts to preserve open spaces—so much so that the National Park Service named the highway between Yellowstone and Grand Teton National Parks in John D. Rockefeller's honor—the Rockefeller family kept this segment of their vast estate pristine throughout their time in the Sleepy Hollow area. In 1983, the Rockefellers gave much of this preserve to the New York State Office of Parks, Recreation, and Historic Preservation, and additional bequests by the family have expanded the original park to more than 1,400 acres. You can come here to enjoy the 30 miles of carriage roads John built here, traveling them on foot, bicycle or horseback; explore the Important Bird Area, where more than 180 species of birds have been spotted; or visit the Peony Monument during its late April/early May bloom time. The 22-acre Swan Lake provides excellent brown trout fishing in season.

Open daily year-round from sunrise to sunset; $6 per vehicle, collected daily Apr through Oct, and on weekends Nov through Mar.

Sleepy Hollow Lighthouse. 299 Palmer Ave.; (914) 365-5109; visitsleepyhollow.com/historic-sites/sleepy-hollow-lighthouse. Visit Kingsland Point Park to see this lighthouse from land, an easy feat now that a landfill from a General Motors factory that once stood here moved the shoreline to within a few feet of the light. In the days when this lighthouse stood a half-mile offshore, it provided a warning beacon to help ships on the Hudson River maintain a safe distance from dangerous shoals. The 1883 light operated for 78 years until the lights on the Tappan Zee Bridge made the 5-story lighthouse unnecessary. Tours are offered on one weekend in July, Aug, Sept, and Oct; visit the website for dates and times; $5 adults, $3 children, no charge to view the lighthouse from shore.

Union Church of Pocantico Hills. 555 Bedford Rd., Pocantico Hills; (814) 631-2069; hudsonvalley.org/historic-sites/union-church-pocantico-hills. The influence of the Rockefeller family brought rare gifts to Sleepy Hollow, not the least of which were the stained glass windows in this neighborhood church. A rose window by world-renowned artist Henri Matisse turned out to be the artist's last work, a commission to honor the memory of Nelson Rockefeller's mother in 1954. Mrs. Rockefeller helped to found the Museum of Modern Art in New York City, and her son's passion for the work of living artists led him to form a relationship with Matisse. Nelson's brother, David, brought Mark Chagall's work to the same church when he commissioned the first of eight windows in the church nave. Over time, all eight windows by Chagall came to memorialize members of the Rockefeller family. Open Apr 2 to early Nov, Wed through Fri and Mon (closed Tues) 11 a.m. to 5 p.m., Sat 10 a.m. to 5 p.m., Sun 2 to 5 p.m.; Nov 10 through Dec 31, weekdays (closed Tues) 11 a.m. to 4 p.m., Sat 10 a.m. to 4 p.m., Sun 2 to 4 p.m.; $7 all tickets; discounts for visitors who have tickets to Kykuit.

where to eat

Blue Hill at Stone Barns. 630 Bedford Rd.; (914) 366-9600; bluehillfarm.com/food/blue-hill-stone-barns. Within the Stone Barns Center for Food and Agriculture, this upscale restaurant sources its ingredients from the fields and pastures of this sustainable, organic farm. There's no menu—instead, you will enjoy a prix-fixe, multi-course farmer's feast, featuring the freshest, most plentiful local ingredients available on the day you dine. Jackets and ties are required for men; no shorts are permitted. Wed through Sat 5 to 10 p.m., Sun 1 to 5 p.m. $$$.

Bridge View Tavern. 226 Beekman Ave.; (914) 332-0078; bridgeviewtavern.com. Ten-ounce burgers served on freshly baked brioche, beer-battered codfish with homemade tartar sauce and chips, dressed-up po' boy and Cuban sandwiches, and a long list of other goodies earned this casual restaurant TripAdvisor's 2014 Certificate of Excellence. Don't miss the view of the Hudson River that gives this tavern its name. Tues through Sun 11:30 a.m. to 10 p.m., Mon 4 to 10 p.m. $$.

Finalmente Trattoria. 31 Beekman Ave.; (914) 909-4787; www.destinationsleepyhollow .org/2010/06/finalmente-trattoria-italiana-wine-bar-.html. You haven't seen entrees like these in your average Italian restaurants: rack of New Zealand lamb; pappardelle in a wild boar, grape tomato, and blueberry grappa sauce; or red snapper in a garlic and clam sauce—accompanied by a substantial list of Italian wines. This intimate restaurant's European feel becomes even more pronounced in summer, when the back patio is open to dining guests. Save room for the ricotta cheesecake. Lunch Tues through Fri, dinner Tues through Sun, closed Mon. $$.

Fleetwood Pizza. 70 Beekman Ave.; (914) 631-3267; fleetwoodpizza.com. Making slices to order usually means that a pizzeria makes a whole pie and reheats the slices, but at Fleetwood, every slice is made when the customer orders it—and the result makes this one of the most popular and highly rated pizzerias in Westchester County. If you want more than a slice—and you will—you can choose from more than a dozen specialty pies, or switch to calzones, rolls, or the famous chicken or meatball Parmigiana sandwiches (or one of many others, all served on fresh Italian bread). The proprietors have made pizza here since 1963, so you can feel confident they've got it right. Mon through Sat 11 a.m. to 10 p.m., closed Sun. $$.

day trip 11

lower valley: new york city

>>> art & soul on the hudson
nyack, ny

nyack, ny

There's something about the light here in Nyack as it comes into town off the Hudson River—something that made painter Edward Hopper spend his life here and paint exactly what he saw. It may be the light that attracted a bevy of famous artists from many different genres to West Nyack in the 1940s, where they founded what is now the Rockland Center for the Arts (RoCA)—luminaries like Aaron Copeland, Helen Hayes, Kurt Weill, Lotte Lenya, Paulette Goddard, and Maxwell Anderson all had a hand in developing this celebration of creativity.

Most of Rockland County is one gigantic bedroom community, but here in Nyack the county gathers up the best of its artistic and cultural offerings and puts them forward—in a town center that makes you want to slow down, stroll through shops, chat with gallery owners, sample some intriguing restaurants, and take in a concert or a show.

getting there

From the north or south, take the New York State Thruway to exit 10 (Nyack), north of the Tappan Zee Bridge on the west bank of the Hudson River. From the exit, follow NY 59 (Main Street) east into town. US 9W also passes through Nyack and North Highland Avenue; take it north or south to Main Street in Nyack, and turn east to reach the town center. **Metro North:** Take the train to the Tarrytown station, and take the Tappan Zee Express Bus to Nyack. The Tappan Zee Express does not run on Sunday.

what to do

Carson McCullers House. 131 S. Broadway, South Nyack. Listed on the National Register of Historic Places, this two-story Second Empire–style home was built in 1880, and received a colonial revival update in 1910. Author Carson McCullers lived here from 1945 until her death in 1967, during which time her novel *A Member of the Wedding* was adapted for Broadway, and she wrote *The Square Root of Wonderful,* based on her experiences related to her husband's suicide in 1953. The house is privately owned, but you are welcome to view it from the street.

Edward Hopper House Art Center. 82 N. Broadway; (845) 358-0774; edwardhopper house.org. The birthplace and childhood home of 20th-century artist Edward Hopper now operates as a nonprofit art center and museum, and you can tour it with a docent if you arrive on a weekend afternoon. Its exhibitions are carefully selected by a volunteer committee of professional artists and curators, and they feature a wide range of artistic styles and media—check the website to see what may be showing during your visit. Wed through Sun, noon to 5 p.m.; closed Mon and Tues; $6 adults, $4 seniors, $2 students, free to students 16 and under; also free to all visitors on the first Friday of each month.

Johnny Apollo Gallery. 88 Main St.; (845) 358-5859; rocklandart.com. The headquarters of RocklandArt.com, Johnny Apollo Gallery presents the work of local artists in a wide range of styles and media. Here you can find an excellent representation of the area's most established and most promising new artists. Tues through Fri 10 a.m. to 6 p.m.; Sat 10 a.m. to 5 p.m.; Sun 1 to 5 p.m.; closed Mon. Free admission.

Pretty Penny. 235 N. Broadway; private phone. The former home of actress Helen Hayes and her husband, playwright Charles MacArthur, this privately owned 19th-century mansion recently listed for $4.9 million when it went up for sale in early 2014. Here Hayes entertained the upper crust of the Hollywood set, including Cole Porter, Laurence Olivier, Vivian Leigh, Marilyn Monroe, and President Ronald Reagan, to name just a few. Rosie O'Donnell bought the home from Hayes's family after her death in 1993 and completed an extensive renovation, and since then it has changed hands several times. Exquisitely maintained and featuring award-winning gardens and a 60-foot swimming pool, the home stands behind a brick privacy wall that Hayes and MacArthur had built for them—but that a subsequent owner raised for additional security. You are welcome to drive by to take a look, but the house is not open to the public.

where to eat

8 North Broadway. 8 N. Broadway; (845) 353-1200; 8northbroadway.com. Taking Mediterranean cuisine to the next level of culinary excellence, 8 North Broadway combines local Hudson Valley ingredients with creativity and presentational style to provide a different kind of dining experience. The menu changes daily based on what's available locally, but there's always a 3-course prix-fixe option as well as the entrees, and the mezze menu at the bar provides a lower-cost, equally tasty alternative while you sip some on-tap wine. Lunch Mon through Fri noon to 3 p.m.; dinner Mon through Sun 5 to 10 p.m.; Sun brunch 11:30 a.m. to 4 p.m. $$.

Casa Del Sol. 104 Main St.; (845) 353-9100; casaofnyack.com. Every day's a festival at Casa Del Sol, where fine Latin cuisine is served in an atmosphere filled with color and south of the border style. Start your dining experience with selections from the tapas menu, and then add a pasta dish—yes, pasta, like the Brazilian moqueca, featuring a wealth of seafood in a saffron-cilantro tomato broth tossed with linguine—or choose something really off the beaten path, like the shrimp Napoleon prepared with a creamy Creole sauce and blue corn tostadas. If your mouth isn't watering yet, you're not paying attention. Open daily noon to late-night closing. $$.

Harry's Burritos. 90 Main St.; (845) 353-5520; harrysburritos.com. Harry's brings Cal-Mex cooking to New York, beginning with a restaurant in New York City in 1987 and expanding to Nyack in 2007. Using only fresh ingredients and swearing against lard or other animal fats, Harry's prepares all manner of traditional Mexican dishes, including tacos, nachos, quesadillas, enchiladas, salads, and chili—not to mention a wide variety of burritos. For a quick, inexpensive meal, Harry's will leave you satisfied. Sun through Thurs 11:30 a.m. to 10 p.m.; Fri and Sat 11:30 a.m. to 11 p.m. $.

Hudson House of Nyack. 134 Main St.; (845) 353-1355; hudsonhousenyack.com. This clever conversion of the 19th-century former village hall and jailhouse results in a 2-story restaurant in a surprisingly elegant setting. The jail cells now house the wine cellar, and the courtroom serves as the upstairs dining room, where contemporary American dishes incorporate styles and flavors from many different regions of the country. Dinner entrees, for example, include Berkshire pork chop and Hudson Valley duck breast, as well as a Carolina low country favorite, shrimp and grits. Tues through Thurs 5:30 to 10 p.m.; Fri 5:30 to 11 p.m.; Sat 11:30 a.m. to 3:30 p.m. and 5:30 to 11 p.m.; Sun 11.30 a.m. to 3:30 p.m. and 4:30 to 9:30 p.m.; closed Mon. $$$.

Murasaki Japanese Cuisine. 138 Main St.; (845) 358-3222; murasakinyack.com. Taking sushi, maki, and classic Japanese dishes a step beyond the traditional, Murasaki offers all the lovely presentation and familiar flavors you expect, but with a variety of new combinations. Lunch Mon through Fri noon to 2:30 p.m.; dinner Mon through Thurs 5 to 10 p.m.; Fri and Sat 5 to 11 p.m.; Sun 5 to 9:30 p.m. $$$.

Olive's. 118 Main St.; (845) 358-3120; oliveboss1.wix.com/olives. Harvesting seasonal organic vegetables from the proprietor's own garden, offering an ample supply of vegetarian and vegan choices as well as dishes for the carnivorous, and bringing it all together with live music nightly, Olive's maintains the hip, indie vibe you came to Nyack to find. Late-night hours make this place a hotspot with locals and visitors alike. Thurs through Sat noon to 4 a.m.; Sun through Wed noon to 3 a.m. Kitchen closes at 12:30 a.m. $$.

Playhouse Market. 20 S. Broadway; (845) 358-3575; playhousemarket.com. Here's the place to relax with a cup of coffee, a freshly baked treat, and strong Wi-Fi. Once the home of the Tappan Zee Playhouse and the Helen Hayes Theatre, this nicely redesigned coffeehouse also offers workshops, cooking demonstrations, live music, and beer and wine tastings. The furnishings, plates, lamps, and even the tables are created by local artists and are all for sale. Shop while you sip. Mon 6 a.m. to 9:30 p.m., Tues through Thurs 6 a.m. to 10:30 p.m., Fri and Sat 6 a.m. to midnight, Sun 6 a.m. to 11 p.m. $.

where to shop

Just about all the shops are closed on Monday. Be sure to schedule your time in Nyack from Tuesday through Sunday.

Finds Sample Sale. 60 S. Broadway; (845) 727-5000; discovernyack.com/business -directory/807/finds-sample-sale. Have you ever wished you could get your hands on manufacturers' samples of the clothing for the upcoming season? You can, here at a store that makes designer samples its entire inventory. There's no telling what you might find here, so come early and think about coming back often, especially if you like discounts of 50 to 70 percent off retail. Tues through Sun 11 a.m. to 6 p.m.; closed Mon.

Hickory Dickory Dock. 43 S. Broadway; (845) 358-7474; discovernyack.com/business -directory/125/hickory-dickory-dock. If you love clocks and appreciate fine handiwork in the European tradition, you may find your heart's desire at this unusual store. Clocks, beer steins, nutcrackers, smoking men, handblown glass, and more come to this establishment from the finest craftspeople in Germany, while the clock inventory also features the best of Chelsea of Boston, Comiti of London, and a number of others. Tues through Sun 11 a.m. to 6 p.m.; closed Mon.

Maria Luisa Boutique. 77 S. Broadway; (845) 353-4122; marialuisaboutique.com. For quality, elegance, style, and comfort—watchwords for Maria Luisa Whittingham, who chooses every item this store offers—shoppers turn to this boutique for the latest in women's fashions. Shoes and accessories are featured just as prominently as the clothing styles, and there's even a baby corner where you can find out what color tutu the well-dressed toddler will be wearing this year. Tues through Sun 10 a.m. to 6 p.m.; closed Mon.

p. ross boutique. 89 Main St.; (845) 348-1767; facebook.com/pages/pross-boutique. Fashion accessories created by local and American designers and a selection of Italian imports make this boutique a must-stop for women and men alike. You'll find the p. ross line of shoes and boots, as well as handbags, jewelry, ties, and clothing that you won't find in your mall's department stores. Tues through Sat 11 a.m. to 6 p.m.; Sun noon to 6 p.m.; closed Mon.

Saffron Trading Company. 14 S. Broadway; (845) 353-3530; saffrontradingcompany .com. For the accents that create a sense of the exotic and eclectic in your home decor, visit this store with its remarkable selection of occasional furnishings, accessories like stoneware and frosted glass, baskets galore, and even scented products for the home and bath. Tues through Sun 11 a.m. to 6 p.m.; closed Mon.

Sanctuary. 60 S. Broadway; (845) 353-2126; sanctuary-home.com. As the name of this shop implies, Sanctuary helps you create your own in-home getaway with scents, hand-made jewelry, organic clothing, soaps, lotions and potions, and other fair-trade items. You'll find plenty of choices to help you bring on the sense of stress release so many of us seek at the end of the day—or even all day. Tues through Sun 11 a.m. to 6 p.m.; closed Mon.

Sign of the Times. 112 Main St.; (845) 353-4059; facebook.com/SignoftheTimesNyack. Here is the store you expected to find in Nyack, a trendy shop that carries tie-dyed cloth-ing and pillows with peace symbols alongside baby onesies and fake moustaches. From stationery to candles, T-shirts to trivets, and Hanukkah stockings to satin robes, this store will satisfy all of your gifting needs. You may want to hang out here just for the music. Tues through Sun 11 a.m. to 6 p.m.; closed Mon.

day trip 12

lower valley: new york city

>>> **meander along the delaware**
port jervis, ny

A startlingly scenic and equally surprisingly unsung area of downstate New York lies between Port Jervis to the east and Hancock to the west—an area with a storied past, a key role in the development of New York, and some of the prettiest views in the northeastern United States.

getting there

From the east, take I-84 south to exit 1. At the end of the ramp, take US 6 (the GAR Highway) west toward Port Jervis. Cross the Neversink River and continue into the town of Port Jervis. **From the west,** take NY 42 south or NY 97 east until the two merge just before Port Jervis. Continue on the merged NY 42/97 into Port Jervis. **From the south,** take I-84 north across the New York/New Jersey border to exit 1 in New York; follow directions above. **From the north,** take US 209 south to the junction with US 6 in Port Jervis. **By train:** Take the New Jersey Transit Port Jervis Commuter Line from Hoboken, NJ or Penn Station in New York City.

port jervis, ny

Your exploration of the Delaware River begins here in this former railroad town, now a hub for outdoor adventure on the Upper Delaware and Neversink Rivers. Known now for its access to canoeing, river rafting, swimming, and kayaking, this city once served as the pivot point for travelers continuing upstate into the Catskill Mountains or heading down into New Jersey and New York on business. With the increase in automobile traffic, passenger railroad faded—but Port Jervis continues to maintain its status as a pivot point, largely because of the sweeping views of its two rivers and the easy access to river sport. Carefully preserved and restored architecture throughout the town provides a look back to Port Jervis's heyday, when wealthy individuals and municipalities built striking homes and public buildings for the railroad, fire department, town offices, and others.

where to go

Erie Railroad Station. Corner of Jersey Avenue and Fowler Street; en.wikipedia.org/wiki/Port_Jervis_(Erie_Railroad_station). This nicely renovated, Queen Anne–style building once acted as the hub for passenger travel from here into the Catskills and along the river, making it one of the busiest stations on the Delaware branch of the railroad. The *Erie Limited* and *Lake Cities* trains ran directly through this station en route to Chicago and Hoboken. Metro North now provides passenger service from here to New York City, and it chose not to use the old station—but the building was added to the National Register of Historic Places in 1980, saving it from possible demolition. Today you'll find a number of shops in the station. Hours vary at the shops within the station.

Fort Decker Museum of History. 127 W. Main St.; (845) 856-2375; minisink.org/forthist.html. Built in 1793 by Lieutenant Martinus Decker, who fought for the Continental Army in the Revolutionary War, this house actually predates the town of Port Jervis, and it remains the oldest structure in the area. It served as a hotel on the Delaware and Hudson Canal during the 1820s and then became a residence, until the Minisink County Historical Society bought it in 1958 and turned it into a museum. Open May through Oct on the last Sat of the month, 1 to 4 p.m., and during special events. Donations encouraged.

Gillinder Glass Factory and Museum. Erie Street; (845) 856-5375; gillinderglassstore.com. Tour the factory where Gillinder glass has been made since 1913, a plant opened well after English artisan William Gillinder made his glass famous at the Centennial Exposition in Philadelphia in 1876. Today you can tour the factory—owned by Charles Gillinder, a member of the sixth generation to create Gillinder glass—to see skilled employees gathering and pressing glass, and using state-of-the-art robotics and equipment to create pieces with technically enhanced color and illumination. Gillinder glass is now used in just about half of all the airport runway lights in the United States, as well as in aircraft lights for the Black Hawk helicopters and C-5A Galaxy transports. Tours Mon through Fri at 10:15 a.m. and at 12:30 and 1:30 p.m. Check the website for dates of special glass-blowing tours. $5 adults, $4 seniors and children. Gift store hours: Mon through Fri 9:30 a.m. to 5:30 p.m., Sat 9:30 a.m. to 4 p.m., Sun noon to 4 p.m.

Park Avenue Observatory. Park Avenue. A 1933 Civilian Conservation Corps project, Park Avenue Observatory was created to give area residents and visitors the best possible access to one of the state's most appealing panoramic views. From this platform on a ridge above the river, you can see mountains in both Pennsylvania and New Jersey, as well as the Upper Delaware River as it winds southward. Look straight out to identify High Point in New Jersey's Skylands region, which at 1,803 feet is the highest peak in the state. Always open, no admission fee.

Port Jervis Fire Museum. 8 Orange St.; (845) 234-0953. The Old Engine Company #1 Fire Station opened as a museum in 2007, and it now features memorabilia from the city's archives and items donated by local residents. It's administered by the Port Jervis volunteer fire department. If it's not open when you visit, call the number below in advance to make an appointment to see inside. Open the last Saturday of the month, May through Oct 1 to 4 p.m., and in July after the fire parade. Free admission, donations encouraged.

Tri-States Monument. Off Main Street in Laurel Grove Cemetery; (845) 858-4000. At the farthest point in the cemetery under the I-84 overpass, the Delaware and Neversink Rivers meet, creating the spot for Port Jervis's most famous landmark. Here you can stand in New York, New Jersey, and Pennsylvania at the same time. A major dispute was settled at this very spot back in 1769, even before the Revolutionary War: With the establishment of this boundary, the colonies of East and West Jersey and New York finally had confirmation of the location of the state line. This ended a bitter war between farmers over the square acreage of their property—one that had caused farmers to burn one another's crops, engage in fistfights, and even schedule a sort of rumble that fizzled when they realized they'd planned it for a Sunday, when the church forbade fighting. King George III finally drew the line along the river, bringing the noisome dispute to a long-awaited close. Always open, no admission fee.

where to go near port jervis

Hawk's Nest Scenic Overlook. Route 97 near Deerpark; portjervisny.com/hawks_nest_in_autumn.htm. About 4 miles west of Port Jervis, one of the most interesting roads in the state emerges suddenly, and it comes as something of a surprise to unsuspecting drivers. This run of curvy, cliff-hugging twists and turns is known as the Hawk's Nest, and it came to be through an accident of ownership. A single lane of dirt road existed along the cliffs here since 1859, as this harrowing but speedy route provided the fastest access between the villages and hamlets along the river and the more densely populated areas to the southeast. When the state planned a new highway through here in the 1930s, however, engineers selected a new route along the river's edge, eliminating the need for a road that followed a precarious cliff ledge. Despite widespread agreement that the new route would be better, the consensus did not reach as far as the Erie Railroad, the owner of this riverside land. The railroad refused to sell, and the engineers had no choice but to design as safe a route as possible high on the cliff face. The result is Hawk's Nest, a delight to drive and a legend among sportscar enthusiasts, motorcycle riders, and bicyclists who love the thrill of curvaceous speed. A low stone wall lines the road, the only barrier between you and a drop of several hundred feet to the riverbed. The posted speed limit here is 55 miles per hour with caution signs that lower this to 25, but few drivers seem to pay any attention to this—so keep your eyes open for drivers taking this route much faster than safety would suggest. Pull-offs allow you to stop and enjoy the magnificent view of the Pennsylvania hills from this lofty perch. Always open, no admission fee.

Roebling Bridge and Delaware Aqueduct. Between Minisink Ford, New York, and Lackawaxen, Pennsylvania; (570) 685-4871; nps.gov/upde/historyculture/roeblingbridge .htm. Named for its designer, engineer John A. Roebling (who would go on to design and supervise the construction of the Brooklyn Bridge), this bridge is the oldest existing wire cable suspension bridge in the US. Roebling designed it as an aqueduct, a key element in the Delaware and Hudson Canal and Gravity Railroad, which transported anthracite coal from northeastern Pennsylvania to the Hudson River, where it was sold to heat homes and businesses in New York City. The bridge, an impressive piece of workmanship, replaced a rope ferry crossing that had slowed traffic at the Delaware River. It opened in 1848 and alleviated the bottleneck, making the D&H Canal competitive with railroads and other canals and sustaining its operation until the canal's closure in 1898. When the National Park Service bought the aqueduct in 1980, it had become a driving bridge and had fallen into disrepair. The park service supervised a restoration that included reconstruction of the superstructure according to Roebling's original plans, returning the bridge to its original design and making it an enduring—and useful—landmark. For a full experience of the bridge and a way to stretch your legs, walk the 1-mile Towpath Trail that begins at the parking area near the bridge. Always open, no admission fee.

Upper Delaware Scenic and Recreational River. Beginning in Port Jervis and continuing up NY 97 west to Hancock, New York; (570) 685-4871; nps.gov/upde. The 73.4 miles of the Upper Delaware River protected here offer opportunities for freshwater fishing, hunting, boating, canoeing, birding, and simply admiring the scenery, but these pristine waters represent much more than a great place to play. This river supported human life as early as 15,000 BC, facilitated timber rafting in the late 1700s—bringing pine and hemlock downstream for use in industry—and became an agricultural center in the 19th century. As New York's economy shifted from agrarian to industrial, the river played an important role in the Northeast's meteoric growth when its waters transported anthracite from Pennsylvania for fuel, and bluestone and other gravels to New York City for use in building roads. Today, the Upper Delaware supplies more than 17 million people with drinking water, and nearly 500,000 come every year to enjoy outdoor sports on and around the river. Most sites on the river are open around the clock; no admission fee.

Zane Grey Museum. 136 Scenic Dr., Lackawaxen, Pennsylvania; (570) 685-4871; nps .gov/upde/historyculture/zanegrey.htm. You wouldn't guess it from the authenticity of his novels—the best remembered of which is *Riders of the Purple Sage*—but Zane Grey did most of his early writing about the American West from his home in New York City, and later from this house in Lackawaxen until he moved his family to California in 1918. Grey became an iconic figure first with Westerns and later in outdoor and adventure writing, and his life was nearly as exciting as those of his characters—a lifestyle made possible by the wealth he generated through his ability to turn out several new books every year. An accomplished deep-sea fisherman, Grey held more than 10 world records for catching large game fish, including his rank as the first person to catch a fish over 1,000 pounds on rod and reel (a 1,040-pound blue marlin in Tahiti in 1930). Whether you're a Zane Grey fan or simply an outdoor enthusiast, you'll find something that will please you on the 20-minute tour of this Lackawaxen home. Open Memorial Day through Labor Day, 10 a.m. to 5 p.m. daily; Sept, Wed through Sun 10 a.m. to 5 p.m.; Oct 1 through 20, Sat and Sun 10 a.m. to 5 p.m.; closed Oct 21 through end of May. No admission fee.

where to eat

Arlene and Tom's. 265 E. Main St.; (845) 856-8488; facebook.com/Meanyburger. For hearty sandwiches, meaty burgers, a nice selection of sides, and big wedges of pie with ice cream, you can't beat a popular diner in a small town. Arlene and Tom's provides all of this in a cozy place with a sense of history—perhaps because of the black-and-white photos of the town's history that adorn the walls. This is the old-school eatery you remember from the 1950s and 1960s, before the chain restaurants took over. Mon 8 a.m. to 4 p.m., Tues through Sat 7 a.m. to 9 p.m., Sun 8 a.m. to 8 p.m. $.

Gio's Gelato Cafe. 31 Pike St.; (845) 858-4467; facebook.com/pages/Gios-Gelato-Cafe. Fresh ingredients and proprietary recipes make this little eatery a favorite with locals and those passing through. You can see your panini and wraps being made, and the variety of options surpasses most small restaurants. Most important, save room for the gelato, all of which is made on premises using local dairy products and fresh fruit, nuts, and flavors. You'll find 24 flavors available just about any time you visit. Mon through Wed 8 a.m. to 3 p.m.; Thurs 8 a.m. to 7 p.m.; Fri 8 a.m. to 9 p.m.; Sat 7 a.m. to 9 p.m.; Sun 7 a.m. to 3 p.m. $.

A Taste of Sicily. 50–52 Front St.; (845) 858-3663; facebook.com/ATasteofSicily. Top-notch Italian food from a chef with more than 30 years' experience—that's what you'll find at this fairly new restaurant, and all at remarkably reasonable prices. Whether you're craving pasta, chicken, veal, or seafood, you'll find your favorites beautifully presented here, and they generate rave reviews from patrons. Tues through Thurs 11 a.m. to 9 p.m., Fri and Sat 11 a.m. to 10 p.m., Sun noon to 8 p.m. $$.

day trip 13

lower valley: new york city

points of view: the hudson highlands
croton-on-hudson, peekskill, beacon, ny

From Storm King Mountain to Dunderberg Mountain, the Hudson Highlands provide some of the finest views of the river and surrounding valley that you will find in downstate New York. It's no wonder that there's a concentration of parks, manor homes, and historic sites here, as this cluster of ridges and daunting expanses of water became one of the most desirable and strategically important areas in the lower third of the state.

getting there

From the north, take I-84 to the Fishkill exit (13S), and take US 9W south 26 miles to Croton-on-Hudson, or 18 miles to Peekskill. **From the south,** take the Henry Hudson Parkway (NY 9A) north, and stay on NY 9A to the Taconic Parkway. Continue to follow NY 9A as it exits in 0.9 miles, and exit toward NY 129. Turn right onto Municipal Place, and take the first left onto S. Riverside Avenue. Continue into Croton-on-Hudson. To reach Peekskill, follow US 9 out of town to the north, and follow US 9 for 8 miles to Peekskill.

croton-on-hudson, ny

Dutch traders chose Croton Landing as a good place for a settlement back in the 1660s, not long after they signed a peace treaty with the local Kitchawanc Indians under an oak tree in what is now Croton Point Park. What began as a farming community became a center of shipbuilding, flour milling, and brick manufacturing by the mid-19th century, and labor eventually turned to the construction of the Croton and New Croton Dams and the New Croton Aqueduct. This brought an influx of Irish, Italian, and German immigrants into the area, many of who remained here and raised families as steady work continued into the 20th century. Writers, artists, musicians, and actors flocked to this area and formed neighborhoods of people in the arts, and the area still maintains a thriving artistic community today. Your visit here takes in the most important industrial developments of the village's rich history, as well as its scenic and artistic merits.

what to do

Brinton Brook Sanctuary. At the top of Arrowcrest Drive off of NY 9A, just before the entrance to Hudson National Golf Club; (914) 666-6503; sawmillriveraudubon.org. Saw Mill River Audubon's largest sanctuary, Brinton Brook spans 156 acres and features a pond, meadows, a red maple swamp, hardwood forests, a rocky slope, and 3 miles of marked trails. Open daily dawn to dusk, no admission fee.

Croton Gorge Park. NY 129; (914) 827-9568; parks.westchestergov.com/croton-gorge-park. This 97-acre park includes Croton Dam, the first large masonry dam in the United States when it was completed in 1842. Many other municipalities used this dam as a prototype for their own water systems throughout the 19th century, until New York City's need for water outgrew this dam and the water distribution industry moved on to larger and more advanced dam architecture. In addition to this glimpse of the past, you can enjoy hiking, picnicking, and fishing here. A trail from the park leads directly to the Old Croton Aqueduct Trail. Open daily 8 a.m. to dusk, $10 parking fee per vehicle May through Sept ($5 with Park Pass).

Croton Point Park. 14A Croton Point Ave.; (914) 862-5290; parks.westchestergov.com/croton-point-park. This peninsula in the Hudson River contains a 508-acre park with charms beyond its views of the river. Here you will find the oldest wine cellars in New York State, part of the farmland purchased by Robert Underhill in 1804 and used to age the wine his son Richard made from vineyards planted here. At the end of the peninsula, archaeologists discovered the oldest oyster-shell middens on the North Atlantic coast, proof that Native Americans inhabited this peninsula as much as 7,000 years ago. Open daily 8 a.m. to dusk, $10 parking fee per vehicle Memorial Day weekend through Labor Day ($5 with Park Pass).

Teatown Lake Reservation. 1600 Spring Valley Rd., Ossining; (914) 762-2912; teatown .org. This 1,000-acre preserve includes 3 lakes, streams, waterfalls, hardwood forests, meadows, and plenty of other green spaces to explore on 15 miles of hiking trails. The Nature Center within the preserve has exhibits with live animals and birds of prey, art exhibitions, a Wildflower Island with more than 230 species of native wildflowers, a working maple-sugar house, and a bee and butterfly garden. Trails open daily dawn to dusk, nature center open Sat and Sun 9 a.m. to 5 p.m. No admission fee; donations encouraged.

Van Cortlandt Manor. 525 S. Riverside Ave.; (914) 631-8200; hudsonvalley.org/historic -sites/van-cortlandt-manor. One of New York's most prominent families lived here in this manor house in the years following the Revolutionary War, and their way of life—which included tenant farming, slaveholding, involvement in debates over the drafting of the US Constitution, religious issues, and all of the challenges of living in 18th-century America. Furnished in both the colonial and federal styles to depict the manor's long history, the house includes one of the largest colonial kitchens in the United States, a garden filled with medicinal and culinary plants, and the expansive grounds. Open July and Aug only, Sat and Sun for timed tours at 10:30 a.m., noon, and 1:30 and 3 p.m. $12 adults, $10 seniors 65 and older, $6 children 3 to 17, free to children under 3.

where to eat

Ocean House. 49 N. Riverside Ave.; (914) 271-0702; oceanhouseoysterbar.com. Have you ever had a mixed dozen oysters? Here at Ocean House, the blue-point gets left in the dust as the proprietors select the best fresh shellfish from all over the east coast—and as far away as Washington state. The house takes a New England–style approach to seafood, with creamy clam "chowda," Maine crab cakes, and lobster rolls, while the menu veers from Moroccan spiced Gulf shrimp to a whole branzino, the sea bass of the Mediterranean. Save room for an apple empanada with warm caramel sauce. Tues through Sat 5 p.m. to closing; closed Sun and Mon. $$$.

Tavern at Croton Landing. 41 N. Riverside Ave.; (914) 271-8020; thetavernatcroton.com. If you happen to be in Croton-on-Hudson on a Tuesday, the tavern offers its wildly popular lobster roll for a special reduced price—as good a reason as any to plan a weekday visit. Burgers, wings, thin-crust pizza, and a generous selection of starters and sides make this an easy, satisfying place for lunch or dinner. Tues through Sun 11 a.m. to 10 p.m.; closed Mon. $$.

Tagine. 120 Grand St.; (914) 827-9393; taginecroton.com. The delights of French Morocco find their way to Westchester at this stylish restaurant and wine bar, where the owners of Umami (see below) flex their culinary muscle in a different direction. A tagine is a meal with meat and vegetables, cooked together in an earthenware pot in the North African style; in addition to a selection of tagines, you'll find kebabs with couscous, a range of French-inspired entrees, and a selection of local and French cheeses as a dessert choice. Best of all, this lovely menu is surprisingly affordable. Tues through Sun 5 p.m. to closing; closed Mon. $$.

Umami Cafe. 325 S. Riverside Ave.; (914) 271-5555; umamicafe.com. Loosely defined as Asian fusion, this imaginative restaurant features a wide range of culinary styles and flavors in an effort to popularize the "fifth taste"—the elusive yumminess known as umami. The macaroni and cheese with truffles is a perfect demonstration of what this cafe strives to achieve, but you're likely to find a number of things on the menu that will satisfy your cravings. Mon through Thurs 5 to 10 p.m., Fri and Sat 5 to 10:30 p.m., Sun 1 to 10 p.m. $$.

peekskill, ny

A town that played host to the Continental Army in 1776, saw attacks by the British army in 1777, and became a critical stop on the Underground Railroad during the Civil War era, Peekskill is popular with tourists these days because of its extraordinary views of the Hudson Highlands. The historic downtown area boasts an artists' district, restaurants, galleries, trendy shops, and a range of fascinating 19th-century architectural styles.

what to do

Blue Mountain Reservation. 45 Welcher Ave.; (914) 862-5275; parks.westerchestergov .com/blue-mountain-reservation. If you brought your mountain bike, Blue Mountain Reservation is the place for you—and if you didn't, you can still enjoy the landscape here or try a hike up Mt. Spitzenberg or Blue Mountain. This 1,538-acre park provides access to the 12-mile Briarcliff Peekskill Trailway, and it also features two comfort stations with historical significance (remarkably *not* because George Washington went here). The Civilian Conservation Corps constructed these two stations in the 1930s, and they represent the same kind of architecture used in America's national parks. Open daily year-round, 8 a.m. to dusk; $10 per vehicle.

Hudson Valley Center for Contemporary Art. 1701 Main St.; (914) 788-0100; hvcca .org. Connecting the community with artists and vice versa, the HVCCA features changing exhibitions and a permanent (free) sculpture garden with installations throughout downtown Peekskill. Indoor exhibitions at the center feature various forms of contemporary art and artists, from sculpture to multimedia. Fri 11 a.m. to 5 p.m., Sat and Sun noon to 6 p.m., Tues through Thurs by appointment; closed Mon; $5 adults, $4 seniors and teachers, $2 students and children 8 and older, free to children under 8.

National Register Historic Districts. Beginning at 16 S. Division St.; (914) 737-2780; downtownpeekskill.com. Two sections of Peekskill are listed on the National Register of Historic Places: the commercial downtown area and Fort Hill, a residential neighborhood north of Main Street. A walk through either neighborhood reveals well-maintained buildings in a number of different architectural styles that represent a range of 19th-century periods. On the south side of Main Street near the corner of Division Street, you will find a plaque where the Birdsall House—headquarters to General George Washington during the Revolutionary War—stood until 1853. You can download a 16-page brochure from the Business Improvement District's website (downtownpeekskill.com) to guide you on your walk. Always open, no admission fee.

Paramount Theater Hudson Valley. 1008 Brown St.; (914) 739-0039; paramounthudson valley.com. This former movie palace dates back to 1930, when it was a 1,500-seat theater owned by Paramount Pictures. Now, thanks to a significant transformation in 2002, this theater hosts top-name music and comedy acts from Foghat to Bob Newhart. Check the website to see what's scheduled during your visit. Times and ticket prices vary with each performance.

Peekskill Museum. 124 Union Ave.; (914) 736-0473; peekskillmuseum.org. This repurposing of a Victorian home provides an opportunity to view 19th-century architecture from the inside as well as out, with its library, parlor, and fireplace with Delft tiles dating back to the house's 1870s origin. Inside, the museum tells stories of local history, with examples of products manufactured in Peekskill during the industrial era—cast iron stoves, Standard Brands and Fleischmann Company products, and items made by the Peekskill Chemical Company, the precursor to crayon maker Binney and Smith. There's a giant ball of string as well, and a velocipede high wheeler—and many other items from the surrounding area. Nov through Mar, Sat 1 to 3 p.m.; Apr through Oct, Sat 1 to 4 p.m. Special tours can be arranged by calling the museum in advance. No admission charge; donations encouraged.

Trinity Cruises. Riverfront Green Park, 30 Hudson Ave.; (914) 589-7773; trinitycruise company.com. Board the *Evening Star* and cruise up the Hudson River for unobstructed views of the Hudson Highlands, the river, and the surrounding lands. Take a sightseeing cruise in the morning (bring your own lunch) or choose a Sunday for a wine-tasting, sangria and salsa, or brews and blues cruise. Check the website for days and times. Spring through fall, sightseeing cruises Thurs through Sun at 11 a.m., sunset cruises Wed through Sat 7 p.m., Sun afternoon cruises at 3 p.m. See website for pricing.

where to eat

Birdsall House. 970 Main St.; (914) 930-1880; birdsallhouse.net. One of the pleasures of exploring smaller cities and towns is the opportunity to sample local craft beers, and you'll find plenty of these here—with as many as 20 on tap and many more in bottles. Pair your selection with a great meal: your choice from a substantial list of charcuterie, a hearty sandwich, an assortment of Hudson Valley cheeses, or one of the generous entrees served after 5 p.m. Open Mon through Wed, noon to midnight (food until 10 p.m.), Thurs through Sat noon to 2 a.m. (food until midnight); Sun 11 a.m. to midnight (food until 10 p.m.). $$.

Kathleen's Tea Room. 979 Main St.; (914) 734-2520; kathleenstearoom.com. Whether you're looking for a staggering selection of teas, scones and raspberry jam, or a delicious smoked salmon sandwich, you'll find this cozy place a welcome retreat in any season—but the working fireplace will make you want to linger in fall and winter. It's right in the middle of historic downtown, making it the perfect lunch spot while you admire Peekskill's architecture. Save room for the mixed berry shortcake. Mon through Thurs 11 a.m. to 5 p.m.; Fri and Sat 10:30 a.m. to 7 p.m. $.

Peekskill Coffee House. 101 S. Division St.; (914) 739-1287; peekskillcoffee.com. Funky, friendly, and comfortable—these three words aptly describe this independently owned coffeehouse, and its uncommonly pleasant staff as well. You'll find robust coffee, sandwiches and panini, and many a sweet treat to enjoy while you chat with friends or use the Wi-Fi, topped off with friendly, helpful service. Mon through Thurs 6 a.m. to 9 p.m. $.

Table 9. 92 Roa Hook Rd., Route 9 at Annsville Circle; (914) 737-4959; tablenine.com. Completely renovated in 2012, this American-style family restaurant gets rave reviews from the locals for everything from burgers to prime rib. The menu is broad enough to provide something for everyone, whether you prefer a casual meal or something more presentational and upscale. Sun through Thurs 11:30 a.m. to 10 p.m., Fri and Sat 11:30 a.m. to 11 p.m. $$.

beacon, ny

Beacon is a town with its own mountain, and it's worth a walk to the top of Mt. Beacon just to enjoy the vistas from a height of 1,611 feet. If hiking up a mountain isn't on your likely itinerary, you can still enjoy the view through Wind Gate, where Storm King Mountain and Breakneck Ridge form the northern gateway to the Hudson Highlands. A stroll through the town's carefully preserved factory buildings and visits to its historic sites—at least one of which predates the Revolutionary War—can fill your day with interesting discoveries.

where to go

Bannerman Castle. Reachable from the ferry docks in Beacon and Newburgh by tour boat; (855) 256-4007; bannermancastle.org. Designed by businessman Frank Bannerman in 1901 as a residence and storage facility for the military scrap and surplus equipment he sold in his Manhattan store, this castle on Pollepel Island in the Hudson River has seen its share of challenges. A munitions explosion in 1920 destroyed part of the structure, and a fire in 1969 took out the roofs and floors, ending tours to the island for decades—and parts of the castle collapsed during Christmas week 2009. Today you can take a ferry from the docks at Beacon and Newburgh (the Beacon dock is across from the Metro-North train station) to see the ruins of the castle up close. Tours leave from May through Oct, Sat and Sun at 11 a.m. from Beacon dock, and 12:30 p.m. from Newburgh dock. $35 adults and $30 children 11 and younger.

Dia: Beacon. 3 Beekman St.; (845) 440-0100; diabeacon.org. "Dia" is Greek for "through," an apt word to describe the Dia Art Foundation's commitment to aiding artists in achieving the visionary projects that might not see the light of day without the foundation's support. Here in Beacon, Dia's art museum showcases the foundation's collection from the 1960s to the present, including a number of new commissions and special presentations. You're likely to recognize the names of some of the artists whose work is displayed here: Joseph Beuys, Andy Warhol, Dan Flavin, Louse Bourgeois, Gerhard Richter, Donald Judd, and many others. Open Jan through Mar, Fri through Mon 11 a.m. to 4 p.m.; Apr through Oct, Thurs through Mon 11 a.m. to 6 p.m.; Nov and Dec, Thurs through Mon 11 a.m. to 4 p.m. Closed Tues and

Wed year-round. Closed Thanksgiving, Christmas Eve, Christmas Day, and New Year's Day. $12 adults, $10 seniors 65 and older, $6 students, free to children under 12.

Hudson Highlands State Park. Route 9D; (845) 225-7207; nysparks.com/parks/9/details .aspx. From Annsville Creek in Peekskill to Dennings Point in Beacon, 6,000 acres of undeveloped land offer unparalleled views of the Hudson River and the surrounding land, and many ways to enjoy the area in its natural state. Fishing, boating, hiking the extensive trail network, and birding are all popular pastimes here, but the most well known adventure is the hike to Breakneck Ridge, a 5.5-mile trek with a 1,250-foot rise in elevation—a trail that Trails.com rates as number one in the country. Why do it? The view is one of the best in the state. Open daily sunrise to sunset, free admission.

Madam Brett Homestead. 50 Van Nydeck Ave.; (845) 831-6533; melzingah.awardspace .com/id5.htm. Built in 1709, this striking home is the oldest standing structure in this part of Dutchess County. It began as the home of Roger and Catheryna Rombout Brett deep in the woods in the midst of the New York wilderness, where they had three sons before Roger died, leaving Madam Brett to defend her homestead and raise her children. Catheryna ran several successful businesses from this home and hired the best surveyor in the area to establish the boundaries of the land she inherited from her father, keeping interlopers away from her property as only a widow of the period could do. Several generations of Bretts raised families in this home, which is now managed by the Daughters of the American Revolution. Open Apr through Dec on the second Sat of the month, 1 to 4 p.m. $5 adults, $2 students.

where to eat

Homespun Foods. 232 Main St.; (845) 831-5096; homespunfoods.com. All the food is made on the premises here at Homespun, and the country kitchen atmosphere makes you want to tuck into a big sandwich or munch a salad filled with local vegetables and dressed with cheese produced just down the road. If you need something hot, there's quiche made fresh daily and macaroni and cheese with just a little chipotle pepper. The desserts are the real stars here, with specials every day based on fresh local ingredients—but you can depend on a selection of bars, chewy cookies, fruit tarts, and vanilla bean cheesecake any time you visit. Mon through Fri 11 a.m. to 5 p.m., Sat and Sun 8 a.m. to 5 p.m. $.

The Hop Beacon. 458 Main St.; (845) 440-8676; thehopbeacon.com. More than 150 craft beers by the bottle, a daily list of 9 beers for tastings, and a menu that features local cheeses, chocolates, pickles, and jams make this just the place you were hoping to find in your travels through the Hudson Valley. The chef makes his own sausages, terrines, and pâtés, so even if you usually skip such delicacies, you'll want to indulge during your visit. Mon, Wed, and Thurs noon to 9 p.m., Fri and Sat noon to 11 p.m., Sun noon to 8 p.m.; closed Tues. $$.

day trip 14

lower valley: new york city

>>>

life beyond the palisades
sloatsburg, ny

Here's some advice from a well-traveled upstater: At some point in your day tripping along the Hudson, it's time to leave the river behind and explore the hills and mountains beyond the Palisades. There's another world waiting for you in the Catskill Mountains region, where the pace slows to an amble and the vistas are vast, untrammeled by crowds, and unendingly green. Secluded lakes, hidden waterfalls, long trails through glacially carved slopes and rises, and spruce-scented air make this part of our state just about as delightful as it gets.

getting there

From the south: Take I-87 north to exit 15A in Ramapo. At the end of the exit ramp, head north/west on NY 17 and continue to Sloatsburg. **From the north:** Take I-87 south to exit 16 in Harriman/Woodbury, and take the exit ramp to US 6. Go west on US 6 to NY 17 in Harriman, and continue south on NY 17 to Sloatsburg.

sloatsburg, ny

A small town with a big history, Sloatsburg played a role in the Revolutionary War when the Sloat House—now a National Historic Landmark—became a headquarters for American troops waiting for action at Ramapo Pass. Sloat House became a tavern on the New York to Albany stagecoach route, serving soldiers, merchants, and passersby as well as General George Washington, who did indeed sleep here. After the war, the Sloat family built a tannery and cotton mill, processing cotton from the southern states into twine at the lightning-fast rate of 8,000 pounds of finished twine per week—an industry that faltered and eventually fell when the Civil War cut off cotton supplies. Iron and lumber became the primary industries after the war until 1903, when a monumental flood wiped out the town's factories along the Ramapo River. Prohibition, the rise of the automobile, and construction of the interstate highway system all had positive impacts on Sloatsburg, bringing people and traffic into the area in steadily increasing numbers. Today the town serves as the gateway to Harriman State Park, one of the most popular parks in New York.

what to do

Harriman State Park. Seven Lakes Road; (845) 786-2701; nysparks.com/parks/145/ details.aspx. Harriman's more than 46,000 acres contain 31 lakes and reservoirs, 200 miles of trails, 2 beaches, scenic roads and vistas, and some of the quintessential downstate hikes. Mixed forest, huge boulders, exposed faces of granite, and metamorphic gneiss line virtually every trail. You may expect old-growth forest here, but most of the trees are second growth, replanted after decades of iron mining stripped this area bare before and after the Civil War. The mines' furnaces required copious amounts of charcoal made from firewood, turning the forest into a continuous raw fuel source for iron ore processing. Mining stopped when Pennsylvania coal and Minnesota iron began to overshadow the Highlands' iron production at the turn of the 20th century. That's when the Harriman family presented the state of New York with 30,000 acres of their private land adjacent to an existing park, turning this area into an outdoor paradise for hikers, campers, boaters, and many others.

The park contains the remains of some of these mines, but they are not easy to spot— in part because the land has recovered so strongly from the mining days. Today the land appears as natural as it may have before the mines, the forests broken only by peaceful blue lakes and silver gray rock faces jutting through the thriving understory. We are particularly fond of the area around Lakes Skannatati and Askoti, especially as viewed from the top of Pine Swamp Mountain—a challenging but entirely possible hike for any healthy individual. The mountains here are minor peaks by Adirondack standards, but with sweeping views of the surrounding Hudson Highlands. You'll be glad you braved the vigorous ascent when you arrive at the top.

where to eat

Auntie El's Farm Market and Bakery. 171 NY 17 South; (845) 753-2122; facebook.com/ auntie.els. This may be the only establishment you spot on your way to Harriman State Park, so let me tell you it's worth the stop. Come for the produce, but stay for the fresh baked goods, especially the big cookies and the pies. You'll want to linger for a cup of coffee and a flaky Danish, or maybe some of the fresh chocolates. Mon and Tues 8 a.m. to 6 p.m.; Wed through Sun 8 a.m. to 7 p.m. $.

Character's. 94 Orange Turnpike; (845) 753-5200; charactersresturant.com. Irish cooking with everything made from scratch—that's the kind of phrase that makes your mouth water. Here's the place to get shepherd's pie, fish and chips, Irish curry and chips, or corned beef and cabbage, all cooked to your liking with solid, friendly service. Sun through Thurs 11:30 a.m. to 10 p.m.; Fri and Sat 11:30 a.m. to 11 p.m. $$.

Rhodes North Tavern. 40 Orange Turnpike; (845) 753-6438; facebook.com/pages/ Rhodes-North-Tavern. A full menu of bar food, a raw bar several nights every week, and live music on most nights make Rhodes North a hotspot with locals. Rhodes maintains an area it calls the Sandy Beach along the banks of the river, where you can enjoy a cheap kamikaze and some soft spring air starting on the first nice evening in May. Open daily 7 a.m. to 4 a.m., food served to 3 a.m. $$.

mid-hudson valley

>>>

day trip 15

mid-hudson valley

>>> **duty, honor, country**
west point, ny

west point, ny

Since 1802, when President Thomas Jefferson chose this spot to establish the United States Military Academy, West Point has occupied this 16,000-acre reserve at an elbow in the Hudson River. Here during the Revolutionary War, Fort Clinton—a fortified site designed by legendary engineer Tadeusz Kosciuszko—guarded upstate New York from British encroachment. While the fort never saw combat, its soldiers were involved in creating and laying the Hudson River Chain, a 500-link iron chain extended across the river to prevent British ships from going any farther north. Today the academy stands as the longest continually operating military installation in America, and the surrounding town—as well as the adjacent town of Highland Falls—provides services to the academy and its guests.

getting there

From the south, take the Henry Hudson Parkway (NY 9A) north and take exit 14 for I-95 and the George Washington Bridge. Follow signs to I-95 Upper Level S and merge onto I-95 S/George Washington Bridge. Cross the bridge and take exit 74 onto the Palisades Parkway. Drive about 34 miles to US 6 east; at the traffic circle, take the third exit onto US 9W north. In about 3 miles, exit onto Main Street in West Point. From the north, take I-87 south to exit 17 (NY 17K/Newburgh). Turn right on NY 300 south (Union Avenue), and follow NY 300 S as it becomes NY 32 south. In about 1.7 miles, turn left onto Quaker Avenue, and then merge onto US 9W south toward Bear Mountain. In about 7 miles, take NY 218 east, and turn right onto NY 218 south/Mountain Avenue. Continue into the town of West Point.

what to do

Black Rock Forest. 65 Reservoir Rd., Cornwall; (845) 534-4517; blackrockforest.org. In 1989, when Harvard University determined it was time to end its 40-year relationship with this 3,830-acre forest, an alliance of local colleges, universities, schools, and scientific institutions came together to preserve and maintain the forest as a living laboratory. The Black Rock Forest Consortium keeps the preserve open to visitors year-round (except during hunting season), while conducting research and education in ecological resource management. The remarkable result of this collaboration is that you and I can hike here, enjoying this verdant forest and its position at the highest part of the Hudson River Highlands, and find our way to Mineral Springs Falls, so named because of the magnetite—the black rock that gives both the falls and the forest its name. While the Continental Army did not require much of the magnetite in this area because they found plentiful supplies farther south, this land still underwent significant changes before and after the war as trees fell to make way for homesteads, orchards, and farms. By the late 1800s this land was unrecognizable as the grand forest it had been, until a wise land steward, Dr. Ernest Stillman, purchased these acres and used scientific forestry techniques to return them to healthy growth. He left the forest to Harvard in his will. Open daily dawn to dusk; free admission.

US Military Academy at West Point Visitor Center. 2107 New S. Post Rd.; (845) 938-2638; usma.edu/Visiting/SitePages/Home.aspx; for tours: westpointtours.com. At the visitor center, you can see videos about cadet life and about the academy, see a full-scale replica of a cadet barracks room, and learn about a cadet's daily life and the academy's academic offerings. If you would like to see the academy itself, bus tours are offered throughout the day: The 1-hour tour stops at the Main Cadet Chapel, Trophy Point (the site of the Hudson River Chain), Battle Monument, and the Plain, while the 2-hour tour explores more of the history of West Point, including all the one-hour tour's stops. Open daily 9 a.m. to 4:45 p.m., closed Thanksgiving, Christmas, and New Year's Day. There are no guided tours during Graduation Week or on football home-game days. Free admission to the visitor center; tours are $14 for adults and $11 for children 2 to 11 for 1 hour, and $16 adults/$13 children for 2 hours.

West Point Museum. 2110 New S. Post Rd.; (845) 938-3590; usma.edu/museum. This museum, adjacent to the West Point Visitor Center, contains the largest public collection of military artifacts in the western hemisphere. Its 7 galleries provide a comprehensive history of warfare and military service, and individual artifacts include the sword of Revolutionary War engineer Tadeusz Kosciuszko, the safety plug removed from the Nagasaki atomic bomb, and George Washington's pistols. Open daily 10:30 a.m. to 4:15 p.m., closed Thanksgiving, Christmas, and New Year's Day. Free admission.

where to eat

Andy's Restaurant. 281 Main St.; (845) 446-8736; andysrestauranthighlandfalls.com. For breakfast, lunch, snacks, or an early dinner, you'll be glad you found Andy's, especially if your hotel breakfast just doesn't cut it. From Reese's Pieces pancakes to the waffle sundae, the menu is comprehensive—and lunch and dinner include all of your diner faves as well. Mon through Fri 5:30 a.m. to 7 p.m., Sat and Sun 6 a.m. to 3 p.m. $$.

Hacienda Mexican Restaurant. 145 Main St.; (845) 446-0406; menuism.com/restaurants/hacienda-restaurant-highland-falls-652211. All of your Tex-Mex favorites are here at very reasonable prices, and you can't beat the decor (the Mexican flag created by hundreds of individual ribbons) and the service. If you're lucky, you'll be there when the mariachi band plays. Have a delicious margarita to get your taste buds ready for what comes next. Lunch and dinner daily. $$.

Maria Bonita. 315 Main St.; (845) 446-5393; facebook.com/pages/Maria-Bonita -Restaurant. Visitors and locals alike talk about the authentic Mexican flavors at this storefront restaurant, where the enchilada suizas draw rave reviews. It's family-owned, and you'll have the feeling that Grandma is in the kitchen as soon as you taste the homemade-style flavors. Lunch and dinner daily. $$.

day trip 16

mid-hudson valley

>>> cycles & revolutions
newburgh, ny

newburgh, ny

For historic landmarks, a cross-section of American history, interesting architecture, and magnificent views of the Hudson River, Newburgh presents a compelling package for the day-tripping tourist. The city contains the second largest historic district in the state in its East End, where you'll find literally thousands of historic buildings narrowly saved from wholesale demolition in the 1980s. Drive or walk Newburgh's downtown streets and see fine examples of Victorian Revival, Federal, Roman, Gothic, Italianate, and turn-of-the-20th-century brownstone architecture, including the newly restored Dutch Reformed Church at 134 Grand St. Today a full-scale restoration of Newburgh's neighborhoods is resulting in new development, including the creation of a waterfront destination with restaurants, shops, and other businesses. Newburgh saw some challenging days in the mid-20th century, but it has found its way back and established itself as a worthwhile day-trip destination.

getting there

From the south, take I-87 to its junction with I-84 at exit 17. Take exit 17 to I-84 east, and continue to exit 10 (US 9W). Take exit 10 and proceed south on US 9W to Broadway in Newburgh. Turn left on Broadway and continue into the city of Newburgh. **From the north,** take I-87 south to its junction with I-84 at exit 17. Take I-84 east and follow the directions above. **From the east,** take I-84 west across the Hamilton-Fish-Newburgh-Beacon Bridge over the

Hudson River. Take exit 10 at US 9W and proceed south on US 9W to Broadway in Newburgh. **From the west,** take I-84 east to exit 10, and follow the directions above (from the north).

what to do

Karpeles Manuscript Library Museum. 94 Broadway; (845) 569-4997; rain.org/~karpeles/ nbgfrm.html. The Karpeles museum in Newburgh is one of a national network of museums that present the holdings of the Karpeles Manuscript Library, the largest private holding of important original manuscripts and documents in the world. The entire system holds more than one million documents, and each museum maintains a general exhibit and a special scheduled exhibition. Thurs through Sat 10 a.m. to 4 p.m., Sun noon to 4 p.m.; closed Mon through Wed. Free admission.

Lawrence Farm Orchards. 39 Colandrea Rd.; (845) 562-4268; lawrencefarmsorchards .com. A visit to this family-owned, pick-your-own fruit and vegetable farm can include a visit with goats and other farm animals, a walk through a Little Village—a replica of an old-fashioned New England farm town—and even a ride in a horse-drawn carriage on weekends. Once you've picked your fruit, get yourself some homemade ice cream and doughnuts before you go. Check the website to see what crops will be available when you visit. Open daily in season 9 a.m. to 4 p.m.; free admission, pay for what you pick.

Motorcyclepedia Museum. 250 Lake St.; (845) 569-9065; motorcyclepediamuseum.org. More than 450 motorcycles from 1897 to present day are in this museum's displays, with galleries dedicated to the military, police, and Harley-Davidson. Here you can see rare vintage motorcycles, enjoy shows in 3 Motordromes, and discover all kinds of memorabilia and artifacts. Open year-round, Fri through Sun 10 a.m. to 5 p.m.; closed Mon through Thurs; $11 adults, $5 children 3 to 12, free to children under 3.

Orange County Choppers. 14 Crossroads Court; (845) 522-5250; orangecountychoppers .com. If you're a fan of the Discovery Channel's reality series *American Chopper*, you know this custom motorcycle shop well—so here's your chance to tour it. Paul Teutul Sr. opened his first bike shop in 1999 as an offshoot of his steel manufacturing business, and he and his crew have since become the most famous bike manufacturers in the United States—and maybe the world. Tours Mon through Sun at 10 a.m., 11:30 a.m., 2 p.m., 3 p.m., and 5:15 p.m.; additional tour Mon through Sat at 7 p.m. Peak hours: $7.50 adults, $3.50 children 4 to 11 and military, free to children under 4. After hours (5 p.m. and weekends): $5 adults, $2.50 children and military. There's a nominal additional charge to have Senior sign your OCC merchandise.

***Pride of the Hudson* boat tour.** Newburgh Landing, Second Street; (800) 979-3370; prideofthehudson.com. Take a 2-hour, narrated sightseeing cruise on the Hudson River to see the Hudson Highlands from the water. Your tour includes Pollepel Island, Cold Spring, Storm King Mountain, Breakneck Mountain, the Catskill Aqueduct, and West Point, as well as a number of impressive homes and other landmarks. The *Pride of the Hudson* is both heated and air-conditioned, and it contains 2 cash bars with light snacks for your tour. Cruises offered May through Oct; check the website for this year's schedule. $22 adults, $20 seniors 65 and older, $18 children 4 to 11, free for children 3 and under.

Washington's Headquarters State Historic Site. 84 Liberty St.; (845) 562-1195; nysparks.com/historic-sites/17/hours-of-operation.aspx. For the last year and a half of the Revolutionary War, General George Washington made his headquarters here at the Hasbrouck family home, a building that became the state's first official historic site in 1850. Here Washington stopped a military rebellion called the Newburgh Conspiracy that might have resulted in martial law, and turned down the opportunity to become king—not president—of the new United States. Here in Newburgh, peace between the Americans and the British was officially declared after the Continental Army's victory in Yorktown. Open Apr to Oct, Wed through Sat 11 a.m. to 5 p.m., Sun 1 to 5 p.m., closed Mon and Tues; Nov through Mar, Fri and Sat 11 a.m. to 3 p.m., closed weekdays; $4 adults, $3 seniors and students, free to children 12 and under.

where to go near newburgh

Knox's Headquarters State Historic Site. 289 Forge Hill Rd., Vails Gate; (845) 561-5498; nysparks.com/historic-sites/5/details.aspx. Just about a mile down the road from the New Windsor Catonment, American artillery commander Henry Knox used this home of John Ellison, built in 1754, as his headquarters on a number of occasions throughout the Revolutionary War. When the catonment was in full operation, Major General Horatio Gates commanded the military encamped here from this Georgian-style house as well. You can still see traces of the mill that operated here, producing flour that Ellison sent down the Hudson River to New York and on to the West Indies throughout the end of the 1700s and into the 1800s. Memorial Day weekend through the end of Oct, Fri and Sat 10 a.m. to 5 p.m., Sun 1 to 5 p.m.; closed Mon through Thurs. Free admission.

New Windsor Catonment State Historic Site. 374 Temple Hill Rd., New Windsor; (845) 561-1765; nysparks.com/historic-sites/22/details.aspx. The Continental Army spent the last winter and spring of the Revolutionary War here, after the British surrender at Yorktown and as the details of peace between the British and the Americans coalesced into the Treaty of Paris. More than 7,000 soldiers and 500 women and children refugees lived here in log huts as they waited for the end of hostilities to be ratified. Today you can see costumed interpreters demonstrating the skills of 18th-century war from Apr to Oct, with additional demonstrators in July and Aug. The National Purple Heart Hall of Fame is here as well. Open mid-Apr through Oct, Wed through Sat 10 a.m. to 5 p.m., Sun 1 to 5 p.m.; closed Mon and Tues. Living history demonstrations are closed Nov through early Apr. Visitor Center is open year-round Mon through Sat 10 a.m. to 5 p.m., and Sun 1 to 5 p.m. Free admission.

Storm King State Park. Bayview Avenue and Storm King Highway; (845) 786-2701; nysparks.com/parks/152/details.aspx. The main activity here is the hike up Storm King, which rises to a height of 1,339 feet above the Hudson River—and those who make the trek will be rewarded with some of the finest views of the Hudson River Valley and the Hudson Highlands you'll find anywhere along the river. The 2.5-mile loop hike includes an 893-foot change in elevation, so plan on about 2.5 hours to complete the loop at a reasonable pace. (The worst of it is in the first half-hour.) The views start fairly early and build to the money spot at the end, where you will want to linger to fully absorb the grand view. There are no amenities or comfort stations in this park, so be prepared to "use the woods." Open daily dawn to dusk; free admission.

where to eat

Billy Joe's Ribworks. 26 Front St.; (845) 565-1560; ribworks.com. Thrice-rubbed meats slathered with homemade sauces bring customers back to this barbecue joint, where acoustic musicians and bands play nightly and an outdoor bar offers a great place to celebrate the arrival of spring. If smoked meat is not your thing, Billy Joe's has a menu of entrees including meatloaf, grilled chicken, and fried catfish. Mon through Thurs and Sun 11:30 a.m. to 10 p.m., Fri and Sat 11:30 a.m. to 11 p.m.; hours may be shorter in winter. $$.

Capri Restaurant and Pizzeria. 410 Broadway; (845) 562-2170; capriofnewburgh.com. All of your traditional Italian favorites are here at Capri, from pasta aglio olio to zuppa di clams, served in a warm, friendly atmosphere. Tues through Thurs 11 a.m. to 9 p.m., Fri 11 a.m. to 10 p.m., Sat noon to 10 p.m., Sun 3 to 9 p.m. $$.

Newburgh Brewing Company. 88 Colden St.; (845) 569-2337; newburghbrewing.com. A long list of craft beers and ales almost dwarfs the food menu in this favorite gathering place. The philosophy employed here is that beer should be "sessionable," or something that you can enjoy over a long period of time, i.e. all evening with friends. Settle in and start sampling, and enjoy a selection of local cheeses or a meal made with local ingredients like farm-raised pork or fresh-caught fish. Wed 4 to 9 p.m., Thurs 4 to 11 p.m., Fri 4 p.m. to midnight, Sat noon to midnight, Sun noon to 5 p.m.; closed Mon and Tues. $$.

Torches on the Hudson. 120 Front St.; (845) 568-0100; torchesonthehudson.com. Not every restaurant features a 6,000-gallon saltwater aquarium in its dining room, in which 30 species of fish swim for your viewing pleasure . . . but the tank seems quite at home here in this mahogany-lined dining room with its nautically themed fixtures. If that's not enough to make you want to stop here, the simple but ample menu should do it. You'll find plenty of seafood here, as well as filet mignon if you're so inclined—and burgers and sandwiches if you'd prefer a smaller meal. Mon through Thurs 11:30 a.m. to 9 p.m., Fri and Sat 11:30 a.m. to 10 p.m., Sun brunch 11 a.m. to 2 p.m., dinner 1 to 8 p.m. $$.

day trip 17

mid-hudson valley

manitoga, boscobel & friends
garrison, cold spring, ny

Across the river from West Point, the towns of Garrison and Cold Spring have served as weekend getaway destinations for New York City dwellers for generations. Not only are these towns brimful of historic sites and restaurants, but they stand as gateways to natural spaces like Breakneck Ridge, Constitution Marsh, and boating on the Hudson River.

getting there

From the south, take the Palisades Parkway north to the traffic circle at the junction with US 6/202. Continue straight on US 6/202 and turn left on NY 9D north. Cross the US 6 bridge over the Hudson River, and continue 5 miles to Garrison. **From the north,** take US 9 south from Fishkill to NY 301, and turn right. Continue on NY 301 to the junction with NY 9D in Cold Spring, and turn left (south). Continue on NY 9D to Garrison. **By train:** Metro North to Garrison station.

garrison, ny

This little Putnam County hamlet has seen its share of celebrity residents, including current homeowners Patty Hearst, poet James Hoch, Facebook cofounder Chris Hughes, Tony-winning theater director Julie Taymor, and former New York governor George Pataki. What attracts them? Perhaps it's the country ambiance, the 10 miles of stubbornly unpaved roads that lead to homes secluded by woods, and the substantial acreage most of the residential properties can claim. Don't expect a lot of shopping and restaurants here, though you'll find plenty to do and see—even if you just drive around to see the rusticated lifestyles of the famous.

what to do

Boscobel Mansion. 1601 NY 9D (Bear Mountain Highway); (845) 265-3638; boscobel.org. This 1808 federal-style mansion on 250 acres of riverfront has had a complicated history since the Dyckman family, who built the home, moved out in the 1880s. In 1955 a group of concerned citizens saved the house from demolition at the last possible moment, but only managed to allow it to be dismantled and stored instead of demolished. A year later, a generous benefactor had the house rebuilt on its current site, but it wasn't until the 1970s that it was restored and decorated in a manner appropriate to the period it represents. Today you will see Duncan Phyfe furniture and other names you may recognize inside. Open Apr 1 through Oct 31, Wed through Mon 9:30 a.m. to 5 p.m.; Nov and Dec, Wed through Mon 9:30 a.m. to 4 p.m.; closed Tues; $17 adults, $14 seniors 62+, $8 children 6 to 14, free to children under 6, $45 for a family of 4.

Constitution Marsh Audubon Center and Sanctuary. 127 Warren Landing Rd.; (845) 265-2601; constitutionmarsh.org. It's one thing to stand on the edge of a marsh and peer into it to see what's going on there, but it's quite another to walk right into the tall grasses and reeds and become part of the action. The boardwalk at Constitution Marsh gives you exactly this opportunity, providing a dry, sturdy, remarkably unobtrusive route into the heart of this freshwater tidal marsh. The visitor center provides interpretive displays and restrooms, and 2 trails into the woods eventually lead to the marsh, with views of the Hudson River just beyond it. The gorgeous cattail marsh resonates with marsh wrens' chattering song, punctuated by calls of the common yellowthroat or red-winged blackbird. Muskrat lodges—piles of sticks and mud—may be visible at the base of the cattails. Open daily 9 a.m. to 6 p.m.; visitor center is open Tues through Sun, 9 a.m. to 5 p.m. Hours may be reduced in winter. Free admission.

Garrison Art Center. 23 Garrison's Landing; (845) 424-3960; garrisonartcenter.org. The arts and arts education find a home in this community art center, founded in 1964 and now hailed as "one of the valley's most active arts meccas" by *Hudson Valley* magazine. Three exhibition spaces feature solo and group shows, educational exhibitions, and juried shows throughout the year, showcasing fine work by local and area artists. Tues through Sun 10 a.m. to 5 p.m., closed Mon. Free admission; donations encouraged.

Manitoga/The Russel Wright Design Center. 584 NY 9D; (845) 424-3812; russelwright center.org. The home of designer Russell Wright, the man who introduced America to the concept of "easier living" with his lines of dinnerware, furniture, appliances, and textiles, this estate protects Wright's modernist house and studio to demonstrate his ability to integrate design and nature. In addition to the fascinating home, 75 acres of landscape offer more than 4 miles of paths through deep forest. Tours May through early Nov, Fri through Mon 11 a.m. and 1:30 p.m.; $20 adults, $15 seniors and students, $10 children under 12.

where to eat

Valley at the Garrison. 2015 US 9; (845) 424-3604; thegarrison.com/restaurants/valley .html. Seasonal American cuisine served alongside one of the finest views of the Hudson Valley you can see from a dining table make the Valley a special place. The menu changes with the season, but it features locally grown ingredients—many of which are grown right here at Garrison Farm in season. Come on Thursday for the "eat local" lounge menu of small-plate items and burgers. Thurs, Fri, and Sat 5 to 9 p.m., brunch Sat and Sun 11:30 a.m. to 2:30 p.m.; closed Mon through Wed. $$$ (less on Thurs).

cold spring, ny

Not to be confused (as it often is) with Cold Spring Harbor on Long Island, this residential village's main street forms the Cold Spring Historic District, a strip of 19th-century buildings on the National Register of Historic Places. Here at the West Point Foundry, workers produced munitions including the famous Parrott gun for use in the Civil War. Cold Spring sits at the deepest point of the Hudson River, and its remarkable scenery has attracted artists, musicians, and outdoor enthusiasts since the middle of the 1800s.

what to do

Putnam History Museum. 63 Chestnut St.; (845) 265-4010; putnamhistorymuseum.org. Find more information about the West Point Foundry and other historic sites in Cold Spring at this museum near the foundry preserve. Changing exhibitions here feature overviews of life in the Hudson Valley, from leisure time to the ebbs and flows of business prosperity. Wed through Sun 11 a.m. to 5 p.m.; $5 adults, $2 seniors and students, free to young children.

Stonecrop Gardens. 81 Stonecrop Lane; (845) 265-2000; stonecrop.org. Twelve acres of landscaped garden once graced the home of Anne and Frank Cabot, enjoying a zone 5 climate at 1,100 feet and presenting an exciting opportunity for a team of passionate horti-culturalists. The expansive grounds include raised alpine stone beds, a cliff rock garden, an English-style flower garden, woodland and water gardens, and structures including a con-servatory, a pit house filled with dwarf bulbs, and a display alpine house. This is a wonderful place for a stroll, especially if you have gardening aspirations or passions of your own. Open spring through Oct, Mon through Sat 10 a.m. to 5 p.m., and some Sundays; $5 adults and children 12 and up; free to children under 12.

West Point Foundry Preserve. 68 Kemble Ave.; (845) 473-4440; scenichudson.org/ parks/westpointfoundrypreserve. Back in 1818, West Point Foundry began supplying the

US military with the artillery that eventually won the Civil War, while creating some of the nation's first steam engines, locomotives, and iron ships. Later this foundry produced the pipes used to build New York City's gargantuan water distribution system. The foundry closed in 1911, but some of its structures still remain, including the casting house and boring mill. You can hike a 0.5-mile trail on this 87-acre site to see the remains and the replica of the 36-foot water wheel that once powered the boring mill. Scenic Hudson now supervises the site. Open daily dawn to dusk; free admission.

where to eat

Hudson Hil's. 129 Main St.; (845) 265-9471; hudsonhils.com. Locals hail Hudson Hil's as the perfect place for breakfast or lunch, and the substantive, reasonably priced menu certainly bears this out. Breakfast is served until 4 p.m., so you can enjoy an omelet whenever the mood strikes you—and with features like a roasted Brussels sprouts salad or a grilled cheese sandwich laden with sliced apples and house-made fig paste, you're sure to find something unexpected and delicious. All ingredients come from the area's organic farms. Wed through Mon 8 a.m. to 4 p.m.; closed Tues. $$.

Moo Moo's Creamery. 32 West St.; (845) 204-9230; moomooscreamery.com. Sixteen flavors of ice cream are served each day at Moo Moo's, selected from more than 100 flavors made on premises from locally sourced, high-quality ingredients. The proprietary family recipe remains a closely guarded secret, but you'll taste the difference, whether you choose a multiflavor variety like cinnabutter pecan spice or walNutella, or a pure flavor like coffee or pumpkin. Mon through Thurs 2 to 9 p.m., Fri 2 to 9:30 p.m., Sat noon to 9:30 p.m., Sun noon to 9 p.m. $.

Riverview Restaurant. 45 Fair St.; (845) 265-4778; riverdining.com. This contemporary American restaurant features a casual atmosphere, fresh local seafood, brick oven pizzas, and amazing views of Storm King Mountain and the Hudson River. Don't miss the Riverview fish and shellfish stew if you like Thai flavors and a little spice; alternately, try the penne with chicken breast and broccoli. The menu is not extensive, but the choices are mouthwatering. Tues through Fri noon to 2:30 p.m. and 5:30 to 9:30 p.m., Sat noon to 4 p.m. and 5 to 10 p.m., Sun noon to 9:30 p.m.; closed Mon. $$.

where to shop

Cold Spring's Main Street. If you're walking the historic district in downtown Cold Spring, you can't miss the shopping: Staley Gretzinger by Art to Wear features clothing for creative professional women; Hudson Valley Outfitters can have you in a kayak in minutes; Cold Spring Train Works provides all kinds of train sets and rolling stock for the railroad hobbyist; and Highland Baskets at the Country Goose provides imported foods and bath products. You'll find plenty of other shops—especially antiques stores—along this fascinating street.

day trip 18

mid-hudson valley

>>> **over the hudson & back**
poughkeepsie, ny

poughkeepsie, ny

Despite the fame bestowed upon it by comedian Chevy Chase, who announced at a 2013 benefit dinner, "Poughkeepsie is the worst name for a city I've ever heard in my life," this small city once provided the ultimate getaway for wealthy bankers and captains of industry. The estates they built lined South Road and other streets in the area, some of them providing public access to allow the community to enjoy their sprawling landscaping, manicured gardens, and meandering carriage trails. While the magnates and millionaires have largely moved on and their estates are now in the hands of preservation groups working to restore them, the attributes that drew so much money here in the 19th century still remain: glorious views of the Hudson River, rolling hills covered with successional forest, and a healthy respect for natural, open spaces rather than the belching smokestacks of heavy industry.

You will find much to explore here in Poughkeepsie, from former estates of the rich and famous to one of the most innovative public parks in the United States, repurposing a railroad bridge into a community asset. The nation's first college for women resides here as well, as it has since 1861—long before most colleges considered women's minds capable of higher education.

what to do

Bridge Music. Mid-Hudson Bridge, US 44; (845) 691-7221; nysba.ny.gov/bridgepages/ MHB/MHBpage/mhb_page.htm. Don't miss the opportunity to walk across the Mid-Hudson Bridge, a highly trafficked segment of US 44 and NY 55 with a pedestrian walkway and an attraction of its own: Bridge Music, the remarkable accomplishment of composer Joseph Bertolozzi. The sounds of traffic crossing the bridge inspired Bertolozzi to write a series of pieces that can be described as percussive funk, created using only the sounds he could generate by making the bridge itself his drum kit. You can listen to a wide selection of these jazzy pieces when you reach the Mid-Hudson Bridge arches, where you will find speakers and buttons to push to hear the Bridge Music. Always open; no toll to cross the bridge on foot.

Clinton House State Historic Site. 549 Main St.; (845) 471-1630; nysparks.com/historic-sites/1/details.aspx. Built in 1765 and expanded after a fire in 1783, this stone house served as the site of the New York state capital from 1777 to 1783, when several branches of state government convened here in Poughkeepsie. The house features 2-foot-thick foundations, fieldstone walls, and gabled ends made of wood. Its name recognizes George Clinton, the first governor of New York. Open year-round Tues through Fri, 10 a.m. to 3 p.m. Free admission; donations are encouraged.

Glebe House. 635 Main St.; (845) 471-1630; dutchesscountyhistoricalsociety.org/visit .aspx. This 1767 rectory served as a residence for the Reverend John Beardsley, minister of Christ Church in Poughkeepsie and Trinity Church in Fishkill. ("Glebe" is the Saxon word for land given to a minister to supplement his income.) Beardsley had no choice but to flee this home in 1777 when his Loyalist position made living in Poughkeepsie untenable as the American Revolution approached the area. He relocated to New York City, which was occupied by the British for the duration of the war. Today the Dutchess County Historical Society operates the house, and community open houses are held at various times during the year. You can schedule an appointment for a tour if you like. Free admission on community open house days; donations are encouraged.

Locust Grove Estate. 2683 South Rd.; (845) 454-4500; lgny.org. Designed for artist and inventor Samuel F. B. Morse by architect A. J. Davis, the 200-acre Locust Grove Estate has graced this spot overlooking the Hudson River since 1851. The Young family rented the house in 1895 and finally purchased it in 1901, expanding it for use as a residence for their daughter, Annette. A tour of the mansion gives you the opportunity to see her extensive collection of artwork and antiques. You are welcome to explore the visitor center, historic gardens, landscaped grounds, carriage roads, and views of the river any time of the year, and to come for a tour of the mansion during the spring, summer, and early fall months. Visitor Center is open year-round, Jan 3 through Apr 6, Mon through Fri 10 a.m. to 5 p.m.; Apr 9 to Dec 31, daily 10 a.m. to 5 p.m. Mansion tours: May 1 through Nov 30 10:15 a.m., 11:30 a.m., 12:45 p.m., 2 p.m. and 3:15 p.m. Tours are $10 adults, $6 children 6 to 18.

Maple Grove. In the St. Simeon property at 24 Beechwood Ave.; (845) 297-4245; maple groverestoration.org. In the 19th century, when Poughkeepsie was the go-to place for wealthy businessmen to move their families away from the summer heat in New York City, a number of opulent country estates lined South Road. Maple Grove—built in 1850—was one of the most impressive, built for banker Charles A. Macy on a high spot in the 35-acre parcel. This brick mansion fell prey to a professional arsonist in 1985 who set a fire in the maids' quarters; while many items were saved through the courage of caretaker Stephen Rendes, the house stood closed for some time. Preservation and restoration did not begin until 2000, when Maple Grove received a Preserve NY grant to assist with the assessment and planning phases of the reconstruction. Today much of the construction has been completed. You can visit Maple Grove from Apr to Nov. Tours from early Apr to early Nov, first Wed of the month, 10 a.m. to noon. To schedule a tour at another time, call (845) 297-4245. Donations are encouraged.

Smith Metropolitan AME Zion Church. 124 Smith St.; (845) 454-1913. This 1910 church, which serves a congregation established here by African Americans back in 1836, now holds a position on the National Register of Historic Places. Guided tours introduce you to the history of prominent parishioners, including the first woman who was ordained a deacon in the Methodist church. You'll also learn about the design, construction, and meaning of the church's stained-glass windows. Tours are by appointment; call the phone number above. Free admission.

Springside National Historic Landmark. 185 Academy St.; (845) 454-2060; springside landmark.org. These 20 acres once served as the country estate of Matthew Vassar, who used the fortune he amassed as a brewing magnate to found Vassar College. Designed by renowned architect Andrew Jackson Downing, the estate was created as an ornamental farm, a landscape meant to be as beautiful as it was functional. It remains largely intact despite the encroachment of development, and a nonprofit preservation organization, Springside Landscape Restoration, has taken on the monumental task of returning it to the stunning condition Downing and Vassar intended. You can wander the carriage trails and hills at your leisure on a self-guided walking tour (pick up a brochure at the kiosk in the parking area), or arrange for a guided tour at your convenience. Open daily dawn to dusk for self-guided walking tours. Free admission; donations are encouraged.

Vassar College. 124 Raymond Ave.; (845) 437-7400; info.vassar.edu. Since 1861, Vassar College has provided a liberal arts education to a carefully selected student body in the Hudson Valley. It began as a college for women founded by Matthew Vassar, a wealthy individual who made his fortune in the beer industry. While it was hailed as "Matthew's Folly" by those who believed that women were not capable of intellectual achievement, Vassar College soon proved the doubters wrong—making its mark as a single-gender college with graduates of the same caliber as the male graduates of Harvard or Yale. Three miles from the center of Poughkeepsie, this 1,000-acre campus features formal gardens, meadows, woodlands, and buildings in a range of architectural styles that offer a timeline of the college's history, from its early collegiate Gothic structures to the modern buildings of the late 20th century. You are welcome to visit to stroll the grounds any time and breathe in the rarefied air of the Ivy League, or to participate in one of the more than 1,650 campus events that take place at Vassar each year. The Vassar Art Center provides an especially interesting experience, housing more than 18,000 works of art from ancient Egypt to today's contemporary styles. The campus is always open; tours and informational visits are offered on weekdays year-round, and on weekends in fall. Tours are free.

Walkway Over the Hudson. 60 Parker Ave.; (845) 834-2867; nysparks.state.ny.us/parks/178/details.aspx. If you only hike one trail in the Hudson River Valley, the Walkway Over the Hudson may be the one to do. You will have no finer opportunity to appreciate the Hudson River and its beautiful valley than from this vantage point. An inspired repurposing of an industrial bridge, the Walkway Over the Hudson puts back into use a 19th-century railroad bridge that served as a major rail corridor for many decades. When fire severely damaged the bridge in 1974, the old structure stood dormant until a group of enthusiastic citizens came together with state and federal governments to repair the bridge and transform it into a new state park.

The wide, smooth, modern walkway opened on October 3, 2009, and now stands as the longest elevated pedestrian bridge in the world. Visitors can stroll 212 feet above the river's surface and admire a spectacular view of the river to the north and south. A sunny summer Sunday can draw thousands of people to the park, making downtown Poughkeepsie a new meeting place for neighbors and friends throughout the Hudson River Valley. Open daily sunrise to sunset; free admission.

where to eat

Aloy's Italian Restaurant. 157 Garden St.; (845) 473-6400; aloysrestaurant.com. Italian food should be delicious, filling, and served with gusto, and Aloy's delivers on all counts. Whether you choose the homemade ravioli of the day, the thin-crust pizza (voted "Best Thin Crust Pizza in the Hudson Valley" by readers of *Hudson Valley* magazine), or the cold antipasto salad—loaded with salami, provolone, and other Italian favorites—you will not leave disappointed. Best of all, it's just 500 feet from the entrance to the Walkway Over the Hudson. Wed and Thurs 3 to 9 p.m.; Fri noon to 10 p.m.; Sat 2 to 9 p.m.; Sun 2 to 8:30 p.m.; Mon 3 to 8:30 p.m.; closed Tues. $$.

Brasserie 292. 292–294 Main St.; (845) 473-0292; brasserie292.com. For a sense of the old world with a commitment to local farmers and fresh ingredients, try this upscale restaurant with its subway tile and polished metal ceiling, and explore its diverse menu. Whether you're looking for the creativity of crab and mascarpone tortellini or a hearty, 12-ounce steak frites, you'll find what you want here—with the added pleasure of a selection of local cheeses or a charcuterie board as the perfect appetizer. Bring three friends and try the prix-fixe brunch, which features eggs Benedict and pumpkin pancakes. Mon through Thurs 11 a.m. to 9:30 p.m.; Fri 11 a.m. to 10:30 p.m.; Sat 2 to 10:30 p.m.; Sun 11 a.m. to 8 p.m. $$$.

PC's Paddock Restaurant. 273 Titusville Rd.; (845) 454-4930; pcspaddockrestaurant.com. You'll find all your American favorites served elegantly in this renovated 1840s barn, with the emphasis on homestyle cooking and fresh local ingredients. The staff includes chefs who graduated from the Culinary Institute of America—which is just up the road, by the way—and everything, including the baked goods, is made here on premises. If you can't make it for lunch or dinner, try breakfast on a Sunday for a hearty, flavorful start to your day. Tues through Thurs 11:30 a.m. to 9 p.m.; Fri 11:30 a.m. to 10 p.m.; Sat 1 to 10 p.m.; Sun 8 a.m. to 9 p.m. $$.

Rossi Rosticceria Deli. 45 S. Clover St.; (845) 471-0654; rossideli.com. If you're looking for a place where you can pick up a really great sandwich before walking across the Hudson, make a point of stopping here. Choose from a wide selection of meats—including all of the Italian favorites, from sopressata to mortadella—and dress it with cheese, toppings, and breads, or pick one of the combinations already imagined by the proprietors. Get here before 12 to avoid the long lines that form every day at lunchtime. Mon through Fri 7:30 a.m. to 6 p.m., Sat 8 a.m. to 5 p.m. $.

where to shop

Adams Fairacre Farms. 765 Dutchess Turnpike; (845) 454-4330; adamsfarms.com. What began as a roadside farm stand has grown to provide 4 locations throughout the Hudson Valley, offering a full-service meat department, seafood, a delicatessen, a variety of prepared foods, a bakery, gourmet sweets and grocery items, a flower shop and garden center, and a nursery for choosing your spring plants. Most impressive is the selection of locally produced foods: dairy, meat, cheeses, and baked goods from local farms and providers. This is a great place to stop for the Hudson Valley's bounty before you head for home. Mon through Fri 8 a.m. to 9 p.m., Sat 8 a.m. to 8 p.m., Sun 8 a.m. to 7 p.m.

Arlington. Centered around Davis and Raymond Streets; arlingtonhasit.org. This neighborhood of shops and restaurants near Vassar College features the specialty retail and unusual boutiques we all hope to find when we travel. From the casual, classic styles at Elizabeth Boutique to the one of a kind jewelry and pottery at Dreaming Goddess, you're sure to find interesting things to bring home. Open daily, hours vary by establishment.

Poughkeepsie Galleria. 2001 South Rd.; (845) 297-7600; poughkeepsiegalleriamall.com. More than 150 stores including all of your brand-name favorites—and some you may only see in the top malls in America—make this über-mall a shopping destination for millions of people every year. Mon through Sat 10 a.m. to 9:30 p.m.; Sun 11 a.m. to 6 p.m.

day trip 19

mid-hudson valley

rock walls, wine & waterfalls
new paltz, ny

Make a trip up through New Paltz to the Shawangunk (pronounced SHON-gunk) Ridge and into the wild countryside beyond it, to park preserves loaded with waterfalls, mountain lakes, and unusually diverse plant life. Here you'll find the little-known Hudson River Apple Trail, a route that takes you to farm markets where you can walk through the orchards and pick your own fruit. You'll love this day trip in any season, but a trip through here during the late summer or fall harvest brings the satisfaction of fresh fruit and vegetables, jugs of apple cider, and the colors of autumn throughout the surrounding hills.

getting there

From the north or south, take the New York State Thruway to exit 18 in New Paltz. At the end of the exit ramp, turn left (west) on NY 299, which is also Main Street in New Paltz, and continue into the town.

new paltz, ny

Settled by French Huguenots in the 1600s, New Paltz is perhaps best known today for the state university that bears its name, but it preserves its own history through the Huguenot Street Historic Site that includes some of the oldest buildings in the Hudson Valley. Very much a college town with a wealth of coffee shops, funky stores, sandwich eateries, and other services, New Paltz attracts tourists by the thousands in fall when the leaves turn crimson and amber and the nearby wineries harvest their grapes. In this chapter, we'll look at some of the natural sites you can enjoy in the area as well as shops and restaurants—if you want to know about the wineries, see the Shawangunk Valley Wine Trail in day trips 20 and 21.

If you've come to the Shawangunks during the height of fall foliage season, you may wait for quite some time in traffic to make your way through New Paltz. We suggest you get on the road early in the day and circle back here for lunch or a leisurely afternoon, especially if it's a sunny Sunday.

what to do

Dressel Farms. 271 NY 208; (845) 255-0693; dresselfarms.com. At this orchard and farm market in the height of the fall harvest, you can pick a dozen different varieties of apples in season, get your Halloween pumpkin, and enjoy fresh doughnuts hot from the fryer and some of the best apple cider we've tasted anywhere. In June, pick your own strawberries, and check the website for the showroom's offerings and other picking opportunities throughout the summer and fall. In winter, get cider, honey, maple syrup, and firewood here. Mon through Fri 9:30 a.m. to 5 p.m., Sat 10 a.m. to 4 p.m., Sun 11 a.m. to 4 p.m.; extended hours in summer and fall.

Huguenot Street Historic Site. Visitor center at 81 Huguenot St.; (845) 255-1660; huguenotstreet.org. This 10-acre historic landmark preserves the neighborhood founded by the earliest European settlers in this area. These founders of New Paltz were families of Walloons as well as Huguenots, 12 families of French-speaking Protestants who followed French theologian John Calvin. They purchased this land from the Esopus Indians in 1677 and built a settlement here; seven of the stone houses and a stone church remain here, dating back to the early 1700s. The graveyard lends itself nicely to nightly ghost walks through the historic site, a particularly entertaining way to absorb this little-known slice of New York history. DuBois Fort Visitor Center: Open daily 10 a.m. to 5 p.m. All-day pass $15 adults, $10 seniors and children 8 to 12, free to military, veterans, SUNY New Paltz students, and children 7 and under.

Minnewaska State Park Preserve. 5281 NY/US 44/55, Kerhonkson; (845) 255-0752; nysparks.com/parks/127/details.aspx. This park rivals North Country hotspots like the Berkshire Mountains and Acadia National Park for aromatic evergreen forests, crystal-clear "sky lakes," and dramatic rock walls with long streams of falling water. The park's special pleasure is its wide, well-groomed carriage roads, created in the days when wealthy visitors from nearby metropolitan areas would ride through this park in horse-drawn carriages to admire the scenery. Today 35 miles of carriage roads (open only to pedestrians) remain in the park, and not surprisingly, they lead to some of the park's most spectacular sights. That's how you'll get to Awosting Falls, a sheer drop from a rock ledge into a wide plunge pool. On weekends from Memorial Day to Columbus Day, entrance to this parking area is

10 miles farther west, directly off US 44/NY 55. Open daily sunrise to dusk; $8 per vehicle on weekends in summer.

Mohonk Preserve. 3197 NY/US 44/55; (845) 255-0919; mohonkpreserve.org. Stop at the visitor center in this preserve for one of the best views in southern New York; it's worth waiting a bit for a parking space if none is available immediately. Once you're parked and out of the car, pick up a map in the visitor center of the short, easy trails that begin here. In addition to the walk to the classic viewpoint, the butterfly garden provides an excellent opportunity to watch monarch, swallowtail, and other colorful butterflies in motion if you're visiting in late spring or summer. If you couldn't park at the preserve, continue for a short distance to a parking area on your left. Here you're at the level of the Shawangunks' rock ridgeline, and the entire Hudson River Valley stretches out before you to the east. Visitor center: Daily 9 a.m. to 5 p.m. Preserve: Open daily, sunrise to 1 hour after sunset. Visitor center and immediate grounds are free; to hike, the day use fee is $12 adults, free for children 12 and under.

Shawangunk Ridge. Part of Minnewaska State Park Preserve (see above), 5281 NY/US 44/55, Kerhonkson; (845) 255-0752; nysparks.com/parks/127/details.aspx. "The Gunks" to people in the know, the north end of the Shawangunk Ridge is visible from New Paltz, and it may be the most striking single natural landmark in New York State, a sudden rocky outcropping among the gently rolling green mountains of the Catskills and the Appalachian range. If you're not into scaling rock faces, however, you may be like most New York residents who have no idea this imposing ridge exists. White quartz pebbles and sandstone, stuck together with a silica conglomerate, overlay the dark gray Martinsburg shale that arrived here about 470 million years ago with the deep ocean that once covered this land. The unique conglomerate arrived later, carried here by braided rivers, and both layers of rock jutted upward during the Permian period some 270 million years ago. When glaciers arrived just a few thousand years ago, they also scoured the ridge and dumped rocks off its east side, the finishing touches on this dramatic rise.

where to eat

For a small town, New Paltz has far more than its share of restaurants. You're sure to discover something you love here on your own, but here are a few of the standouts to help you narrow your choices.

A Tavola. 46 Main St.; (845) 255-1426; atavolany.com. Limiting its menu to a tight selection of starring dishes, this restaurant scores both on the quality of its food and on the exemplary service. Using fresh local ingredients, the chef has created an assortment of unusual choices in the Italian style, like the grilled octopus appetizer with chickpeas and olives, and the roasted local beets with whipped local goat cheese. Pasta dishes can be ordered as entrees or half-size starters (which may be plenty for smaller appetites). Most important, you'll feel like you made friends in your time here. Thurs through Mon 5:30 p.m. to closing; closed Tues and Wed. $$.

Mexicali Blue. 87 Main St.; (845) 255-5551; mexicali-blue.com. This is primarily a take-out restaurant, so if you're heading up into the Gunks, grab some fish tacos before you go. These are no ordinary tacos: they're blue corn tortillas loaded with catfish, tuna, salmon, or shrimp, paired with unusual ingredients like mango salsa, jicama, red onion, and cole slaw. If tacos aren't big enough for you, the burritos are just as interesting. Sun through Thurs 10 a.m. to 9 p.m., Fri and Sat 10 a.m. to 10 p.m. $–$$.

Main Street Bistro. 59 Main St.; (845) 255-7766; mainstreetbistro.com. Brave the crowds and get in here for the breakfast that was voted the best in the Hudson Valley. American and vegetarian dishes range from breakfast burritos with broccoli instead of bacon (or bacon instead of broccoli), or the Zoo Canoe, a pile of eggs, bacon, tomato, and cheese in a wedge of walnut citron bread. Pancakes are served with real maple syrup, the French toast can be smothered in your favorite fruit, and the choice of omelet ingredients is staggering. You can enjoy lunch here as well, but come for breakfast. Mon through Fri 8 a.m. to 4 p.m., Sat and Sun 7 a.m. to 6 p.m. $.

Rock and Rye Tavern. 215 Huguenot St.; (845) 255-7888; rockandrye.com. With its focus on "tried and true ways of taking care of people," as its website states, this establishment does its best to recapture the sense of what a tavern might have been like before we all started rushing through meals—back when going out to dinner was an event instead of a way to get out of cooking. The menu demonstrates a passion for good food, offering a wealth of small plates that feature local artisan cheeses and fresh produce, and entrees that cast a wider net to Tasmanian pepperberries and Prince Edward Island mussels. You won't go home hungry. Tues through Sun 5 p.m. to closing; closed Mon. $$.

where to stay

Mohonk Mountain House. 1000 Mountain Rest Rd.; (855) 883-3798; mohonk.com. One of the most famous inns in New York State had its humble beginnings in 1869, and today accommodates up to 600 guests in turn-of-the-20th-century style. The hotel fills a Victorian castle that rivals Downton Abbey, but with the modern conveniences today's guests expect from a luxurious hotel with a gasp-inducing view of the Hudson River Valley. As you might guess, the price of a room will elicit a gasp or two as well, especially from working-class folks like us. $$$.

where to shop

The Awareness Shop. 180 Main St.; (845) 255-5756; secure.awarenessshop.com. What is it about a day out of town that makes us want to explore our mystical selves? Here in this enticing metaphysical center, you can peruse the selection of tarot decks, crystals, books, incense, candles, blended essential oils, other scented products, and items used in spell rituals. Mon, Wed, Fri through Sun 11 a.m. to 6 p.m., Tues and Thurs 11 a.m. to 9 p.m.

Heady Teddy's Outfitters. 19 Front St.; (914) 373-1897; headyteddys.com. With a slant toward the groovy, this shop carries clothing, jewelry, and accessories you may not have seen since Woodstock, including licensed merchandise for the Grateful Dead, the Beatles, Jimi Hendrix, Bob Marley, and many more of your nostalgic faves. Open daily noon to 6 p.m.

Waterstreet Market. 10 Main St.; (845) 255-1403; waterstreetmarket.com. This little shopping village offers more than 20 shops and restaurants in one concentrated area, from the serenity of Himalayan Art to the contemporary fashions at Eden Boutique. A gallery of local artist G. Steve Jordan's photographs of the Hudson Valley, a cheese shop that provides a comprehensive introduction to the area's farm-raised bounty, and Maglyn's Dream, a shop that features the work of 80 local and regional artists, will keep you busy all afternoon. Hours may vary by establishment.

day trip 20

mid-hudson valley

>>> shawangunk hudson valley wine trail:
south
warwick, highland mills,
washingtonville, ny

Discover a wine region that produces world-class wines just up the road from Manhattan or down from Albany—an area with a centuries-old agricultural heritage and the ideal climate for growing viniferous and American grapes. The first half of your Hudson Valley wine tour begins 60 miles north of New York City and spans an area from Warwick to Washingtonville, north and south of NY 17.

getting there

To begin your tour in Warwick, take I-87 to exit 16 for NY 17 west. Merge onto NY 17 west and continue about 7 miles to exit 127, Greycourt Road/Sugar Loaf/Warwick. At the end of the exit ramp, turn left onto Lehigh Avenue, and left again onto county road 13/Kings Highway. Continue about 6 miles to Maple Avenue, and turn right. Take the first left onto Grand Avenue, and continue 0.5 mile to Pine Island Turnpike. Demarest Hill Winery in Warwick will be on your left.

warwick, ny

The sizable town of Warwick supplies this area with a measure of Revolutionary War history, serving as the site of a Continental Army encampment and hosting the iron works at which the Hudson River Chain was forged (see day trip 15). George Washington slept here at the home of John Hathorn in 1783. New York Yankees shortstop Derek Jeter owns a home here in Warwick, and a number of artists, authors, and musicians have chosen this scenic place for their homes since the 19th century. The town may be most famous for its annual Applefest, held on the first Sunday in October, and considered to be one of the top 100 events in North America (so says the American Bus Association, which transports more than 35,000 people to this festival annually).

what to do

Demarest Hill Winery. 81 Pine Island Turnpike; (845) 986-4723; demaresthillwinery.com. Winemaker Francesco Ciummo selected this spot for his winery after perfecting his skills in Molie, Italy, and in countries all over the world. Today Demarest produces its regionally famous Warwick Black Pearl Local and a range of reds including cabernet sauvignon, merlot, bacchus noir, red zinfandel and varietals, as well as a number of whites and a series of wines from other fruit. Beyond wines, Demarest offers vinegars grappa, brandy, and its own limoncella and orancella, luscious after-dinner drinks. Open daily 11 a.m. to 6 p.m., closed Christmas and New Year's Day.

Warwick Valley Winery & Distillery. 114 Little York Rd.; (845) 258-4858; wvwinery.com. Growing both European and American varietal grapes to create nearly a dozen wines, Warwick Valley also produces its line of American Fruits brandies and liqueurs from apples, pears, black currants, and sour cherries. The distillery's deliberately rustic Warwick Gin features coriander, angelica, root, and anise in addition to the traditional juniper berries. Open daily 11 a.m. to 6 p.m., closed Easter Sunday, Thanksgiving, Christmas, and New Year's Day. $5 wine tasting (6 wines and a winery glass).

Clearview Vineyard. 35 Clearview Lane; (845) 651-2838; clearviewvineyard.com. One of the newest wineries in the Hudson Valley, Clearview is the dream of its owners, Frank and Karen Graessle, who introduced their first vintages in 2011. Now producing boutique amounts of 8 varieties, they use their own organically grown grapes and purchase some from selected vineyards in the Finger Lakes for entirely New York State vintages (the Estate varieties are Clearview's own grapes). Tastings Fri and Sat noon to 5 p.m., or weekdays by appointment. $5 tasting (6 wines and an 11-ounce wine glass).

Applewood Winery. 82 Four Corners Rd.; (845) 988-9292; applewoodwinery.com. Producing limited-edition wines including chardonnay, cabernet Franc, and barrel-fermented reds, Applewood was one of the first wineries in the area to grow viniferous grape varieties. The apple orchard here predates the vineyard, however, finding its roots (literally) in 1949 when Donald B. Hull purchased the farmland to fulfill his dreams of becoming a fruit grower. Today the farm's apples are used to make Naked Flock Hard Cider and its Apple Blossom wine, which you can sample during your visit. Mar through Dec, Fri through Sun 11 a.m. to 5 p.m.; July and Aug, open until 6 p.m. on Sat; closed Jan and Feb. Tasting $6.

where to eat

Bellvale Farms Creamery. 385 NY 17A; (845) 988-1818; bellvalefarms.com. Fifty flavors of ice cream are made in small batches daily; call ahead if you've got a favorite to find out if it's available that day. The cream comes from the resident herd of Holstein and Jersey cows, and you can tour the farm on Sun at 12:30 p.m. from June to Oct if you'd like to meet them (call for a reservation). Locals swear this is the best ice cream in the Hudson Valley, served against a backdrop of an unbeatable valley view. Open daily Apr through Oct at noon—Apr and May until 8 p.m., end of May to end of June until 9 p.m.; July, Mon through Wed until 9 p.m., Thurs through Sun until 10 p.m.; Aug, daily until 9 p.m.; day after Labor Day until end of Oct, Mon through Wed until 8 p.m., Thurs through Sun to 9 p.m. $.

Pané Bakery Cafe. At Warwick Valley Winery & Distillery, 114 Little York Rd.; (845) 258-4858; wvwinery.com/pane. Fresh bread baked from scratch, pizzas, sandwiches, a marvelous fruit and cheese starter, and salads are the lunchtime and afternoon fare at this charming eatery on the winery grounds. Enjoy your lunch in the wood-paneled dining area or outside on the brick terrace overlooking the glorious Hudson Valley. You are welcome to open the wine you purchased at Warwick Valley to enjoy with your meal. Fri noon to 4 p.m., Sat and Sun noon to 5 p.m. $, cash only.

Yesterday's Irish Pub. 29 Main St.; (845) 986-9933; yesterdaysnet.com. Visitors swear by the Reuben at this tavern, but you won't go wrong with any of the Irish specialties: English beef stew, shepherd's pie, fish and chips, or the many variations on your American favorites. Sun through Thurs 11:30 a.m. to 10 p.m., Fri and Sat 11:30 a.m. to 11:30 p.m. $$.

highland mills, ny

North of Warwick, the hamlet of Highland Mills serves as an upscale bedroom community between Woodbury and Cornwall, with a cluster of businesses and restaurants along NY 32 on the way to Palaia Vineyards.

what to do

Palaia Vineyards and Winery. 10 Sweet Clover Rd.; (845) 928-5384; palaiavineyards .com. Farming land that has been used for agriculture for more than 200 years, Palaia produces wines on the lower level of its heroically restored barn with the tasting room above it. Working with the grapes that grow in their more than 10 acres of vineyards, Palaia is known for its cabernet franc, merlot, and traminette—but you can taste its mead, strawberry mead, and blended wines as well. Check the website for the live entertainment scheduled during your visit. Memorial Day to Dec 31, Mon through Thurs noon to 6 p.m., Fri noon to 11 p.m., Sat 11 a.m. to 11 p.m., Sun 11 a.m. to 6 p.m.; Jan 1 through Memorial Day, Fri noon to 11 p.m., Sat 11 a.m. to 11 p.m., Sun 11 a.m. to 6 p.m., closed Mon through Thurs.

where to eat

Mario's Restaurant. 503 NY 32 and County 105; (845) 928-2805; mariosny.com. All of your basic Italian favorites are here, cooked with the traditional recipes that make Italian food so comforting. The menu extends from antipasti to cannoli with plenty of Parmigiana, Bolognese, saltimbocca, and mellanzane to fill in all the spaces in between. Sun through Thurs 11:30 a.m. to 2 a.m., Fri and Sat 11:30 a.m. to 4 a.m. $$.

Taco Express and Deli. 514 NY 32; (845) 928-5305; tacosexpressdeli.jigsy.com. The tacos here get rave reviews from locals and visitors alike, as do the enchiladas for their authentically Mexican flavors. There's a full menu of entrees served with rice and beans, so if a taco or two doesn't fill you up, there's plenty more to come. The wall murals and tile floor give the place a sense of south-of-the-border style we don't often find in upstate New York. Mon through Sat 11 a.m. to 10 p.m., closed Sun. $$.

washingtonville, ny

Legend has it that General George Washington watered his horse in a trough under a big elm tree in the center of the village of "Little York," a tale that led village businessmen Samuel Moffat and John Jaques to rename it Washingtonville in 1818. Today the 2.5 square miles of Washingtonville house about 1,500 families around the crossroads of NY 94 and NY 208.

what to do

Brotherhood Winery. 100 Brotherhood Plaza Dr.; (845) 496-3661; brotherhood-winery .com. The underground cellars used for storage and fermentation here at Brotherhood are reputed to be the oldest winemaking cellars in the United States, originally dug in 1839 for Huguenot vintner Jean Jaques. The winery takes its name from an experimental utopian society that once lived here in the Hudson Valley, for whom Jaques supplied grapes to improve their wine vintages. If all this history is not enough to make you want to stop at this unusual winery, consider the possibilities of tasting wines that have been in production since the early 1800s, like a holiday wine that was served in colonial taverns. Jan through Mar, Fri through Sun 11 a.m. to 5 p.m.; Apr through Dec, daily 11 a.m. to 5 p.m., Sat until 6 p.m. $10 tour and tasting pass, $7 tasting flight.

where to eat

Kokopelli Cookie Company Bakery and Cafe. 9 Goshen Ave.; (845) 614-5665; face book.com/kokopellicookies. Handmade cookies, cakes, cupcakes, and more make this place a favorite with locals and visitors, especially for its breakfast pastries and French toast on Sat and Sun. If you like what you have here, you can order gift baskets or get a bag of cookies to nibble between wineries. Wed and Thurs 10 a.m. to 5 p.m., Fri 10 a.m. to 7 p.m., Sat 9 a.m. to 3 p.m., Sun 9 a.m. to 2 p.m. $.

Vinum Cafe at Brotherhood Winery. 100 Brotherhood Plaza Dr.; (845) 496-9001; vinum cafe.com. Here on the ground floor of the 1839 winery building, you can enjoy fine French cuisine in the restaurant's Copper Room, or lighter fare in the cafe. In warm weather, the outdoor patio with its two historic chimneys provides a one-of-a-kind setting for a romantic dinner. The restaurant also features a full bar with a wine and cheese happy hour until 7 p.m. Open Wed through Sun noon to 9 p.m. $$.

day trip 21

mid-hudson valley

>>> shawangunk hudson valley wine trail: north
marlboro, pine bush, new paltz, gardiner, ny

The Hudson Valley wine region produces world-class wines in an ideal climate for grape varieties that originated in Europe, and a number of new ones that were bred to do well in the temperate summers and frigid winters of New York State. The second half of your Hudson Valley wine tour begins in Marlboro and continues north to Gardiner.

getting there

To reach the first winery on this tour from the north or south, take the New York State Thruway (I-87) to exit 17 (I-84). Merge onto I-84 east and continue 2.5 miles to exit 10 (US 9W). At the end of the ramp, turn left onto US 9W. Continue 5 miles to Conway Road/Highland Avenue. Benmarl Winery will be on the right in about a mile.

marlboro, ny

During the 1800s, Marlboro was the principal supplier of fresh fruit to the residents of New York City—and today this rich agricultural heritage lives on through the fruit farms and wineries that flourish here. In addition to the winery tours and tastings you will find in this fertile area, the Marlboro area overflows with pick-your-own orchards, fruit farms, and farmers' markets to explore.

what to do

Benmarl Winery. 156 Highland Ave.; (845) 236-4265; benmarl.com. Producing wines in small batches has not kept Benmarl from growing—its production has tripled over the last six years, and the winery's view of the Hudson River Valley attracts many visitors to its tasting room. The vineyard on this 37-acre site is the oldest in America, and today it grows baco noir and cabernet franc grapes, while Benmarl sources Riesling from the Finger Lakes and merlot from Long Island's North Fork. Jan through Mar, Fri through Sun noon to 5 p.m.; Apr through Dec, daily noon to 6 p.m. Closed Thanksgiving, Christmas, New Year's Day through Jan 10, and Easter. $8 tasting includes 6 wines; $2 additional charge to keep the glass.

Stoutridge Vineyard. 10 Ann Kaley Lane; (845) 236-7620; stoutridge.com. The focus at Stoutridge is on sustainability, from its use of waste heat from its stills to heat the winery building to its use of gravity in its winemaking instead of pumps or filters. What this means for the wines is that you will find a little more sediment and a little less clarity, and the reds need to be decanted for several hours before drinking . . . but you will experience a boost in flavor. The winery stands on the site of the pre-Prohibition-era Morano Winery, which closed in 1919. Open all year, Fri through Sun 11 a.m. to 6 p.m. Call for this year's tasting price.

Glorie Farm Winery. 40 Mountain Rd.; (845) 236-3265; gloriewine.com. Producing wine at the boutique level of just 1,000 cases a year, the proprietors of Glorie Farm turned to wine in 2004 as a natural extension of their fruit farm's capabilities. Today they offer wine tastings of their new vintages and some unique blends—and an unusual DeChaunac, a grape usually found in blends that takes on a Chianti-like character here. Open Apr to Aug and Nov and Dec, Fri through Sun 11:30 a.m. to 5:30 p.m.; Sept and Oct, Fri through Sun 11:30 a.m. to 6 p.m. $5 for tasting of 5 wines and a souvenir glass.

pine bush, ny

Baldwin Vineyards. 176 Hardenburgh Rd.; (845) 744-2226; baldwinvineyards.com. Patricia and Jack Baldwin planted their first grapes here in 1982, and today the winery spans 35 acres and took the Hat Trick medal in the Finger Lakes International Wine Competition in 2013—not for its wines made from grapes, but for its strawberry, raspberry, and Trilogy (another raspberry) dessert wines. All three of these wines took medals again in 2014. Come for the fruity reds and the creamy chardonnay, but stay for these delicious desserts. May through Dec, Thurs through Sun noon to 5 p.m.; closed Thanksgiving and Christmas. Call for this year's tasting price.

Brimstone Hill Vineyard. 61 Brimstone Hill Rd.; (845) 744-2231; brimstonehillwinery.com. Brimstone Hill sold its first wines in 1980, creating wines from grapes planted in 1969. Since then the vineyard has grown to more than 13 acres, and the winery produces 9 wines including a sparkling wine in the "Methode Champenoise" tradition, and a Noiret—a fairly recent New York State grape variety that has already netted Brimstone Hill a bronze medal. Memorial Day weekend to Columbus Day weekend: daily 11:30 a.m. to 5:30 p.m. After Columbus Day to before Memorial Day: Sat and Sun 11:30 a.m. to 5:30 p.m., closed weekdays. Call for this year's tasting price.

where to eat

Cup and Saucer Diner. 82 Boniface Dr.; (845) 744-5969; facebook.com/CupAndSaucer Diner. Here's where you can fill up on a good breakfast before you head to the wineries. If you need a snack in the middle of the day, come back here for some stuffed grape leaves or wings; in the evening, there's roast turkey with stuffing or sugar-cured ham with fruit sauce. Every town needs a good, all-purpose diner. Daily 6 a.m. to 10 p.m. $.

Paraiso Latino. 72 Main St.; (845) 787-2451; paraisolatinopinebushnymexicanfood.com. For dependably good Mexican food on the Tex-Mex side of the spectrum, this eatery gets high marks from locals and visitors. Tacos, tamales, tostadas, and all the larger plates are here; don't miss the house's special queso blend. Mon through Wed 4:30 to 8:00 p.m.; Thurs 11:30 a.m. to 8 p.m.; Fri and Sat 11:30 a.m. to 9 p.m. $.

Thorndale Dairy Bar. 143 Maple Ave.; (845) 744-5382; yelp.com/biz/thorndale-dairy-bar-pine-bush. Don't miss this delicious stop on the corner of NY 52 and NY 302, where you can order from nearly two dozen flavors made on the premises. The banana cream pie ice cream bursts with fruit flavor even as it provides satisfying crunchiness with chunks of graham cracker crust, and the brownie chocolate-chip cookie dough would actually be too chocolaty if such a thing were possible. Birthday cake ice cream has become a staple at a lot of creameries, but here it's loaded with swirls of frosting and chunks of actual cake. Order mix-ins, sundaes, shakes, or any of your other favorite treats here as well, and enjoy them at outdoor picnic tables while you take in the remarkable Shawangunk area views. Open daily in season; call for this year's hours. $.

new paltz, ny

Here are the wineries to visit in New Paltz. For more information on what to see and do in this college town, see day trip 19.

what to do

Adair Vineyards. 52 Allhusen Rd.; (845) 255-1377; adairvineyards.com. Wines made from estate and local grapes with some unusual blends make Adair's cocktail wines—called "kir" after the French wine and fruit cocktail—particularly interesting. Be sure to try the black currant kir rouge and the kir peche during your visit. May through Oct, Sat and Sun 11 a.m. to 6 p.m.; Nov through mid-Dec, Sat and Sun 11 a.m. to 5 p.m. Closed mid-Dec through Apr. Call for this year's tasting price.

Robibero Winery. 714 Albany Post Rd.; (845) 255-9463; rnewyorkwine.com. This young, 42-acre winery produces artisan wines in limited amounts—sometimes no more than 40 cases—and sells them only at the vineyard or online, so a visit here is an opportunity to try some fairly rare vintages. Jan and Feb, Sat and Sun 11 a.m. to 6 p.m.; Mar through Jun and Dec, Thurs through Sun 11 a.m. to 6 p.m.; July through Nov, Thurs through Mon 11 a.m. to 6 p.m. Closed New Year's Day, Thanksgiving, and Christmas. $10 tasting of 5 wines and a souvenir glass; $15 for cellar tour and tasting.

gardiner, ny

The last leg of your wine tour takes you to Gardiner, where you'll find a number of antiques stores, farm markets, and the striking Gardiner Reformed Church, established in 1890, with its newly repaired and restored steeple. From here, you're just down the road from the magnificent Minnewaska State Park Preserve, described in detail in day trip 19.

what to do

Whitecliff Vineyard. 331 McKinstry Rd.; (845) 255-4613; whitecliffwine.com. One of the largest vineyards in the Hudson Valley, Whitecliff began as an outgrowth of owner Michael Migliore's degree in organic chemistry and his family's experience making wine at home. With his wife, Yancey, he experimented with grapes and growing until he found the winning combinations, and today Whitecliff has a globally recognized wine—its Riesling—that took a Best White Wine in Show Award in the San Francisco International Wine Competition. Open Feb through May, Nov, and Dec, Thurs through Mon 11:30 a.m. to 5:30 p.m.; June through Oct, daily 11:30 a.m. to 5:30 p.m., Sat until 6 p.m.; Jan, Sat only 11:30 a.m. to 5 p.m. $10 tasting of 6 wines and a souvenir glass ($8 with wine purchase), or $15 for a Crystal Tasting including 10 wines ($13 with wine purchase).

where to eat

Mountain Brauhaus Restaurant, 3123 US/NY 44/55; (845) 255-9766; mountainbrau haus.com. In the shadow of the Shawangunk ridgeline, this traditionally German restaurant may be best known for its extensive German beer and wine list. You'll find all of your favorites here, from bratwurst to jaegerschnitzel with spaetzle. If German food isn't for you, there's a nice burger menu as well. Wed through Sat 11:30 a.m. to 9 p.m., Sun 11:30 a.m. to 8:30 p.m.; closed Mon and Tues. $$.

Tuthill House at the Mill Restaurant and Tavern. 20 Grist Mill Lane; (845) 255-4151; tuthillhouse.com. A restaurant in a National Historic Landmark, Tuthill repurposes the Tuthill-town Gristmill—built in 1788—by featuring Italian and American country cooking. Ingredients are locally sourced and present many of the finest artisan products in the area. Sun, Mon, and Thurs 11:30 a.m. to 9 p.m.; Fri and Sat 11:30 a.m. to 10 p.m.; closed Tues and Wed. $$.

day trip 22

mid-hudson valley

>>>

hudson's 7 lights
new york city to athens, ny

Did you know there are lighthouses on the Hudson River? If you've never had to navigate the waters of a rushing river while heading upstream against the current, then it may surprise you that ships making their way between the banks of the Hudson required lighthouses to help them find their way. Just as navigational aids are necessary on the Great Lakes and the oceans, these beacons helped keep ships from running aground along the shorelines, and they let captains know where cities and towns were along the river's length. Today you can drive from one lighthouse to the next, from close to the river's mouth in Manhattan all the way up to Athens, New York.

getting there

The day trip begins in Fort Washington Park in northern Manhattan. From Riverside Drive at 181st Street, walk west and take the walking path into the park across the footbridge and down to the Hudson River. Look for the red lighthouse on the banks of the river, just under the George Washington Bridge.

what to do

Little Red Lighthouse (Jeffreys Hook Lighthouse). Fort Washington Park, Greenway, New York City; (212) 628-2345; hudsonlights.com/littlered.htm. Featured in the children's book *The Little Red Lighthouse and the Great Grey Bridge* by Hildegard H. Swift, this easily found light is actually the second to be built on this site. It was commissioned in 1922, but its useful life turned out to be short, as the construction of the George Washington Bridge made a navigational device unnecessary here. Thanks to Swift's book, however, the lighthouse became a popular landmark and the city made the decision to let it remain instead of demolishing it when it was decommissioned in 1947. Tours are offered once a month, June through Oct; call for this year's schedule. No admission fee.

From here, drive south on Riverside Drive to the ramp onto NY 9A north. Stay on this as it becomes the Henry Hudson Parkway, and then the Saw Mill River Parkway north. In about 10 miles, merge onto I-87 north. Take exit 9 toward US 9/Tarrytown/Sleepy Hollow. At the end of the ramp, turn left onto White Plains Boulevard, and then right onto South Broadway (continue to follow US 9). In about 2 miles, turn left onto Pierson Avenue, and right onto Bellwood Avenue. Take the third left onto Palmer Avenue. Turn left at the end of the road and enter Kingsland Point Park.

Tarrytown Light/1883 Lighthouse at Sleepy Hollow. Kingsland Point Park, Route 9, Sleepy Hollow; (914) 366-5109; hudsonlights.com/tarrytown.htm. This is the lighthouse you can see from the Tappan Zee Bridge anytime you drive to or from New York City. Shoals on the eastern shore of the Hudson River could be dangerous to ships navigating through this area, so the Tarrytown Lighthouse became a necessity by the middle of the 19th century. It took more than 30 years, however, for politicians and landowners to settle the controversy surrounding the purchase of the valuable land at Kingsland Point—a prosperous vineyard at the time—and to choose, at last, the spot offshore in the river itself. Pieces of the lighthouse came partially assembled by barge, and the lighthouse began assisting with navigation in 1883. It served its purpose until 1961, six years after the Tappan Zee Bridge rendered it unnecessary, and it became a point of controversy once again as citizens rallied to save it from demolition. Finally, on October 1, 1983—exactly 100 years since its original commission—it reopened to the public for tours. Tours are by appointment only or during periodic public visiting hours; call for details and fees.

Cross the Tappan Zee Bridge on I-87/287 and continue about 8 miles to exit 13N for the Palisades Parkway North. Merge onto the Palisades and continue about 10 miles to exit 15: Gate Hill Road and Stony Point. At the end of the ramp, turn left onto NY 210. In about 2.7 miles, turn left onto S. Liberty Drive. Continue to Park Road, and turn right. Go straight into the Stony Point Battlefield.

Stony Point Lighthouse. Stony Point Battlefield State Historic Site, Battlefield Road, Stony Point; (845) 786-2521; hudsonlights.com/stonypoint.htm. (For more on Stony Point Battlefield, see day trip 5.) Built in 1826 when river traffic increased after the opening of the Erie Canal, this is the oldest lighthouse on the Hudson River. Lighthouse keepers here had to be mindful of fog as well as shoals and other hazards, and often spent a foggy day or night hand-ringing a bell near the shoreline to guide navigators up and down the river. The light functioned here for just under 100 years, and in all of that time only one ship ran aground (in March 1901), and not a single life was lost at this point in the river. While the lighthouse was decommissioned in 1925 and replaced by a steel tower close to the shoreline, this light remained on post, eventually becoming part of the historic site and receiving a complete restoration. It opened to the public in 1995, and tours are available on weekends from mid-April through Labor Day. Open Apr 15 to Oct 21, Fri and Sat 10 a.m. to 5 p.m. No admission fee.

From the battlefield, turn right onto Park Road and right again onto US 202 east/US 9W north. Continue about 56 miles on US 9W north to Ulster Park, New York. Turn right on River Road in Ulster Park and drive 1.4 miles to the lighthouse.

Esopus Meadows Lighthouse. 255 CR 24, Ulster Park; (845) 848-1569; hudsonlights .com/esopus.htm. This small lighthouse sits in the middle of the river, surrounded by water on a foundation of 250 40-foot-long poles driven into the riverbed. The area required a lighthouse at this spot because of mud flats to the west on the river, which presented a potential hazard for boat traffic. This lighthouse was constructed in 1871 with a 53-foot-high light tower, and it's the only remaining lighthouse on the river with a wood frame. Extensive renovations have restored this building to its original structural integrity and design, with some modernization to ensure its continued sturdiness. It's not open to the public, as the structure is not safe for visitors.

Take Union Center Road to NY 213 east and turn right. Drive 3.8 miles to Broadway and turn right. In about 500 feet, turn left onto Rondout Landing. Continue to the Hudson River Maritime Museum.

Rondout Lighthouse. Hudson River Maritime Museum, 50 Rondout Landing, Kingston; (845) 338-0071; hudsonlights.com/rondout.htm. (For more information on restaurants and things to do in Historic Kingston, see day trip 25.) Two lighthouses preceded the one you see here: one made of wood in 1837 that barely lasted a winter, and another built in 1867, for which you can still see the circular base. The lighthouse you can visit today was constructed from 1913 to 1915, and it marks the end of the Delaware and Hudson Canal here in Kingston. Here workers unloaded canal barges laden with Pennsylvania coal transported through the Shawangunk Mountains, transferring the coal to riverboats that took it down to New York City. As technology improved and the lighthouse became automated with electricity in the 1940s, the need for a lighthouse keeper ended—but this light continues to serve as a navigational aid even though it's now part of the Hudson River Maritime Museum. As of this writing, the lighthouse is not open for tours; check the museum's website at hrmm .org/explore/rondout-lighthouse for current information.

Return to US 9W north and continue about 13 miles to Saugerties. Continue on US 9W north to Clermont Street and turn right. Turn right again on Post Street. Continue to Lighthouse Drive and go straight to the lighthouse.

Saugerties Lighthouse. 168 Lighthouse Dr., Saugerties; (845) 247-0656; saugertieslight house.com. The Saugerties Lighthouse Conservancy stepped in to buy and restore this aging light, which was commissioned in 1869 and served its purpose until the light was automated in 1954. Today it's a bed-and-breakfast establishment on the edge of a 17-acre nature preserve, making a visit here a particularly delightful experience. Take the 0.5-mile trail to the lighthouse (check the tide schedule first) or a forked trail to a picnic area along the river, and enjoy a 20-minute tour of the lighthouse and the climb to the top of the tower. Tours offered Memorial Day through Labor Day on Sun afternoons, or by appointment. $5 donation requested, $3 for children.

Return to US 9W and drive north to NY 23 north of Catskill. Turn right on NY 23 east and cross the Rip Van Winkle Bridge. Turn left on NY 23 east and continue about 2.5 miles to NY 9G north. Turn left and continue about 2 miles to Mt. Merino Road; turn left. Take this road to the end to reach a good viewing spot for the lighthouse.

Hudson-Athens Lighthouse. Visible at the end of Mt. Merino Road, Athens; (518) 828-5294; hudsonlights.com/hudson.htm. Standing in the middle of the river between Hudson and Athens, this light emerged at the end of a long petitioning process to convince the US Congress to allocate funds for its construction after the Civil War. This part of the river contains the Middle Ground Flats, a hazardous section that made navigation particularly risky— so eventually, Congress yielded and construction took place. The light was built to last, with a front end resembling the bow of a ship to ward off ice floes, and pilings driven some 50 feet into the riverbed to keep the light permanently embedded. Restored in 1990 to its full glory by the Hudson-Athens Lighthouse Preservation Society, this Second Empire–style lighthouse remains an impressive landmark, and its beacon continues to operate under the supervision of the US Coast Guard. Boat tours are available on the second Saturday of July, Aug, Sept, and Oct, departing from Henry Hudson Riverfront Park in Hudson; check the website at hudsonathenslighthouse.org/events.html for details. $25 adults, $10 for children under 12, includes boat ticket.

day trip 23

mid-hudson valley

>>> **lifestyles of the rich & powerful**
hyde park, rhinebeck, ny

Back in the days when industrial giants roamed the Hudson Highlands, the most spectacular views of the Hudson River quickly became the property of the wealthiest families in the nation. Families with names including Roosevelt, Vanderbilt, Mills, and Astor laid claim to thousands of acres of hilltop landscape and built magnificent mansions that captured the area's sweeping vistas through their expansive windows. The captains of industry are long gone today, but their estates remain—and the families of a number of the original owners had the foresight to make arrangements for these manor homes to be maintained in perpetuity as monuments to opulent living. Your visit to Hyde Park and Rhinebeck will not be complete without tours of these remarkable homes.

hyde park, ny

Here in the cradle of genteel 20th-century civilization, the ultra-wealthy Vanderbilt family built its fabulous mansion, the Roosevelts preserved many acres of natural land and used Hyde Park as a northern White House, industrial leader Ogden Mills built the family's Greek Revival estate home, and a descendant of the Beekmans and the Livingstons, two prominent families of the 17th and 18th centuries, constructed a Queen Anne–style country house with one of the finest views on the river. This is the place to discover how the wealthiest 0.001 percent lived in the times of our nation's greatest growth.

getting there

From New York City, take the Henry Hudson Parkway (NY 9A) to the Saw Mill River Parkway. Continue 10 miles on the Saw Mill, and merge onto I-87 north. Take exit 9 toward US 9. Continue about 45 miles on US 9 to Hyde Park.

what to do

Clinton Vineyards. 450 Schultzville Rd., Clinton Corners; (845) 266-5372; clintonvineyards .com. If you feel the need to extend the sense of the luxurious life beyond your tour of the mansion, make a stop at Clinton Vineyards, a quick trip northeast of Hyde Park on your way to Rhinebeck, and sample the gold medal–winning cassis, a full-bodied black currant dessert wine. The vineyard's seyval blanc, a single-grape white wine, is a well-reviewed favorite, while its Jubilee and Seyval Naturel use seyval blanc grapes to create a sparkling wine in the traditional Champagne-style method. Open Oct through Jan and Mar 15 through beginning of Apr, Fri through Sun noon to 5 p.m.; closed in Feb and through Mar 15. Open Apr through Sept, Fri through Sun 1 to 6 p.m. Wine tasting is $10.

Eleanor Roosevelt National Historic Site. 54 Valkill Park Rd.; (845) 229-9422; nps.gov/ elro. First Lady Eleanor Roosevelt also maintained a home of her own, called Val-Kill, and the National Park Service now preserves this modest house. Here the wife of the president established Val-Kill Industries, a factory that provided rural families with income during the winter, making furniture, cloth, and pewter items right here in the First Lady's household. The program became a model for some of the initiatives Roosevelt would enact as part of the New Deal. Mrs. Roosevelt turned the factory into her home after the Great Depression, moving into it permanently after her husband's death. This is where she lived while she served as the first chair of the United Nations Commission on Human Rights, and as chair of the Presidential Commission on the Status of Women under President John F. Kennedy. Open May to Oct, daily 9 a.m. to 5 p.m.; Nov through Apr, guided tours Thurs through Mon at 1 and 3 p.m., closed Tues and Wed. $10 adults, children 15 and under are free.

Home of Franklin Delano Roosevelt National Historic Site. 4097 Albany Post Rd.; (845) 229-5320; nps.gov/hofr. This National Park Service unit sits adjacent to the **Franklin Delano Roosevelt Presidential Library and Museum,** so if you're an FDR fan or if you want to learn more about the president who held the office longer than any other person in history, you can immerse yourself in Roosevelt information for days at this site. Roosevelt gave us Social Security and the Federal Deposit Insurance Corporation, dug the country out of the Great Depression with a number of stimulus programs, put people back to work through the Works Progress Administration and the Civilian Conservation Corps, and saw the US through World War II. While he ran into many of the same kinds of controversies over his policies that we see in our own Congress today, he accomplished a great deal—including the New Deal—for working-class Americans, all of it after polio placed him in a wheelchair in 1921. He died on April 12, 1945, just a few weeks after his inauguration to his fourth term as president, and he and his wife, Eleanor Roosevelt, are buried here on the grounds of the estate. Take the 1-hour guided tour to understand what home life was like for a president of the United States who governed from a wheelchair—and see the actual hearth where he delivered his famous Fireside Chats. Open daily 9 a.m. to 5 p.m., closed Thanksgiving, Christmas, and New Year's Day. $18 joint admission ticket to both the home and the FDR Presidential Library; children 15 years and under are free.

Mills-Norrie State Park. 9 Old Post Rd., Staatsburg; (845) 889-4646; nysparks.com/parks/171/details.aspx. A pair of adjoining parks created from the estates of Margaret Lewis Norrie and Ogden and Ruth Livingston Mills, these 1,000 acres provide walking and cycling trails, woods, a marina and boat launch on the river, and some of the best panoramic views of the countryside that you'll find in the Hudson Valley. Open daily year-round, sunrise to sunset; $8 entrance fee on weekends in summer.

Staatsburgh State Historic Site, Old Post Road, Staatsburg; (845) 889-8851; nysparks.com/historic-sites/25/details.aspx. Just outside of Hyde Park to the north, you'll find the former home of Ogden Mills and his wife, Ruth Livingston Mills. The Mills family made their money in banks, railroads, and mines, investing in promising enterprises and seeing those investments pay off, and Ruth Livingston inherited this property originally acquired by her great-grandfather Morgan Lewis, the third governor of New York State. Today you can tour this sprawling, 65-room Beaux-Arts mansion with its French-style interior design and its many pieces from the 1600s and 1700s, and get a sense of the period called the American Renaissance. The gift shop here, by the way, is one of the top-rated in the county by local residents. Apr 17 through Oct: Open Thurs through Sun and holiday Mondays, 11 a.m. to 5 p.m.; closed Tues and Wed; closed Easter. Nov 1 through Thanksgiving: Closed for holiday decorating. Fri after Thanksgiving through Dec: Open Thurs through Sun noon to 4 p.m. Closed Christmas Eve and Christmas Day. Open every day Dec 26 to 31. Jan through Mar: group tours only by appointment. $8 adults, $6 students and seniors, free for children 12 and under.

Vanderbilt Mansion National Historic Site. 119 Vanderbilt Park Rd.; (845) 229-7770; nps.gov/vama. In sharp contrast to Eleanor Roosevelt's understated home, the Vanderbilt Mansion National Historic Site may be everything you might expect of the home of one of the nation's richest industrial magnates. This mansion is one of the region's oldest estates on the Hudson River, built in the late 1800s in the classic American Beaux-Arts style and still furnished with many of the pieces purchased by the Vanderbilts themselves. Just visiting the formal gardens gives you an idea of the kinds of lives the elite class could live at the time, but you really must go inside and take the tour to fully comprehend the divisions between the very wealthy people of the Gilded Age and the rest of us. In addition to this marvelous estate, the historic site also owns the original estate records, ledgers, diaries, and photos that inform the preservation of the buildings and grounds, lending a superlative level of authenticity to the park service's management of the estate as a historical resource. Open Apr through Oct daily by guided tour only; tours are given throughout the day. The visitor center is open 9 a.m. to 5 p.m. In Nov and Dec, and March 9 to 31, open daily; tours are given at 10 a.m., noon, and 2 and 4 p.m. Closed Thanksgiving, Christmas, and New Year's Day. Jan through early Mar, closed on Wed and Thurs; open Fri through Tues by tour only; tours are given at 10 a.m., noon, and 2 and 4 p.m. The grounds are free and open daily from sunrise to sunset. $10 adults; children 15 and under are free.

where to eat

Culinary Institute of America. 1946 Campus Dr., Hyde Park; (845) 471-6608; ciachef .edu/newyork. Recognized by many as the premier college for chefs in the entire world, the CIA draws the next generation of top chefs to learn their craft here—and you have the opportunity to sample their creativity and admire their skill by dining in one of several restaurants on campus. All restaurants keep the same hours: Tues through Sat, lunch 11:30 a.m. to 1 p.m.; dinner 6 to 8:30 p.m.; closed Sun, Mon, and major holidays.

> **American Bounty Restaurant.** Using the freshest local ingredients and focusing its menu on the Hudson Valley, this restaurant demonstrates how enlightened culinary skill and farm-to-table procurement can work together. Roasted chicken from KNK Farm gets a boost from butternut squash bread pudding and lemon chutney, while Hudson Valley Moulard duck breast becomes a delicacy when combined with applejack brandy sauce and sweet-potato puree. Best of all, you'll find a nice variety of New York State wines complementing the dishes. As for dessert, how about chestnut cake with white chocolate caviar? $$$.

> **Apple Pie Bakery Cafe.** You can enjoy fresh-baked delicacies and casually elegant fare at this cafe without a reservation. For breakfast, you'll find a selection of scones, bagels, croissants, buns, and muffins, while lunch includes soups, salads, and a variety of savory dishes including a cheese selection and an assortment of meats and condiments. Save room for a caramel éclair or a raspberry tart. Mon through Fri 7:30 a.m. to 5 p.m. $.

> **Bocuse Restaurant.** Billed as "a culinary journey through France," this extraordinary restaurant takes the culinary high road in preparing traditional dishes with contemporary flair—and even technology. You'll feast on dishes like slow-cooked guinea hen with a green pea and lemongrass puree, or braised beef short rib with hibiscus-infused parsnips. Be sure to order the ice cream made tableside using liquid nitrogen. $$$.

> **Ristorante Caterina de'Medici.** Dine in a Tuscan-style villa, either in the sophisticated dining room overlooking the Hudson River, or in the casual Al Forno

Trattoria bistro. Your dinner may begin with zuppe di ortiche—barley and nettle soup—or gnocchi in a pecorino and saffron fondue, followed by a lamb loin chop with dandelion greens or roasted veal with porcini mushrooms and spring onions. If you choose Al Forno, you can enjoy a traditional wood-fired pizza or a panini involving ingredients like goat cheese, chickpea hummus, parmacotto, or fontina cheese and herb mayonnaise. Either way, you're sure to have a delicious experience. Ristorante $$$, Al Forno $$.

rhinebeck, ny

Rhinebeck became the center of international attention in the summer of 2010 when Chelsea Clinton, daughter of former President Bill Clinton and former Secretary of State Hillary Rodham Clinton, married Marc Mezvinsky at Astor Courts, on John Jacob Astor IV's former **Ferncliff estate.** If you'd like to see the mansion where the wedding took place, turn left onto Montgomery Street in Rhinebeck, and take the first left onto Astor Drive. The property is privately owned and is not open for tours; please respect the owners' privacy.

Even on the heavily trafficked US 9, one extraordinary home after another slides into view, most of them repurposed as bed-and-breakfast establishments, inns, and shops. More than 400 homes in this town are listed on the National Register of Historic Places, and the town itself is a designated National Landmark District—and part of the Hudson River Valley National Heritage Area, just to give it some extra panache. Dutch settlers arrived here in 1686, including Henry Beekman and Casper Landsman, two men whose names are still on many landmarks in the area. William Traphagen built the first tavern here on what would become US 9 back in 1706, and his son relocated the tavern in 1766. The Bogardus Inn, as it was known then, changed hands a number of times until it became the Beekman Arms Inn—albeit with extensive renovations. Today the Beekman Arms is the oldest continually operating inn in the US.

what to do

Dutchess County Fairgrounds. 6550 Spring Brook Ave.; (845) 876-4000; dutchessfair .com. From May to Oct, there's a special event every month at this central meeting place for the entire county. The Dutchess County Fair in August is the second largest fair of its kind in New York State, bringing nearly half a million people to the fairgrounds' 144 acres to see thousands of farm animals, horticultural and agricultural displays, and free shows and music acts. May brings the Rhinebeck Antiques Fair, June features the Hudson Valley Brew Festival, and the lure in October is the Sheep and Wool Family Festival, one of the most popular fiber arts fests in the state. Ticket prices vary for a wide range of events. Visit the website for days, times, and admission fees.

Hudson River Valley Greenway. Headquarters at 625 Broadway, 4th Floor, Albany; (518) 473-3835; hudsongreenway.ny.gov. Thirteen counties border the Hudson River, and a total of 264 communities live within these counties. In an effort to bring all of these civic units together to preserve and protect the Hudson River and the land throughout its watershed, the state of New York created the Hudson River Valley Greenway Act of 1991, a process for cities and counties to become partners in protecting green space and historic resources along the river. There is no central place where you can "visit" the Greenway, but it's a good thing to keep in mind in your travels throughout this region—more than 250 communities are working together to provide the pristine landscapes, extensive views, and nuggets of historical significance you enjoy on your day trips.

Old Rhinebeck Aerodrome. 9 Norton Rd.; (845) 752-3200; oldrhinebeck.org. If you have a passion for World War I and Lindbergh-era aircraft or the pioneering crafts that preceded them, a visit to this museum is a must. Here you can see original aircraft including a 1909 Bleriot XI from France, a Burgess-Collier Model M Flying Boat built in 1913, a Curtiss JN-4H that has survived since 1917, and dozens of other original planes and skillfully crafted reproductions. If you visit on a Sunday from June to Oct, you can see some of these planes take to the air—and you can even take a ride in a biplane. Open May to Oct, daily 10 a.m. to 5 p.m. Closed Nov to Apr. Weekday admission: $10 adults, $8 seniors 65+ and teens 13 to 17, $3 children 6 to 12 and Scouts in uniform, free to children under 5. Weekend airshows: $20 adults, $15 active military, seniors 65+, and teens 13 to 17, $5 children 6 to 12 and Scouts in uniform, free to children 5 and under.

Wilderstein Historic Site. 330 Morton Rd.; (845) 876-4818; wilderstein.org. Take a left onto South Mill Road and drive through a wooded neighborhood to reach perhaps the most unusual of the mansions-turned-museums in this area, because of its Queen Anne style. When Thomas Holy Suckley bought this land in 1852, he and his wife prized the natural setting with its varied terrain and its stunning views of the river, and they built an Italianate villa on the site. Nearly four decades later, the Suckleys' son and his wife transformed the villa into the elaborate home we see here, with its 5-story circular tower and its multi-gabled attic. When you see the outside, you will want to know how the inside fits together and how New York City decorator Joseph Burr Tiffany made the most of the design with his interior choices. Grounds are open year-round, 9 a.m. to 4 p.m. daily. Mansion tours: May through Oct, Thurs through Sun, tours every half-hour from noon to 3:30 p.m. Closed Mon, Tues, and Wed. The mansion is closed Nov through Apr. $10 adults, $9 students/seniors, free for children under 12.

where to shop

A.L. Stickle 5 & Dime Store. 13 E. Market St.; (845) 876-3206; alstickle.com. Where can you buy a paddle-ball game, alpaca-wool yarn, a cap gun, and collapsible drinking cups, all in one place? Here at Stickle's, you'll find these items and thousands more, most of them for prices close to what we older folks remember from the neighborhood five-and-dime back in the 1960s. You'll want plenty of time to explore this place, especially if you knit or crochet—in the Knitting Garage, you'll find yarns here from brands like Blue Sky Alpaca, Jade Sapphire, Spud & Chloe, and many others. Try to schedule your visit around a wine and yarn tasting, when Stickle's pairs its yarns with wines of the same region. Mon through Sat 9 a.m. to 5 p.m.; Sun 11:30 a.m. to 4 p.m.

Gatehouse at Old Mill Antiques. 7085 NY 9; (845) 876-0685; gatehouseatoldmill.com. This popular antiques store specializes in furniture and accessories from the late 18th to the early 20th centuries. This is the place to go for primitives, Americana, and one-of-a-kind pieces. Wed and Fri 11:30 a.m. to 4 p.m.; Sat and Sun 11 a.m. to 5 p.m. Closed Tues and Thurs; call for a Mon appointment.

Hammertown Barn. 6420 Montgomery St.; (845) 876-1450; hammertown.com. With a commitment to helping you "love where you live," Hammertown features carefully chosen furniture and housewares that work together to create a store you'll want to come to again and again. Owner Joan Osofsky looks for high-quality local products and items made in America, as well as the products of companies that place enlightened reasoning and concern for the environment within their operating philosophy. The result is what locals call "Hammertown style," including many products you may not have seen before, from bedding and bath products to rugs and lighting. Mon through Sat 10:30 a.m. to 5:30 p.m.; Sun 11 a.m. to 5 p.m.; open later in summer.

Montgomery Row. This is the place to go for all kinds of unusual shops, boutiques, restaurants, and seasonal events. Hailed as the best shopping block in the valley by *Hudson Valley* magazine, this district features many locally owned and one-of-a-kind stores, from the unique canine apparel at Pause Dog Boutique to the specialty kitchen experience at bluecashew Kitchen Pharmacy. Hours vary per establishment.

day trip 24

mid-hudson valley

>>> **the lost towns of rondout**
peekamoose road, rondout reservoir,
ellenville, ny

Clean water: It's a mainstay we take for granted as it comes out of our taps and fills our sinks, bathtubs, drinking glasses, and ice cube trays. In New York City in the late 19th and early 20th centuries, however, clean drinking water was a luxury for the well-to-do and the middle class, while the vast majority of residents—immigrants arriving by the hundreds of thousands every week—struggled to find usable sanitation facilities in the slums of lower Manhattan. The City of New York examined its options and determined that there was plenty of clean water up in the Catskill Mountains, in that magical land they referred to only as "upstate." The city's leaders needed a way to collect the water flowing through rivers and creeks in the Catskill region, so plans began to build a vast network of reservoirs throughout the green region.

This was all well and good for the poor and suffering residents of New York City, but the decision to create reservoirs and export the water to the metropolitan area meant that some of the Catskills' small towns would have to make the ultimate sacrifice. The city planned to build Merriman Dam, a barrier across Rondout Creek, allowing the water to back up behind it and cascade into an enormous lake basin 6.5 miles long and 175 feet deep at its lowest point. The sudden appearance of a lake-size reservoir required much more land than the creek did before it, so entire small towns would be submerged. How this may have been presented to the residents is anyone's guess, but all of these residents agreed to move (eventually). As you drive along the reservoir, watch for signs that note the previous locations of Lackawack, Montela, and Eureka, all of which were condemned and flooded.

Your day trip begins with a pleasant drive down Peekamoose Road, one of the Catskills' rare gems with more than its fair share of waterfalls. I recommend that you continue from the end of Peekamoose to the Rondout Reservoir, and then on to Ellenville, where you'll find plenty of services and a number of restaurants.

peekamoose road, ny

This little-known but much loved roadway follows Rondout Creek and provides great looks at a number of waterfalls tumbling down the Catskill Mountains on either side of the road. It's a great way to start an exploration that leads you around the reservoir for excellent water views.

getting there

From I-87 south, take exit 19 (Kingston), then take NY 28 West 16.3 miles to the junction with NY 28A and bear left (west) onto NY 28A. Continue 3 miles to Watson Hollow Road and turn right. In 7.8 miles, Watson Hollow Road becomes Peekamoose Road.

what to do

Here in the midst of the protected lands of Catskill Park, Peekamoose Road stretches along the bottom of a heavily wooded valley nestled between Woodstock to the northeast and Grahamsville to the southwest. With the Ashokan Reservoir at one end and the Rondout Reservoir at the other, Peekamoose Road passes over a number of small waterways including Rondout Creek, Buttermilk Falls Brook, and tributaries and side streams that seem to have no names. As a result, this road provides us with access to at least six stunning waterfalls—and probably more in the high-water seasons. Rugged outdoor people use these falls for ice climbing in winter, bear-watching in spring and summer, and as the icing on the foliage cake during autumn leaf-peeping season.

You might think that such a popular place would have all of its attributes carefully mapped, named, and labeled, but Peekamoose Road has managed to keep it loose for many decades. Some of the falls may not be flowing on the day you visit, but others might be raging torrents in that season. Rest assured that whenever you choose to explore Peekamoose Road, you will see waterfalls. Drive slowly and keep an eye out at every opening in the trees or bridge crossing on the south side of the road, and you will spot the falls.

rondout reservoir, ny

Sundown Creek meets Rondout Creek on the left side of Peekamoose Road at Sundown Wild Forest, where you will find trailheads, a campground, and other amenities in season. As you come into the town of Sundown, homes begin to appear along the road. This is the end of the waterfall portion of this drive, but you can continue on County Route 46 as it becomes NY 55A, and turn left on NY 55A for a very pleasant drive along Rondout Reservoir.

Built from 1937 to 1954, Rondout Reservoir provides water to New York City—in fact, it's one of six reservoirs in the Catskills constructed for this purpose. Today Rondout Reservoir contains 49.6 billion gallons of water, which reaches New York City through the 85-mile-long Delaware Aqueduct—the world's longest continuous underground tunnel.

Merriman Dam marks the southeastern end of Rondout Reservoir, and NY 55A soon joins NY 55 as it follows the southern end of Rondout Creek all the way down to Honk Lake. Here the road enters the town of Ellenville and NY 209, ending the scenic drive.

ellenville, ny

At the junction of US 209 and NY 52, turn left and enter Ellenville. Here in the Rondout Valley, the Shawangunk Ridge rises in the east, and the Catskill Mountains appear in the west, surrounding this small town with scenery. It's no wonder that settlers moved into this area before the Revolutionary War, though the village itself did not start to take shape until 1798. It takes its name from Ellen Snyder, who convinced the town leaders to name it after her when they reached a stalemate in a meeting on the subject.

what to do

Cragsmoor Historic District (formerly Evansville). On NY 52 near the top of the Shawangunk Ridge; (845) 647-4611; cragsmoor.info. It may not surprise you that artists have found inspiration from these spectacular mountain views and the diversity of plant and animal life here for centuries. Nearby, the Cragsmoor Historic District once housed an artists' colony that included the popular rural nostalgia painter Edward Lamson Henry, as well as figure and landscape artist George Inness Jr. The entire district was named to the National Register of Historic Places in 1996. A short drive or a stroll through the 19th-century cottages will give you a sense of what it must have been like to live among those who shared a passion for capturing this natural landscape on canvas. The town is always open to the public; many buildings are privately owned and not available for tours, but you are welcome to walk the town's streets at your leisure. No admission fee.

North Gully Falls. On NY 52 after the junction of NY 209 and NY 52; (845) 647-7080; villageofellenville.com. At the junction of NY 209 and NY 52, turn left (east). The big white steeple in front of you is Ellenville Reformed Church, probably the most easily identifiable landmark in town. Continue up NY 52 as it curves to the left and begins to climb. As you cross Rondout Creek, look to your left to see North Gully Falls, a particularly attractive waterfall set back into the crevasse the flowing water has created here. In a moment, there's a pull-off area from which you can enjoy a terrific view of the valley. Be warned, however, that you are likely to encounter a rather shocking amount of trash and debris here, as people seem to stop here to admire the view and drop their beer cans, paper cups, cigarette butts, and whatever else they are holding before getting back into their cars. There's quite a lot of this kind of abuse of natural spaces the closer you get to New York City; this is a sad fact of downstate life. Always open; be careful in winter. Free admission.

Sam's Point Preserve. 400 Sam's Point Rd., Cragsmoor; (845) 647-7989; nature .org/ourinitiatives/regions/northamerica/unitedstates/newyork/placesweprotect/easternnew york/wherewework/eastern-sams-point-preserve.xml. Here at the highest point of the Shawangunk Ridge, you can enjoy one of the most spectacular views of the Catskill Mountains in the entire region. When masses of conglomerate separated during some major tectonic event, the movement produced deep gaps between the vertical layers, creating places like this one. If you want to see the deeper canyons, the Shingle Gully Ice Caves in Sam's Point Preserve offer challenging hiking and remarkable views. For those who may not be up for climbing into ice caves, Sam's Point also offers one of the best examples of ridgetop dwarf-pine barrens in the world, according to the Nature Conservancy—and because of this and the preserve's protection of nearly 40 rare plant and animal species, the conservancy has made this place one of its highest priorities for conservation in the US. If you visit from Thurs to Sun, stop into the preserve's conservation center to check on recent sightings, find out the condition of trails, and get information that will help you make the most of an afternoon or a day spent here. Open daily. Summer hours (May 1 through early Oct): 9 a.m. to 7 p.m. Winter hours: 9 a.m. to 5 p.m. Conservation Center: Mid-Apr through Nov, Thurs through Mon 9 a.m. to 5 p.m. $10 parking fee per vehicle.

where to eat

Aroma Thyme Bistro. 165 Canal St.; (845) 647-3000; aromathymebistro.com. With a firmly stated commitment to sound environmental practices, this Certified Green restaurant (the certification comes from the Green Restaurants Association) creates its menu from local produce and dairy products, meats from local farms that raise free-range, grass-fed animals, wild-caught seafood and fish from sustainable fisheries, and selections like a shot of fresh pressed organic wheatgrass juice as an appetizer. The result is an award-winning restaurant with a varied menu that features many vegetarian choices alongside spicy seafood dishes, beef and chicken, and hearty soups and salads. Mon through Wed 5 to 10 p.m., Thurs 5 to 11 p.m., Fri 3 to 11 p.m., Sat and Sun noon to 11 p.m. $$.

Gaby's Cafe. 150 Canal St.; (845) 210-1040; gabyscafe.com. Mexican dishes prepared with plenty of style make this restaurant a favorite with locals and tourists. You'll find all of your favorites, but with lots of flair: guacamole prepared tableside, fajitas that include lobster tails with beef (filet mignon) or calamari and chorizo as well as chicken, 7 kinds of quesadillas, and platters that are as tasty as they are substantial. Bring your friends and your appetite. Open daily 11 a.m. to 10 p.m. $$.

day trip 25

mid-hudson valley

>>> **the world's largest kaleidoscope**
kingston, hurley, mount tremper,
phoenicia, ny

If you live in New York State and you've driven upstate from New York City or down from the Chautauqua or Great Lakes regions, you may have passed through Catskill Park on NY 17 and admired the scenery as it whizzed past. This day trip gives you the opportunity to slow down and savor this truly magnificent area, one of two massive preserves in New York State that contain both private and public land.

About 100 miles north of New York City and 40 miles south of Albany, Catskill Park forms the northeastern end of the Allegheny Plateau, a mountain range that extends all the way to Kentucky and as far west as Ohio. The mountains begin dramatically on the shores of the Hudson River, where they rise sharply, and then they roll gradually through the southeastern part of the state until their height begins to decline as they join the plateau to the west and blend into the Poconos to the south. The Catskills are among the oldest mountains on the North American continent, the result of the erosion of the Acadian Mountains to the north around 395 million years ago.

Modeled after European parks in which highly valued natural land areas coexist with the people who live within their borders, Catskill Park became a protected area in 1885 in an effort to save the region's natural beauty from destruction. Logging, bluestone quarrying, and other unregulated harvesting threatened to strip and clear-cut the 98 peaks' forests and mountains, leaving a denuded landscape in place of the heavily forested mountainsides we enjoy today. The effort has not only paid off, but it has saved nearly 10 times the originally protected land mass: While the Catskill Forest Preserve began with 34,000 acres, it now shelters nearly 300,000 pristine acres that will "be forever kept as wild forest lands," as the

New York State Constitution states. "They shall not be leased, sold or exchanged, or be taken by any corporation, public or private, nor shall the timber thereon be sold, removed, or destroyed."

kingston, ny

The seat of Ulster County, Kingston briefly served as the capital of New York State during the Revolutionary War in 1777, when Albany—which had just been named the capital of the free State of New York—was under threat of British attack. Relocating the seat of government to Kingston seemed like a prudent move, but like so many precautionary measures, this one ended ironically: The Continental Army stopped the British at the Battle of Saratoga, so the enemy never made it to Albany . . . but they did burn Kingston on October 16, 1777, by coming up the Hudson River and entering the city near Rondout Creek. The joke was on the British, however, because the residents of Kingston knew the British were coming and evacuated the area, fleeing down the road to Hurley. If you happen to be passing through the area in October of an odd-numbered year, you can see a dramatic, town-wide reenactment of this historic event.

getting there

From the south: Take I-87 north to exit 19. On the exit ramp, follow I-587 to Kingston. At the junction with NY 28, turn left (east) to go to Kingston, or right (west) to continue on the Onteora Trail through Catskill Park. From the north: Take I-87 south to exit 19 and follow the directions above.

what to do

Chestnut Street District. W. Chestnut Street to 87 W. Chestnut, East Chestnut Street, Broadway north for 1 block from Chestnut, and Stuyvesant Street; (845) 331-9506; kingston-ny.gov/filestorage/708/710/720/KingstonHistDist.pdf. The top of the hill on W. Chestnut Street became the neighborhood of the affluent in the 1850s, and the homes they built provide fascinating viewing in a self-guided walking tour of this area. You'll see homes ranging from Italian villa to Colonial Revival, as well as more modern styles as the neighborhood flourished into the 20th century. Your walk also takes you past some impressive viewpoints for Rondout Creek, the Kingston-Rondout Lighthouse, and a number of bridges. Always open, no admission fee.

Fair Street District. On Fair Street from St. James Street to Franklin Street; (845) 331-9506; kingston-ny.gov/filestorage/708/710/720/KingstonHistDist.pdf. Take a walk down Fair Street to see the 1893 St. James Methodist Church, a remarkable example of the Richardsonian Romanesque style, and a number of homes built in the 1850s in a range of period styles: Italianate, Second Empire, Queen Anne, Greek Revival, and Colonial Revival.

The houses are privately owned and not open to the public, but you are welcome to look. Always open, no admission fee.

Hudson River Maritime Museum. 50 Rondout Landing; (845) 338-0071; hrmm.org. Kingston served as the most important 19th-century port on the Hudson River between New York and Albany, so it became the logical place to establish a museum to tell the story of the shipping industry that once dominated the river. In two galleries—one with changing exhibits—the museum provides a glimpse of American industrial history, from the ships that traveled the river to ice harvesting, commercial fishing, brick making, and boat build-ing. From here, you can take a boat tour to see the **Kingston-Rondout Lighthouse,** an 86-year-old structure that helped guide ships through a tricky part of the river. Open May through Oct, daily 11 a.m. to 5 p.m. Closed Nov through Apr. $7 adults, $5 seniors 62+ and children 5 to 18, free to children 4 and under.

Kingston Stockade District (Uptown Kingston). Bounded by North Front Street, Green Street, Main Street and Clinton Avenue; (845) 331-9506; kingston-ny.gov/filestorage/708/710/720/KingstonHistDist.pdf. Look for the replica of the 1658 stockade on North Front Street, and you'll find your way into this 8-block area that was once the original vil-lage of Kingston. Here you can see a whopping 21 of the original 17th- and 18th-century limestone buildings, including four at the intersection of John and Crown Streets—the only place in the United States with four 18th-century stone buildings on all four corners. Stop at the visitor center at 308 Clinton Ave. to get information about the self-guided walking tour, so you won't miss things like the Ulster County Courthouse—where George Clinton, the first governor of New York, was sworn in, and Sojourner Truth won her case to gain her son's freedom from Alabama slavery in 1821—and the burying ground at the Old Dutch Church, where you'll find the graves of many Revolutionary War soldiers. You'll also find many res-taurants, galleries, and shops here. Always open; no admission fee.

Rondout-West Strand District. 1 Broadway; (845) 331-7517 or (800) 331-1518; ci.kingston .ny.us/content/102/112/default.aspx. If you're looking for a place to spend your day with a good meal, an attractive view, some fun shopping, and maybe a lesson or two in history, Kingston's waterfront can provide the entire package. More than a dozen restaurants offer everything from Hudson Valley produce and cheeses to Mexican, Japanese, and Italian deli-cacies, and antiques stores and galleries tempt shoppers with unusual finds. Complete your afternoon or evening with a quiet stroll along Rondout Creek on a brick walkway, watching the ducks and the occasional boat pass by on the water.

Trolley Museum of New York. 89 East Strand; (845) 331-3399; tmny.org. Take a ride on a real trolley car, visit the rail yard and restoration shop, and learn about the history of rail transportation and its impact on the growth of the Hudson Valley. Your 45-minute ride takes you from the foot of Broadway—the former rail yard of the historic Ulster and Delaware Railroad—to picnic grounds on the Hudson River, about 1.5 miles away. In the rail yard, you can see trolley, subway, and rapid transit cars from the US and Europe, and even watch technicians work to restore older cars. Open weekends and holidays, May 10 through Oct 13, noon to 5 p.m., plus special events. $6 adults, $4 seniors 62+ and children 6 to 12, free for children 5 and under.

where to eat

You will find more than 150 places to eat in Kingston, from casual coffeehouses serving fair-trade brews to wildly creative menus from top chefs. Here are just a few standouts to help you explore the area's cuisine.

Dolce. 27 Broadway; (845) 339-0921; tripadvisor.com/Restaurant_Review-g48003-d837749 -Reviews-Dolce-Kingston_New_York.html. Dolce has the breakfast that brings people back over and over—for the sweet or savory crepes, the goat cheese omelet and other egg dishes, the gourmet egg sandwiches, the inspired sandwich combinations (like cranberries with tuna salad), and much more. Even the coffee and tea choices exceed expectations. Come early, or expect to wait for a table. Wed through Sun 8 a.m. to 3 p.m., closed Mon and Tues. $, cash only.

Ecce Terra. 288 Fair St.; (845) 338-8734; ecce-terra.com. The Mediterranean-themed menu (don't miss the grilled haloumi cheese) draws residents and tourists alike to the heart of Kingston to dine at Ecce Terra, but the service gets even more enthusiastic reviews. Down-home hospitality makes the difference, pushing this restaurant to #1 on TripAdvisor's rankings of Kingston's eateries. Lunch Mon, Thurs, and Fri 11:30 a.m. to 3 p.m.; dinner Mon through Thurs 5 to 9 p.m., Fri and Sat 5 to 10 p.m. $$.

Hoffman House. 94 N. Front St.; (845) 338-2626; hoffmanhousetavern.com. Dining in a stone house built before 1679 just has to be interesting, and Hoffman House lives up to that expectation. It stands on a corner of the Stockade district where it once served as a lookout against Indian attacks, and its 1970s renovation maintained the large fireplaces, dry rubble construction, and floorboards of random widths. Not surprisingly, the fare here is largely continental—but with modern twists, like the coconut-encrusted chicken with peach apricot sauce, or seafood cioppino in a spicy sauce. You will find a quesadilla and a Rangoon of the day on the specials menu—and the tavern menu offers sandwiches, burgers, salads, and other lighter fare. Open daily, lunch 11:30 a.m. to 4 p.m., dinner 4:30 p.m. to closing, tavern 4 p.m. to closing. $$.

Ship to Shore. 15 West Strand; (845) 334-8887; shiptoshorehudsonvalley.com. One of the most talked-about restaurants in Kingston, this American bistro offers an inventive menu using fresh, local ingredients, making every dish out of the ordinary. The name suggests a robust seafood menu, and you will indeed find remarkable choices: seafood macaroni and cheese with shrimp, sea scallops, clams, and a 4-ounce lobster tail; gluten-free penne pasta with white Gulf shrimp, sea scallops, and a riot of fresh vegetables and herbs; and grilled

Atlantic salmon with a house-squeezed orange juice and basil reduction, just to choose a few. At the same time, you'll find an old-fashioned steakhouse menu of choice cuts and chops, with your choice of sauces and sides. If you like seared tuna, don't miss the tuna stack—the appetizer that draws the most oohs, ahhs, and yums. Open daily 11 a.m. to 11 p.m.; Sun brunch 10 a.m. to 3 p.m. $$.

where to shop

Rondout-Strand District. In between the museums and the restaurants, you'll find lots of opportunities for antiquing, gallery-hopping, and boutique-browsing. **TheGreenSpace** (73B Broadway; 845-417-7178; shopthegreenspace.com) helps you buy local by offering a wide variety of food and drinks produced in New York State, from Saratoga Spring Water to Queen Majesty Hot Sauces. At **Mezzanine Antiques** (79 Broadway; 845-339-6925; mezzanine.us), you can find vintage jewelry and mid-century home decor, as well as glassware and ceramics dating back to the early 1900s. If you're in search of high fashion, try **Next Boutique** (17 West Strand; 845-331-4537; nextboutique.com), where the historic building creates a sense of romance as you browse the latest styles. At **Karmabee** (73A Broadway; 845-443-3358; karmabee.com), you'll discover the illustrations of local artist Karen Berlowitz on baby clothes and note cards, as well as a selection of artwork by other local artists as part of Karen's localism approach to business.

Uptown Stockade District. You'll find a wealth of shopping experiences uptown, especially on Wall Street, where shops and galleries line both sides of the road and offer all kinds of merchandise, often in unlikely combinations. For example, **Blue-Byrd's Haberdashery & Music** (320 Wall St.; 845-339-3174; kingstonuptown.org/BlueByrds_Haberdashery) provides a wide variety of CDs and hats, as well as other fashion accessories; **Bop to Tottem** (299 Wall St.; 845-338-1800; boptottem.com) brings together fashion and functional items from around the globe to bring you a mix that goes well beyond eclectic—you never know what funky thing you may find here. Nearby on John Street, The **Edelweiss Soap Company** (38 John St.; 845-514-2709; facebook.com/pages/The-Edelweiss-Soap-Company/) provides handmade goat's milk soap, massage lotions, bubble bath, and—what else?—rubber ducks. These are just a few of the fun shops you'll find in this area, so explore as you discover the history of the state's first capital city.

hurley, ny

After your exploration of Kingston, Hurley provides the small-town charm you may have expected to find on your day trip into the Catskills. Settled for the first time in 1661 and then again in 1669—after an attack by Esopus Indians in 1663 destroyed the village and drove the residents away—this primarily agricultural community became the military headquarters for American General George Clinton's army in 1777, briefly holding the title of capital of

New York State. The area continued to supply grain to the northern colonies until the 1830s, when bluestone—a valuable building material used to construct sidewalks, building facades, and curbs—was discovered in the forests north of town, and the quarry industry became the dominant source of income for villages in and around Hurley. This continued until 1917, when New York City's requirements for clean water outweighed its need for bluestone, and these quarry towns were condemned and flooded to create Ashokan Reservoir. (Two of the towns—Glenford and West Hurley—were relocated to the north shore of the reservoir.)

Today Hurley's Main Street occupies a position on the National Register of Historic Places because of its stone houses—some of which are more than 300 years old—that still serve as residences.

getting there

From Kingston, take NY 28 west US 209 south. Continue 2.5 miles to Wynkoop Road in Hurley. To reach the historic district, turn right on Wynkoop Road and take the first right onto Main Street.

what to do

Hurley Heritage Society. In the Col. Jonathan Elmendorf House, Main Street; (845) 338-1661; hurleyheritagesociety.org. If you'd like to know more about the stone houses and other local history, this museum provides historical displays, including artifacts collected in and around the town. You can also pick up the self-guided walking tour brochure here. Open weekends May through Oct, Sat 10 a.m. to 4 p.m., Sun 1 to 4 p.m. Closed Nov through Apr. Free admission.

The Stone Houses. Main Street; stonehouseday.org. How old are America's oldest private homes? The 10 Stone Houses in Hurley were built between 1685 and 1786, and you can reach them all on a 0.25-mile walking tour. More importantly, a number of these houses played significant roles in history and continue to stand to tell the tale. The Van Etten/Dumond House, the oldest colonial house in town, served as a guard house for prisoners of the Continental Army in 1777, including an alleged spy who was detained in a dungeon in the basement. Part of the Ostrander-Elmendorf House became a popular tavern during the Revolutionary War. The VanDeusen House took the most prestigious place of all the houses when it became the New York State capitol building for several months in 1777, with its parlor serving as the meeting room for the New York State Committee of Safety. While these houses are all private residences and are not open to the public for 364 days of each year, on the second Saturday in July the homeowners open their doors to tourists for Stone House Day, a town-wide event with house tours, costumed reenactors, a Revolutionary War military encampment, demonstrations of 18th-century skills and crafts, and other festivities. Visit stonehouseday.org for dates, tickets, and other information.

mount tremper, ny

Defined not as a town or a hamlet but as a "populated place," Mount Tremper's uncommonly lovely location on Esopus Creek in the midst of the Catskills has made it a choice spot for retreats in many forms. Here the Mountains and Rivers order of Zen Buddhists maintains the Zen Mountain Monastery, a repurposing of the former Camp Wapanachki. Mount Tremper Arts, a relatively new arts organization, hosts residencies for aspiring artists and enlivens summers here with its annual arts festival, bringing contemporary art and performance to the area on weekends in July and Aug.

getting there

From Hurley, continue west on NY 28. As Esopus Creek comes into view on your left and the Migliorelli Farm stand appears, you have reached Mount Tremper.

what to do

Catskill Mountain Railroad. 5401 NY 28; (845) 688-7400; catskillmtnrailroad.com. Take a scenic train ride along Esopus Creek from Mount Tremper aboard a restored railroad car from the 1920s, or in an open gondola car that allows riders to enjoy sunshine and fresh air as they admire the Catskill scenery. Some parts of the route suffered major damage in 2011 during Hurricane Irene, so the railroad offers a shortened, 5-mile round-trip route while the track undergoes a multiyear repair. Even so, this ride provides plenty of stunning scenery in just about any season—but especially in fall. Trains run on weekends from late May through late Oct; check the website for this year's times. $14 adults, $8 children 2 to 11, free for children under 2 with paid adult fare.

The World's Largest Kaleidoscope and Emerson Resort and Spa. 5340 NY 28; (877) 688-2828; emersonresort.com. Easily spotted as you approach Mount Tremper, the Emerson Resort provides upscale boutique shopping, high-quality antiques, and the Kaleidostore—a shop dedicated almost entirely to kaleidoscopes. The resort is a fairly new addition to the area's hospitality scene, and it features a fine restoration of a number of older buildings, as well as some new construction to accommodate guests in 53 rooms and suites. The Catamount Restaurant and the Emerson Spa add to the complete package, making this a highly rated getaway spot for a weekend or longer.

As if luxury pedicures and rustic-chic guest rooms weren't enough, The Emerson features a one-of-a-kind attraction: **Kaleidoscraper,** the world's largest kaleidoscope, built within the large silo on the Emerson's grounds. Not surprisingly, the nearly 60-foot-tall kaleidoscope has a multidimensional past: Built in 1996, the scope was designed by Charles Karadimos (a name you will recognize if you're a kaleidoscope aficionado), and the video used to create the scope's imagery came from the psychotropic brain of 1960s artist Isaac Abrams and his son, computer artist Raphael Abrams. You can enjoy a trippy

10-minute show by stepping into the silo, lying on the ground or leaning on a support platform designed for this purpose, and looking up. A 37-foot-tall, 2.5-ton assembly of mirrored surfaces reflects Abrams's artwork and makes the prismatic images. The kaleidoscope is open during the Kaleidostore's hours: Sat through Thurs 10 a.m. to 5 p.m., and Fri 10 a.m. to 6 p.m. $5 per person.

phoenicia, ny

Driving west on NY 28 from Mount Tremper, relax with sweeping views of Belleayre, Hunter, and Panther Mountains and watch for the sign on your right to Phoenicia. Recently named "one of the 10 coolest small towns in America" by *Budget Travel* magazine, Phoenicia offers a remarkable assortment of galleries, shops, restaurants, and services for a town of its size, with just enough quirkiness to make visitors smile.

what to do

Empire State Railway Museum. 70 Lower High St.; (845) 688-7501; esrm.com. The 1899 Phoenicia Junction railroad station, a stop of the Ulster and Delaware Railroad when rail traffic brought people from the stuffy, overheated city to breathe the clean mountain air, now serves as a museum dedicated to preserving the railroad's history. You can visit the museum in summer to view artifacts and photos of rail's heyday in the region, and see the ongoing restoration of classic train cars from the early to mid-1900s. Most recently, the museum became the home of the Catskill Mountain Live Steamers, a small live steamer club with a 750-foot large-loop single-track mainline (as of this writing—expansion may have taken place since). Open Memorial Day through Oct 31, weekends and holidays, 11 a.m. to 4 p.m. Closed Nov 1 through the end of May. Free admission, nominal fees for children to ride the live steamers.

where to eat

Mama's Boy Market. 7 Church St.; (845) 688-3050; mamasboymarket.com. For a cozy lunch in a Catskill cottage or a leisurely al fresco breakfast, this casual eatery serves some of the best locally roasted coffee around, as well as a range of sandwiches, sliders, homemade baked goods, and breakfast specialties. Whatever else you eat here, be sure to leave room for dessert—because you must have Jane's Ice Cream here in the town in which this rich confection was invented. It's made in Kingston now, but the best restaurants in the Hudson Valley now serve it (including those at the Emerson Resort and Spa in Mount Tremper). Jane's delivers some of the most intense flavors we've found in New York State: Killer Chocolate serves up as much cocoa flavor as a high-end candy bar, while the White Pistachio bursts with the aroma and essence of freshly picked and ground nuts. Mon through Thurs and Sun 8 a.m. to 7 p.m.; Fri and Sat 8 a.m. to 9 p.m. $.

Ricciardella's Restaurant. 54 Main St.; (845) 688-7800; ricciardellas.com. A mainstay in Phoenicia for more than 50 years, Ricciardella's offers fine dining with creative twists on favorite dishes. Your fried calamari appetizer can feature a sweet sauce rather than spicy, a traditional rigatoni dish involves wild mushrooms, ravioli features a short rib filling and an osso bucco cream sauce. If the menu doesn't surprise you, the presentation certainly will—check out the photo gallery on the website. Wed and Thurs 5 to 10 p.m.; Fri and Sat 5 to 11 p.m., Sun 4 to 10 p.m., closed Mon and Tues. $$.

Sweet Sue's. 49 Main St.; (845) 688-7852. Can eating pancakes be a transcendent experience? They can here, because of the secret recipe that draws people who will wait in line for a table for as long as it takes, just to get their plateful. Order one plate and split it with a friend so you can try the omelets, inch-thick toast, and other specialties. Bring cash; Sweet Sue's doesn't take credit cards. Thurs through Mon 8 a.m. to 2 p.m. Closed Tues and Wed. $$.

where to shop

Main Street. Phoenicia has one main thoroughfare, and it's lined with shops and markets between the restaurants—most of which feature antiques, vintage clothing, or the kinds of items you expect to find in small-town country stores. **The Nest Egg** (84 Main St.; 845-688-5851; nesteggshop.com), for example, provides everything from Minnetonka Moccasins to stick candy, as well as soaps, candles, local maple syrup and honey, and souvenirs. **Tender Land Home** (64 Main St.; 845-688-7213; tenderlandhome.com) showcases rustic, contemporary home accessories in country style, offering pottery, rugs, pillows, soaps and candles, and furniture. **Mystery Spot Antiques** (72 Main St.; 845-688-7868; lauralevine.com/mystery-spot/index.php) calls itself an "odditorium" because of its ceiling-to-floor stacks of eclectic, previously enjoyed merchandise. The shop **60 Main** (60 Main St.; 845-688-5395; babytoes.com) offers clothing and other items made in and around Phoenicia by local residents. As you stroll Phoenicia's very walkable town center, you're sure to discover artists, businesses, and items you would not necessarily find unless you wandered off the main routes and into towns like this one.

day trip 26

mid-hudson valley

>>> **the road to woodstock**
woodstock, bethel, ny

If you want to see the famous farmer's fields that became the site of the Woodstock Music Festival on August 15 to 18, 1969, you may be surprised to discover that the festival did not take place in Woodstock at all, but on the farm owned by Max Yasgur in Bethel, 43 miles southwest of the town of Woodstock. This fact does not diminish the pleasure of a day trip to this area, however, as the town of Woodstock provides the not-quite-hippie arts vibe that you may still expect to find here more than 45 years after the festival. In Bethel, the Woodstock Museum at Bethel Woods brings the entire event back to life for you through memorabilia and news coverage.

getting there

From the north, south, or east, take I-87 to exit 20 in Saugerties. At the end of the exit ramp, turn west on NY 212 and continue 10 miles to the town of Woodstock. **From the west,** take I-88 east to exit 8, and merge onto NY 206 east. Continue on NY 206 for 22 miles to NY 10 north, and turn left. Follow NY 10 about 23 miles to NY 28 south, and take NY 28 south 35 miles to Woodstock.

woodstock, ny

Woodstock's history as an arts colony predates the music festival by more than 60 years, beginning in 1902 with the founding of Byrdcliffe. Here the Arts and Crafts movement of the turn of the 20th century flourished, giving rise to a new style of architecture and home furnishings that celebrated the clean, simple lines and structures found in nature and sought to blend manmade structures with their natural surroundings. Byrdcliffe continues here today, the last intact colony from the Arts and Crafts movement and a fine place to discover some of its remaining practitioners—as well as painters, writers, sculptors, potters, and others in many genres who make Woodstock their home.

what to do

Historical Society of Woodstock. 20 Comeau Dr.; (845) 679-8111; woodstockarts .com. Founded in 1929, the historical society maintains the historic Eames House, where it mounts exhibitions and stores its permanent collection of art, books, manuscripts, photos, and other media. Open in summer and fall, Sat and Sun 1 to 5 p.m.; closed winter and early spring. Donations encouraged.

HITS-on-the-Hudson. 454 Washington Ave. Extension, Saugerties; (845) 246-5515; hitsshows.com/saugerties/hits-saugerties-series. Top-level horse shows in which equestrians compete for more than $2 million in prize money take place in Saugerties—just 7 miles down the road from Woodstock—on weekends from Memorial Day through Labor Day. Check the website for show dates and special events. Horse shows are Wed through Sun 8 a.m. to 4 p.m. Free admission Wed through Sat; Sun is $5 adults, free to children under 12.

Woodstock Farm Animal Sanctuary. 35 Van Wagner Rd., Willow; (845) 679-5955; wood stocksanctuary.org. If you love meeting farm animals, the ones who live here could use some love—they're all rescued from abuse or neglect and brought here for rehabilitation. You will meet cows, goats, pigs, chickens, sheep, ducks, turkeys, and rabbits, and perhaps even a mule. Early Apr to end of Oct, Sat and Sun only, 11 a.m. to 4 p.m. $10 adults, $5 seniors and children, toddlers free.

Woodstock Museum. 13 Bach Rd.; Saugerties; (845) 246-0600; woodstockmuseum .com. About 7 miles north of the town of Woodstock, this museum captures the history and heritage of Woodstock as an arts colony, with a nod to the music festival and the 1960s counterculture. While you'll see plenty of interesting artifacts here, what's equally interesting is the museum's emphasis on using solar-generated electricity to power its activities, and on educating the public about sustainable energy, organics, questioning authority, and marijuana. Open Memorial Day weekend through Labor Day, weekends noon to 4 p.m.; call for tours on weekdays. $7 adults, $3.50 children under 12.

where to eat

Cucina. 109 Mill Hill Rd.; (845) 679-9800; cucinawoodstock.com. Located in a restored farmhouse as you enter Woodstock, this fairly new restaurant offers contemporary Italian cuisine based on seasonal, local ingredients. You'll find the atmosphere casual and the service professional, whether you dine indoors or on the expansive wraparound porch. Open nightly and for Sunday brunch; call for hours and reservations. $$.

Garden Cafe on the Green. 6 Old Forge Rd.; (845) 679-3600; woodstockgardencafe .com. Fresh, organic, vegetarian meals are exactly what you would expect to find here in Woodstock, so the Garden Cafe more than amply meets your expectations. Salads, soups, and sandwiches are the fare of the day, with an opportunity to choose your own bowl of rice, tofu or tempeh, greens, and beans for a healthy entree. At the very least, stop here for fruit crisp or pie as you browse through the galleries. Mon and Wed through Fri 11:30 a.m. to 9 p.m.; Sat 10 a.m. to 9:30 p.m.; Sun 10 a.m. to 9 p.m. $$.

Joshua's Cafe. 51 Tinker St.; (845) 679-5533; joshuascafe.com. Joshua's has been here for more than 40 years, attracting locals and tourists with an ambiance that makes artists and writers feel at home. The full menu covers breakfast, lunch, and dinner with a wide variety of creative and homestyle options. You will most definitely find meat on the menu here. Mon, Tues, Thurs, and Fri from 11 a.m.; Sat and Sun from 10 a.m.; closed Wed. $$.

where to shop

Art museums and galleries. Nearly 20 galleries and small museums provide opportunities to see and buy the work of local artists, as well as a selection of work from the national and international art communities. Download the walking map at the Woodstock Chamber of Commerce and Arts at woodstockchamber.com/walking-map.html to help you find the stops you'd like to make along the town's Tinker Street (NY 212), on Waterfall Way, and up Rock City Road. You'll find hand-woven carpets and kilims, fine art, handcrafted furniture, eco-friendly products, jewelry, and other art objects to decorate your home. Hours vary by establishment, but all are open on weekends and for extended hours on summer evenings.

bethel, ny

Fifty-seven miles down the road from Woodstock, Bethel was the site of the Woodstock Music and Art Festival in 1969, and the town has since built the Bethel Woods Performing Arts Center there—with an amphitheater that can accommodate 15,000 spectators. It also features the Museum at Bethel Woods, dedicated to the exploration of the social, political, and cultural aspects of the 1960s that preceded and followed the Woodstock festival.

getting there

From Woodstock, take NY 375 south about 3 miles to NY 28 east. Turn left onto NY 28 and drive 5 miles to US 209 south. Merge onto US 209 and drive south for about 40 miles to NY 17 west. Turn right on NY 17 and drive 11.2 miles to exit 104, for NY 17B. Take exit 104 and turn left onto NY 17B west. Continue for 9 miles to Bethel.

what to do

Woodstock Monument at the Site of Woodstock Music and Art Festival. Crossroads of Hurd and West Shore Roads, Bethel; (866) 781-2922; bethelwoodscenter.org/plan-your-visit/campus-map. Bethel Woods surrounds the farmer's field in which the Woodstock Music and Art Festival took place in August 1969, and a monument—a stone tablet—erected by the property owners stands a short distance from the location of the stage at the three-day concert. You are welcome to pick up a map and walk the grounds to see where many of the famous landmarks were located at the festival. Grounds are open when the museum is open (see below).

Woodstock Museum at Bethel Woods. 200 Hurd Rd.; (866) 781-2922; bethelwoods center.org/the-museum. Newly opened in 2008, the museum's main exhibit is "Woodstock and the Sixties," an immersive multimedia experience with interactive displays, music, film, and personal narratives that describe not only the festival, but its place in the context of a turbulent decade. Whether you remember Woodstock firsthand or you've only heard about it from your parents, you will come away with a stronger understanding of the importance of this event and the transformations taking place during this period of American and world history. Open Apr through Dec. Summer: Open daily 10 a.m. to 7 p.m. Fall: Open daily 10 a.m. to 5 p.m. Oct 14 through Dec 31: Thurs through Sun 10 a.m. to 5 p.m. Closed Jan through Mar. $15 adults, $13 seniors 65+, $11 children 8 to 17, $6 children 3 to 7, free to children 2 and under.

day trip 27

mid-hudson valley

>>> **birthplaces of american art**
catskill, hudson, palenville, haines falls, ny

It's one thing to drive through the Catskill Mountains and take in all the lovely views from your car, but it's quite another to walk in the footsteps of the painters who created the first uniquely American style of artistic expression: the Hudson River School. Back in the mid-1800s, a young artist named Thomas Cole became the founder of an art movement that interpreted the natural landscape, long before photography allowed every traveler to document each pretty view in the blink of an eye. Transplanted from England by his parents in 1818, Cole discovered the Catskill wilderness in 1825 and made it his home beginning in 1832, renting a small studio at the Cedar Grove home that is now a National Historic Landmark. With the goal of creating a legacy to help Americans, in his words, "know better how to appreciate the treasures of their own country," Cole created paintings of wild, unspoiled scenery, with gnarled trees, sweeping clouds, dense forests, and tumbling waters—all the elements that artists had smoothed out of their paintings in favor of pristine landscapes for many generations. Cole's work inspired other painters of his era to join in this new American style of art, and their paintings continue to persuade others to seek personal renewal through the beauty of the nation's landscapes.

The Thomas Cole National Historic Site put together this driving and hiking tour of eight sites at which Cole and his contemporaries found the scenes they made famous. Now you can stand in the same places and see mountains, lakes, trees, and waterfalls that appear markedly similar to the way they were more than 150 years ago, perhaps in tribute to the artists who showed us that these places had value just as they were when they captured them in watercolor or oils.

To see some of these iconic places, you will need to do some walking. The trail to Kaaterskill Falls requires a 0.5-mile uphill hike, though the Adirondack Mountain Club maintains and stabilizes the path to make it passable for any healthy person with good hiking shoes. Likewise, the Sunset Rock viewpoint appears at the end of a gentle 1-mile hike with some uphill slopes. The one promise we can make is that the scenes at the end of these hikes are oh-so-worth the effort—and if you think about what it took for Cole and his compatriots to reach these points in the 1820s and 1830s without the benefit of paved roads, maintained trails, and walking shoes loaded with technology, the energy you expend will seem almost trivial in comparison.

catskill, ny

Once considered the crossroad town between northern and southern New York State, Catskill served as a meeting place for travelers, a retreat for city dwellers eager to escape the heat and smells of summer in Manhattan, and a stop for businesspeople journeying on to Albany or Montreal. As superhighways replaced the Hudson River and railroads as the primary modes of travel, Catskill became the peaceful village it is today, with a Main Street lined with historic buildings and a clear understanding of its place in the modern landscape.

getting there

From the north or south, take I-87 to exit 21. Follow the exit ramp into the village of Catskill.

what to do

Cedar Grove, the Thomas Cole National Historic Site. 218 Spring St.; (518) 943-7465; thomascole.org. When you see the view of the Hudson River from the front yard and the upstairs windows of this hillside mansion, you will know exactly why Cole chose to make this place his home. At the time, Cedar Grove's property extended all the way to the river, an advantage that his descendants continued to enjoy for many decades after his death. Four years after renting the studio (which stood where Temple Israel is now) and shortly after he completed some of his best-known paintings in a series he titled "The Course of Empire," Cole married Maria Bartow and the Coles moved into the big house. Years later he designed the ultimate studio and had his New Studio built in 1846, a marvelous Italianate structure that has since been demolished—though the National Historic Landmark has plans to construct a replica based on photos and drawings of the original building. Look for the brown-and-white Rubbing Medallion sign positioned next to the interpretive boards. On it, you'll see a QR code that allows you to "check in" at the viewpoint, to let the Thomas Cole National Historic Site staff know that you visited the spot. These check-ins help the site tabulate the number of people using the art trail, which in turn will help them raise the funds they need to expand the trail, rebuild Cole's New Studio, and preserve the history of the Hudson River School.

hudson, ny

Once the fourth largest city in New York State, Hudson hosted the first law office of future president Martin Van Buren, who would settle upriver in Kinderhook. By the mid-19th century, however, this town on the banks of the river had become a notorious center of vice, with more than 50 drinking establishments and active whorehouses openly flaunting the law. All of this came to an abrupt end in 1951, when Governor Thomas E. Dewey ordered raids that exposed local policemen among the customers of these houses of ill repute. Today's Hudson bears little evidence of those days, with its city center bustling with nearly 70 antiques shops and dealerships, its active arts scene, and many services for tourists.

getting there

From the parking area at Cedar Grove, turn right onto Spring Street and cross the Hudson River on the Rip Van Winkle Bridge. Bear right on NY 9G south. Your goal is Olana State Historic Site, 1 mile south of the bridge on the left.

what to do

Olana State Historic Site. 5720 NY 9G; (518) 828-0135; olana.org. Thomas Cole inspired a number of painters to capture the Catskill landscape, including Frederic Edwin Church, who became one of the most famous of the Hudson River School artists. In many ways, his glorious Olana became another of his many masterpieces, a Persian-style mansion created not only to take best advantage of the landscapes and views around it, but to contribute to and become one with these natural wonders. Tour the home, walk through the lush gardens as they take full advantage of each season, and stop on your way out as you wind down the carriage road at the Hudson River view (you'll see the interpretive sign and rubbing medallion there). Today's view from here sports more foliage than it did in Church's day, and the three radio towers have been provided as a courtesy of modern progress, but you can still appreciate the splendid panorama of the Hudson River and surrounding hills. Open for tours Apr through Nov, Tues through Sun 10 a.m. to 4 p.m., closed Mon. Grounds are open daily year-round 8 a.m. to sunset. $9 adults, $8 seniors and students with ID, free to children under 12.

where to shop and eat

Warren Street. Six walkable blocks of antiques stores, art galleries, gift shops, and specialty stores line Hudson's main thoroughfare, truly leaving no need unmet if you're shopping for housewares, clothing, or the perfect period item for your perfect period room. Well merchandised and enticingly decorated, these are the shops of interior designers and style spotters, making this concentrated area especially fun to explore. Between the shops and dealerships are a wealth of restaurants, both upscale and casual, many of them with outdoor dining in season so you can continue to enjoy the street scene with your meal. Visit hudsonantiques.net before you visit to peruse dozens of shops and their wares, to help you narrow your focus as you explore this decorator's paradise.

a quick stop: the view on catskill creek

*Before heading into the mountains, make a quick return to Catskill to see one of the most iconic views in the entire Hudson River School compendium. As you leave Olana, turn right and continue to the Rip Van Winkle Bridge. Cross the bridge and continue straight on NY 23 west for 0.5 mile. Turn left onto NY 9W south, and drive about 1,000 feet past the ramp to Jefferson Heights. Continue to the bridge across Catskill Creek. Just before you reach the bridge, pull into the parking area for **Tatania's Restaurant** (601 Main St., Catskill; 518-943-1528; facebook.com/Tatianas ItalianCuisine). You'll see the next stop just past the restaurant alongside the creek, where there's a gazebo and an interpretive sign.*

Both Thomas Cole and Frederic Church painted this scene a number of times, capturing it in different seasons and at both sunrise and sunset. The historic site has done us a courtesy by putting up a white wooden frame to let us know just where to stand to see the famous view the way the artists saw it. The view faces west, so Church in particular worked to reproduce the "magic hour" that so fascinates artists and photographers with the quality of the glow in the sky just before twilight.

Note the sharply pointed mountain in the painting, and stand where you can position this mountain in the right place in the wooden frame. This is the best way to see today's landscape as it compares with the way Cole and Church saw it. It's particularly interesting to note, however, that Cole's first painting of this scene had little to do with its actual appearance—the painting was commissioned by Jonathan Sturges, who specifically asked Cole to paint Catskill Creek as he wished it looked. At the time, the area had become an industrial center crowded with gristmills, sawmills, carding machines, factories, ironworks, and tanneries. Knowing this, we can be even more impressed with the skill of these artists to create such a fancifully natural landscape out of this chaos of manufacturing.

From here, continue south on NY 9W to pick up NY 23A south of Catskill. Begin traveling west on NY 23A.

palenville, ny

The town of Palenville—a gas station, a general store, and a sign for Hunter Mountain—comes up quickly, and it's likely that one thing will catch your eye here: Palenville considers itself the home of fictional character Rip Van Winkle. If you read the short story Washington Irving wrote in 1819, or if you've seen any of the film adaptations dating back to 1905 or the episodes of animated television shows that parody the story, you know the tale—but here's a quick refresher: A mild-mannered man falls asleep in the Catskill Mountains and wakes up 20 years later, unaware that he slept for a generation. Based on Irving's vivid description of the town and its surroundings, Palenville chose to adopt the character and take his village's identity. As Irving had never actually been to the Catskill Mountains when he wrote the story, he could not possibly have had a particular town in mind, so no village is slighted by Palenville's adoption of the story as its own. Likewise, NY 23A became the modern designation for what was known as Rip Van Winkle Trail.

what to do

Kaaterskill Clove and Kaaterskill Falls. NY 23A west of Palenville. Shortly after passing through Palenville, you will cross the "Blue Line" and enter Catskill Park. The road begins to wind through the mountains at this point, signaling that you're in for a treat—this scenic route offers unsurpassed natural beauty, rivaled in New York State only by the Adirondacks' High Peaks Scenic Byway. Pass Fawn's Leap, a narrow waterfall in **Kaaterskill Creek,** and begin watching for Bastion Falls. This massive waterfall appears on your right at a 90-degree bend in the road. Drive on by and into the parking area on the left side of the road about a third of a mile past Bastion Falls. You won't miss it; on any nice day, the parking area will be crowded with visitors from all over the world who have come to enjoy the view of Kaaterskill Clove and to hike to New York State's tallest waterfall, Kaaterskill Falls.

As many of the people parking here have stopped just to see the view and grab a quick photo, a spot probably will open up for you in a few minutes. Once you're parked, take a good look at the view. The deep valley called Kaaterskill Clove, created by a network of creeks and streams winding between mountains, dives downward from here for as much as 2,500 feet. Whatever the weather, this view has the power to thrill visitors with its startlingly majestic mountain slopes and its enchanting hues, but fall really turns the clove into a cavalcade of color, light, and shadow.

Not surprisingly, Kaaterskill Clove inspired a number of artists of the Hudson River School to immortalize it. In addition to Thomas Cole, artists Asher Brown Durand and Sanford Gifford painted this landscape, and artist Jennie Augusta Brownscombe had a studio nearby.

From here, walk east on NY 23A to Bastion Falls, following the road carefully along the left side and stepping over guardrails to stay away from traffic as much as you can. Oncoming cars zip around this bend, making caution a good idea. When you reach the falls, there's plenty of room to step away from the road and admire the 30-foot cascade to your heart's content. Bastion serves as a sort of aquatic appetizer to the main course farther up: Kaaterskill Falls, a 264-foot, two-part drop at the end of a rocky but well-constructed 0.5-mile trail. (There's a detailed description of this hike in our book *Hiking Waterfalls in New York,* with photos.)

If you choose to make the trek up to the big falls—and I did it, which means that any healthy person can do it—you will see one of the most painted sights in the entire Catskill region. The falls splits into two distinct sections, the first a stunning, sheer drop from a notch at the top of the gorge, and the second pouring in half a dozen torrents from a hanging valley to a boulder-clogged pool below. From here, Lake Creek (a tributary of Kaaterskill Creek) flits and frills down the mountain, creating shallow rapids and whitecaps as it trips along to Bastion Falls. You can linger in front of Kaaterskill Falls, sitting on large, flat slabs of rock to observe the hypnotizing glitter of water in the sun, or you can do what some folks enjoy and take the trail next to the falls to get to the hanging valley and stand behind the cascade. Some people climb to the top of the falls, but I can't see any good reason for doing that, ever.

The trail to Kaaterskill Falls involves climbing a series of stone and/or wooden stairs up the mountainside, with some short, level walks between them. We completed the trek up in about 15 minutes, and took more time going down—the rock steps can be slippery if it's rained in the last few days. All in all, plan an hour of your day to reach and enjoy Kaaterskill Falls. We think you'll be glad you did.

When you've left the falls, walked along the roadside, and returned to your vehicle, continue west on NY 23A.

haines falls, ny

The gateway hamlet to Hunter Mountain ski resort and North South Lake Campground, Haines Falls once thrived as a support community for the Catskill Mountain House, about which you'll read more in a few minutes. With the demise of that once-distinguished hotel of the very rich, however, this little town became a sleepy hamlet that becomes marginally more lively when the skiers arrive in winter.

what to do

North-South Lake Campground. 2 miles north of Haines Falls on CR 18; (518) 357-2289; www.dec.ny.gov/outdoor/24487.html. Get a map from the ranger at the entrance, as getting around the park can be a little confusing. Once you're in the campground, bear left toward North Lake Beach, and turn right at the stop sign. Drive down the hill and park in the small parking area near the Recreation Center. You'll see a short, level path directly across the parking area from the Recreation Center; take this path about 250 feet. Look across South Lake for the head of Round Top, the mountain rising above South Mountain. This is just about where Cole stood when he sketched the area for his painting "Lake With

Dead Trees." The dead trees themselves are long gone, replaced by successional forest as the area regained its mantle of deciduous trees, so the view may seem even more attractive than Cole's painting had already led us to believe.

From here, your next view is at Sunset Rock, reachable with a walk through pine trees and flat rocks for 0.9 mile. Many consider this view to be the single best panorama in the Catskill Mountains, so if you're willing to put in the effort (it's not nearly as challenging as the hike to Kaaterskill Falls), you will be rewarded at the end. Starting from the North-South Lake beach parking area, begin the hike at the bulletin board just before the North Lake Beach parking lot. Follow the short trail with yellow markers into the pine forest, and join the Escarpment Trail in 0.1 mile. Begin to follow the blue trail markers to the left. Scramble up a ledge to the trail register, and walk over some flat slabs of rock from one viewpoint to the next until you reach Artist's Rock (you've gone 0.3 mile at this point). The trail levels out here until you reach another short uphill stretch at 0.7 mile. Turn right at the trail junction and follow the yellow markers to Sunset Rock. Enjoy the magnificent view of North and South Lakes, the Hudson River, and the surrounding peaks and valleys, just as Thomas Cole, Sanford Gifford, and fellow artist Jasper Cropsey did when they paced this trail to capture this sight.

Catskill Mountain House site. In North-South Lake Campground. You have one more spot to explore before leaving this most excellent park. Return to the Escarpment Trail (the one with blue markers) and walk east to the grassy, open area where you'll see interpretive signs about Catskill Mountain House. This exquisite mansion once served thousands of guests in "season," as wealthy city dwellers made the journey to the mountains to escape the heat and odors of summer in Manhattan. The hotel operated here until 1941, when World War II and the growing popularity of the Adirondacks finally eclipsed the Mountain House's supremacy. The building fell into disrepair and eventually was demolished in a controlled burn by the state conservation department in the winter of 1963, but while the hotel no longer drew guests here, the view of the mountains, lakes, and Hudson River from this spot never ceased to attract admirers. Perhaps it goes without saying that such a view would also attract artists: The Catskill Mountain House became a favorite resort for painters of the Hudson River School, who came here to make the most of the amazing scenery and the genteel clientele. Thomas Cole himself came here often and produced many great works from this spot, not the least of which was his "A View of Two Lakes and Mountain House, Catskill Mountains, Morning," which now resides in the Brooklyn Museum. Jasper Cropsey, William Henry Bartlett, and Frederic Church all painted this view from a number of different angles, some of which they sold to hotel guests as expensive keepsakes of their visit. Both James Fenimore Cooper and Washington Irving wrote of this place in their novels and stories. Even 18th-century botanist and explorer John Bartram, considered the father of American botany, purportedly collected specimens and wrote about this area.

This is your last stop on this tour of sites that inspired America's first school of landscape painting.

day trip 28

mid-hudson valley

>>> **adventure in the taconics**
austerlitz, hillsdale, taconic state park,
millerton, ny

If you're looking for a more pleasant drive than the New York State Thruway through upstate's flowers, hills, and foliage, this day trip from Austerlitz to Millerton will do the trick. Here on New York's border with New England, forest-covered mountains rise to the east while small towns loaded with country charm cluster to the west. Towns along this route hold fairs and community events for every holiday, country stores and farm markets offer wares that grew on vines and stalks hours before, and carefully preserved homes, churches, and storefronts harken back to times we remember as simpler.

austerlitz, ny

Loaded with the country charm of a fairly genteel agricultural community, the town of Austerlitz contains a number of buildings that date back to the early to mid-1800s, most of them in the Spencertown Historic Site. According to local 19th-century historians, Austerlitz itself almost was named for the dozen Spencer families who settled in this area in 1818, but State Senator Martin Van Buren (who would later become the nation's eighth president) demanded an amendment to the bill naming the town. His motivation: exacting revenge on a colleague who had managed to get a town in upstate New York named for Napoleon Bonaparte's last battleground in Waterloo. Van Buren insisted that the new town be named Austerlitz, after Napoleon's 1805 victory near the Austrian Empire town of that name. If nothing else, this tale serves as an excellent reminder that politics have been petty for hundreds—perhaps thousands—of years.

getting there

From I-90 between Albany and the Massachusetts border, take exit B3 (Austerlitz/New Lebanon), and head south on NY 22.

what to do

Circle Museum. 11005 NY 22; (518) 392-7156; cargocollective.com/circlemuseum/welcome. Here at the home and studio of artist Bijan Mahmoodi, you can view more than 100 different large-scale works of art installed on the lawn, apparently created from whatever materials the sculptor happened to find. At the very least, these works of art are enough to make visitors wonder about the workings of the mind who saw art in scrap metal; at best, many of them reveal imagination and vision that deserve a place in a finer gallery. Inside the garage/studio, Mahmoodi shares a selection of his oil paintings as well. This open-air museum is always open, but please respect that Mahmoodi lives on premises. Free admission.

Old Austerlitz Historic Area. 11550 NY 22; (518) 392-0062; oldausterlitz.org. This living history museum contains buildings originally constructed from the late 1700s to the mid-1800s, moved and reconstructed here to create a village. Post-and-beam construction and Shaker design elements demonstrate homebuilding methods over several generations. The ongoing restoration and preservation of the buildings makes this an interesting place to visit several times over a period of months or years, to see progress and enjoy new buildings added to the collection. Today Old Austerlitz contains a one-room schoolhouse, a Methodist church, a blacksmith shop, a granary, and several residences. The area is part of town and is always open for walking around; some buildings are open on special event days. Free admission; donations are encouraged.

Steepletop. 436 E. Hill Rd.; (518) 392-EDNA (3362); millay.org. The home of Pulitzer Prize–winning lyrical poet and playwright Edna St. Vincent Millay, Steepletop began as a 635-acre blueberry farm. Millay and her husband, Jan Boissevain, lived here from 1925 until their deaths a year apart in 1949 and 1950, and the couple added a writing cabin, a vegetable garden, a barn they built from a Sears Roebuck kit, and a tennis court. The property became a museum in 2010, along with 230 acres of land that includes Millay's gardens. Open for tours from end of May to end of Oct, Fri through Mon 11:30 a.m. and 12:30, 2:30, and 3:30 p.m., with an additional tour on Sat and Sun at 1:30 p.m. Garden tours are available Fri through Mon at noon and 3 p.m. House tour $16, garden tour $16, combination tour $25.

hillsdale, ny

Established in 1788. Hillsdale clearly has made an effort to remain small and charming, with its wealth of buildings that date back to the early 1800s, and its village square with a general store, farm-fresh restaurant, and ice cream parlor. The Hillsdale Historic District—added to the National Register of Historic Places in 2010—features a number of carefully preserved buildings in architectural styles including early Federal, Gothic Revival, Greek Revival, Victorian Italianate, Picturesque, and Victorian Second Empire.

getting there

From Austerlitz, continue south on NY 22 to the crossroads with NY 23. Turn right on NY 23 to reach Hillsdale's town center.

where to eat

CrossRoads Food Shop. 2642 NY 23; (518) 325-1461; crossroadsfoodshop.com. At this farm-to-table restaurant, the menu changes seasonally according to what's fresh from local fields, making every new visit a locavore's delight. You'll find choices loaded with fruits, vegetables, whole grains, the area's best cheeses, and a nice list of beers from local and regional breweries—though nearly all of the wines are European imports. Breakfast and lunch Wed through Sun 8:30 a.m. to 2:30 p.m.; dinner Thurs through Sat 5:30 to 9:30 p.m., Sun 5:30 to 9 p.m. $$.

Mount Washington House Historic Tavern. 2627 NY 23; (518) 325-4631; mtwashington house.com. While a large part of downtown Hillsdale is now listed on the National Register of Historic Places as part of Hillsdale Hamlet Historic District, Mount Washington House stands out for its striking architectural character. Built in 1881, the imposing Victorian mansion once hosted guests throughout the summer. The house has undergone a meticulous renovation, and it now serves as a casual restaurant with a menu of burgers, quesadillas, wraps, salads, and so on. Mon through Sat 4 p.m. to closing; closed Sun. $$.

Village Scoop. 2642 NY 23; (518) 325-6455; villagescoop.com. If Almond Joy, pumpkin spice, and apple spice ice cream all sound like heaven to you, schedule a stop at Village Scoop, next to Hillsdale General Store at the town square in Hillsdale. Not only can you put together the sundae of your dreams here, featuring Jane's Ice Cream—one of the best brands in the Hudson River Valley—but you can top it off with a downstate favorite, Sweet Sam's Baking Company cupcakes, cookies, and brownies. Here's an idea: a Sweet Sam's chocolate chunk brownie with Jane's Killer Chocolate ice cream, whipped cream, and a cherry. Thurs and Sun noon to 6 p.m.; Fri and Sat noon to 8 p.m. Closed Mon through Wed. $.

where to shop

Hillsdale General Store. Village Square Plaza, 2642 NY 23; (518) 325-3310; hillsdale generalstore.com. This emporium in the historic town of Hillsdale provides a stroll through antiques, china, household items, old-fashioned toys and games, items selected by local interior designers, and local food products including maple syrup. The building has been a retail store since the late 19th century, serving as a central part of Hillsdale life as a grocery store, sports shop, and even a video store until it became this nicely appointed general store in 2009. Thurs through Mon 10 a.m. to 6 p.m., closed Tues and Wed.

taconic state park

The Taconic Mountain Range is to your left as you head south on NY 22. The State of New York has had the good sense to preserve 16 miles of this imposing ridgeline on the New York–Massachusetts border as a park, maintaining its natural state and its historical significance as a center of iron production beginning in the 1850s. Within the park you'll find waterfalls, the Harlem Valley Rail Trail, a museum about the old ironworks, and well-equipped cabins if you decide you'd like to stay a night or two.

getting there

As you continue down NY 22 from Hillsdale, signs direct you to the left at Copake Falls, sending you toward one of the entrances to Taconic State Park.

what to do

Bash Bish Falls. Within Taconic State Park; (518) 329-3993; nysparks.com/parks/83/details.aspx. A series of cascades that create a 200-foot waterfall just over the New York state border in Massachusetts, Bash Bish is one of the most famous waterfalls in the New York State park system. The falls tumbles through a gorge on Mount Washington, and it can be viewed from Falls Road—the continuation of NY 344 in Massachusetts—so if you're not up for hiking, you can still enjoy this impressive cascade and its dramatic gorge.

Copake Iron Works. Just east of the campground on NY 344. The iron works began in 1845 as an opportunity to maximize local resources—water power from Bash Bish Brook, charcoal made from the area's abundant forests, and limestone from the mountains. Its founders may have had the foresight to know that this production compound would become one of 40 sources of pig iron in what was known as the Salisbury district. Ironworks from southern Vermont to northwestern Connecticut provided the material for cannonballs, rifle barrels, and wheels for railroad cars throughout the Civil War and well beyond.

Harlem Valley Rail Trail. Within Taconic State Park; (518) 789-9591; hvrt.org. This (mostly) paved trail someday will be 46 continuous miles long, but as of this writing, 16.2 miles in two sections have been completed and are open for foot and bicycle traffic. Most recently, a 0.5-mile segment reached completion, running from Copake Falls to Orphan Farm Road. The foot/bike trail replaces the tracks of the New York & Harlem Railroad, which ran 125 miles northward from Manhattan to Chatham, connecting to other railroads to take people and goods to Albany, Montreal, Boston, and beyond. When the line was abandoned in 1981, the railroad company—the New York State Metropolitan Transportation Authority (MTA) by that time—removed the track, later giving up the land to allow the linear corridor to be repurposed for public use. Always open; free admission.

millerton, ny

The town of Millerton signals the south end of Taconic State Park. Here is a town that could just as easily have become nothing more than a whistle stop on the railroad route between New York City and Albany, were it not for centuries—literally—of forward-thinking leadership. Back in 1851, the town's founding fathers decided to expand the village and add a commercial center with plenty of services for travelers, proving to the railroad that this town could support massive increases in tourism. More than 100 years later, after the railroad left the area, Millerton came to life once again with a thriving downtown area loaded with shops, restaurants, and lodging choices. The strategy worked once again: *Budget Travel* magazine named Millerton one of the "10 coolest small towns in America."

where to shop

Main Street. Pick out some locally made alpaca apparel at **Copper Star Alpaca** (20 Main St.; 518-592-1414; copperstaralpacafarm.com), browse through artworks at **Eckert Fine Art** (34 Main St.; 518-592-1330), **Gilmor Glass** (2 Main St.; 518-789-8000), or **Lady Audrey's Gallery** (52 Main St.; 518-592-1303), search for the perfect lamp or table in half a dozen antiques stores, or step back into the 1920s at **Terni's** general store (42 Main St.; 518-789-3474). These are just a few of the many options you'll find when you slow down your pace and poke through the offerings along Millerton's main thoroughfare.

McEnroe's Organic Farm Market. 194 Coleman Station Rd.; (518) 789-3252; mcenroe organicfarm.com. As you leave Millerton and head south on NY 22, watch for a farm market that has the good sense to be entirely enclosed, making it possible to stay open even when winter comes early. Farming more than 1,000 acres here in the Harlem Valley, the farm provides fruits, vegetables, poultry, beef, lamb, and pork for sale, as well as soups, prepared foods, fresh baked goods, sandwiches, and ice cream from its kitchen. At any time of year, you'll find eggs, honey, dairy products (including goat cheese from local goats), breads, cookies, pies, doughnuts, and a wide selection of regional and specialty products in the country store.

upper hudson valley

>>>

day trip 29

upper hudson valley

>>> **hudson-berkshire beverage trail**
ghent, chatham, clermont, valatie,
castleton-on-hudson, ny & richmond, ma

How often have you sped down the Thruway east of Albany in a dash to reach Boston, and wondered what might be happening in the rolling hills of this well-forested part of New York State? This trip gives you the opportunity to slow down and discover a corner of the state that has only begun to receive its fair share of visitors. Sample the bounty provided by the farms, vineyards, and distilleries in the area between Albany and the Massachusetts border.

getting there

From the Albany area, head east on I-90 (the New York State Thruway Berkshire Connector) to exit 12 (US 9). At the end of the ramp, turn right to head south on US 9. Continue on US 9 south to NY 203 in Chatham. Turn right and take NY 203 for about 7 miles to Ghent. Watch for the junction with NY 66, and head south on NY 66 briefly to the Hudson-Chatham Winery, on your right. **From the south,** take the Taconic Parkway to the exit for NY 82 (Ancram/Hudson). Turn right on NY 82. In about 5 miles, turn right onto NY 23 east/NY 9H north. Continue for 7.5 miles, and turn right onto NY 66 north. The Hudson-Chatham Winery in Ghent will be on the left.

ghent, ny

The views of the Hudson River Valley and the Catskill Mountains in this little town would be enough to warrant a stop here, but there's much more going on in Ghent than its size would lead you to believe. Here you'll find enlightened farmers demonstrating a new generation of agricultural practices, raising wholesome food while maintaining harmony between the farm and the land. At the same time, there's a remarkable arts center here that attracts painters, writers, and sculptors from all over the world to create their art here in the Hudson Valley. If you love 18th-century history, the former Van Valkenburgh-Isbister Farm (now the privately owned Ten Barn Farm) features buildings that date back to 1790, placing it on the National Register of Historic Places. Today it functions as an organic farm that provides community-supported agriculture (CSA) shares to area residents.

what to do

The Creamery at Twin Maple Farm. 416 Schnackenberg Rd.; (518) 672-7650; twin maplefarm.com. Specializing in just two small-batch, artisanal cow's milk cheeses it calls Hudson Red and Hudson Gold, Twin Maple farm has nonetheless put its products on the map—the award-winning Hudson Red is now served at top Manhattan restaurants. It's firmly described as "funky" by just about everyone who tastes it, while Hudson Gold is available as bags of cave-aged curds, a favorite snack food in dairy states. Check the website to be sure the farm's self-service cheese shop is in season and open when you plan to visit. Free admission.

Hawthorne Valley Farm. 327 CR 21C; (518) 672-7500; hawthornevalleyfarm.org. If you've never heard of biodynamic farming, here's a place where you can see it in action and learn about its place in what the people of Hawthorne Valley call "Agriculture 3.0." This is a farm that can produce everything it needs from within its own resources, balancing the right mix of plants and animals to be entirely self-sustaining. The store here—open 7 days a week—features food made fresh on the farm, and you can take a self-guided tour to enjoy the grounds and the barn, and to meet some farm animals. Daily 7:30 a.m. to 7 p.m.; free admission, but donations are encouraged.

Hudson-Chatham Winery. 1900 NY 66; (518) 392-WINE; hudsonchathamwinery.com. It's fitting that you begin your exploration of the area's wines here at the first winery founded in Columbia County. Your tasting will take place in a farmhouse built in 1780, and the wines you discover here have the specific characteristics of the *terroir*—the land, climate, and soils in which the grapes are grown, and the selection of grape varieties that fare best in these conditions. The handmade, small-batch wines you sample here are truly local in every possible way. Enjoy Hudson-Chatham cheeses, drizzles, jams, and caviar, and Sugarmaker's Reserve maple syrups here as well. Wed through Sun noon to 5 p.m. Call for this year's tasting price.

OMI International Arts Center and Sculpture Garden. 59 Letter S Rd.; (518) 392-7656; artomi.org. Begin your visit to this unusual artists' retreat and arts center at the Charles B. Benenson Visitor Center and Gallery, where you can learn about the artists in residence, explore the 1,500-square-foot gallery, and gain an orientation to the fascinating sculpture garden. The 90-acre outdoor Fields Sculpture Park features a walking trail loop that takes you through all 6 areas of the park, to be sure that you don't miss any of more than 40 examples of installation art. Plan to spend at least an hour walking the grounds. Visitors Center and Gallery: Apr through Oct, 11 a.m. to 5 p.m. daily; Nov through Mar, Thurs through Mon 11 a.m. to 4 p.m.; closed Tues, Wed, and major holidays. Sculpture Park, Architecture Omi, and Visitor Center: Open every day year-round, dawn to dusk.

where to eat

Kozel's Restaurant. 1006 NY 9H; (518) 828-3326; kozelsrestaurant.com. In business since 1936, Kozel's serves old-fashioned comfort food in a comfortable, 1960s-style atmosphere. You'll find a robust menu of steaks, veal, pork, lamb, seafood, and poultry, and while there are no culinary innovations here, you're sure to enjoy a well-prepared, cooked-to-order, hearty meal. If you'd rather order from the sandwich menu, you can do that at any time of day. Weekdays 11 a.m. to 10 p.m. or later, Fri and Sat until "late," Sun noon to 10 p.m.; closed Tues. $$.

chatham, ny

Chatham served as a railroad hub back in the early 20th century, but now this town provides a break from the pulse of big-city life for the 4,000-plus people who live here. Visitors may find live music performed in parking lots in midsummer, independent bookstores still holding their own in the town center, and a place to enjoy a cup of coffee and a gluten-free pastry (appropriately called the Gluten Free Bakery, at 54 Main St.).

what to do

Chatham Brewing. 59 Main St.; (518) 697-0202; chathambrewing.com. Good beer often comes from a couple of guys with a dream, so make a point of stopping at this microbrewery for a taste of the latest batch. You'll find the house's award-winning porter, a light-tasting IPA, and amber, blonde, golden, and Scotch ales that reflect Jake and Tom's sensibilities about the taste of a good beer. Thurs 4 to 7 p.m., Fri 3 to 8 p.m., Sat 11 a.m. to 7 p.m., Sun noon to 4 p.m.; Mon through Wed by appointment. $.

Old Chatham Sheepherding Company. 155 Shaker Museum Rd.; (518) 794-7733; blacksheepcheese.com. Who knew that the largest sheep dairy farm in the United States would turn up in Old Chatham, New York? Founded in 1993 with 150 ewes and a few rams, this lovely farm now hosts more than 1,000 East Friesian purebred and crossbred sheep, and the ewes provide milk for cheeses that can be found in specialty stores throughout New York City, upstate New York, and as far away as Texas and California—as well as in Wegmans Food Markets and Whole Foods Market. Visit anytime to meet the sheep and purchase cheese at the self-serve cheese store, at the Shaker Barn on the farm lane. Open daily year-round, dawn to dusk. Free admission.

clermont, ny

In the early 18th century, the Livingston family, prominent Dutch citizens who were among the first to come to the New World, established their manor home here on 160,000 acres of prime Hudson Valley land. They built Clermont Manor on a 13,000-acre section of the family homestead, and the Livingston dynasty began to expand and grow in the new United States. Philip Livingston was a signer of the Declaration of Independence, and his brother William Livingston became the governor of New Jersey. While the original Clermont Manor burned during the Revolutionary War, it was reconstructed after the war and now remains a National Historic Landmark and a New York State Historic Site. (You can visit the site at 1 Clermont Ave. for guided tours from mid-Apr through Oct; call 518-537-4240 or visit nysparks.com/historic-sites/16/details.aspx for this year's hours.)

After the revolution, the land that had been Clermont Manor became the town of Clermont, and seven generations of Livingstons inhabited Clermont over the centuries until 1962. Harriet Livingston, a descendant of Philip, married an inventor named Robert Fulton who would become the first person to build a commercially viable steamboat—originally called the *North River*, but later known as the *Clermont*—thus launching the era of steam power.

Today it's hard to fathom that this small town had such an impact on American civilization, with its quiet country setting and thousands of acres of farmland. A drive through town will bring a number of 18th- and 19th-century buildings to your attention: The Bouwerie dates back to the days of Dutch dominance in the area, while St. Luke's Church and the Old Parsonage were constructed in 1867. A number of residences date back to the early to mid-1800s; watch for interpretive signs.

what to do

Hudson Valley Distillers at Spirits Grove Farm. 1727 US 9; (518) 537-6820; hudson valleydistillers.com. Just opened for business in 2014, this brand-new distillery makes vodka from apples grown on premises, and even grows its own botanicals and flavorings for its gin. So far the partners have created a vodka, an applejack, and a bourbon named for Chancellor Robert Livingston, a signer of the Declaration of Independence. By the time you read this, a gin and a whiskey are expected to be on the beverage list as well. Fri through Sun noon to 6 p.m. Call for this year's tasting price.

valatie, ny

Known best for its cluster of waterfalls—in fact, the town name is Dutch for "little falls"—Valatie was a center of textile manufacturing in the early 19th century, harnessing the waterpower to run the mills. Today its falls inspire musicians, authors, painters, and other artists who leave New York City and Albany to settle here in the country. While you stop here, make a point of seeing Beaver Mill Falls, where Harry Houdini's silent film *Haldane of the Secret Service* was produced, and of strolling through the town center to see the latest merchandise at Beaver Mill Antiques or Great Finds at the Millhouse.

what to do

Harvest Spirits Farm Distillery at Golden Harvest Farm. 3074 US 9; (518) 253-5917; harvestspirits.com. Making vodka by distilling hard apple cider three times, Harvest Spirits has devised a vodka with a bright floral nose—not what you expect when you're used to the potato variety. Flavored vodkas using macerated fruit grown here at the farm; brandies made from peaches, cherries, and pears; and some bourbon-like applejack all make this a fascinating and fun place to stop. Tastings Sat and Sun noon to 5 p.m. Call for this year's tasting price.

castleton-on-hudson, ny

Imagine the seafaring life of English explorer Henry Hudson, sailing on his ship *Half Moon* in 1609 on behalf of the Dutch United East India Company to find a passage to the exotic lands to the east. In mid-voyage, the waters of Europe's northern seas became too treacherous, and Hudson made the choice to turn west, setting sail for the New World and whatever he might find there. Eventually he found the mouth of the river that would one day bear his name . . . and here in Castleton-on-Hudson, on the northern end of Schodack Island, Hudson claimed this land in the name of the Dutch. You can visit this island today; it's a state park with some terrific hiking trails, and it's one of the best features of this small bedroom community just 15 miles outside of Albany.

what to do

Brookview Station Winery at Goold Orchards, 1297 Brookview Station Rd., (518) 732-7317, brookviewstationwinery.com. Not only can you sample award-winning wines here, but you also can enjoy the bounty provided by an award-winning apple producer. Daily 9 a.m. to 5 p.m.

Schodack Island State Park. 1 Schodack Way (NY 9J south of Castleton-on-Hudson); (518) 732-0187; nysparks.com/parks/146/details.aspx. On a slim island flanked by a major river and a wide creek, you may expect excellent water views from this park—but the views only become visible in the leafless seasons. Otherwise, you'll find yourself surrounded by dense foliage until you reach Schodack Creek on the island's east side, where a picnic table provides a pleasant place to relax and enjoy the view. Otherwise, enjoy vibrant foliage in fall, and plenty of wildflowers and flowering trees in spring and summer. Open daily year-round; free admission except for weekends and holidays mid-Apr through mid-Oct, $6 per vehicle.

richmond, ma

Dip a toe into Massachusetts with a quick trip over the border to the last of the wineries on the Hudson-Berkshire Beverage tour route. While the topography is much like what you've seen in this part of New York State, the farms and orchards dominate this area, leaving little trace of the ironworks that provided jobs to this area for nearly a century. Its link with greatness today is Deval Patrick, governor of Massachusetts as of this writing and former assistant US attorney general under President Bill Clinton, whose personal home is here in Richmond.

what to do

Furnace Brook Winery at Hilltop Orchards. 508 Canaan Rd. (MA 295); (413) 698-3301; furnacebrookwinery.com. Excellent views of the Berkshire hills of western Massachusetts make this orchard and winery an even bigger treat to visit than it already is. Taste a range of reds and whites as well as a honey mead that has received a number of medals, and an apple ice wine made from fruit grown, pressed, and cryo-concentrated right here at the winery. The hard ciders here are aged in oak barrels. Open daily 9 a.m. to 5 p.m. First wine tasting is free; 5 additional wines for $5.

day trip 30

upper hudson valley

>>> **old kinderhook's president**
kinderhook, ny

Martin Van Buren, the eighth president of the United States, became a public figure from his home here in Kinderhook, and some say that the iconic "OK" expression originated here because he signed his correspondence with the letters O.K.—meaning Old Kinderhook. While this origin story doesn't really hold up to close scrutiny, it's just one of the many anecdotes that make Van Buren one of the most colorful characters of the early 19th century. You can tour his home and see just what kind of environment turned out a top political leader back in the 1830s.

getting there

From the New York Thruway Berkshire Connector (I-90 east of Albany), take exit 12 to US 9 toward Hudson. At the end of the exit ramp, turn left to follow US 9 south. Continue 5 miles on US 9 south to Kinderhook. **From the south,** take the New York State Thruway north to I-90, and continue in I-90 east to exit 12; follow the directions above.

kinderhook, ny

First settled before 1651 by Dutch colonists, Kinderhook (which means "children's corner" in Dutch) is loaded with bits of history. Aaron Burr hid here for a short time after killing former Secretary of State and Treasury Alexander Hamilton in a notorious pistol duel in July 1804. Benedict Arnold spent time recuperating here after being wounded at the Battle of Bemis

Heights in 1777, and British General John Burgoyne spent a night here as a prisoner of war in 1777 as well. You'll find a number of historic homes here, some of which are open in summer for tours, and most of which have historical markers that describe their background and architecture.

what to do

Luykas Van Alen House and Ichabod Crane Schoolhouse. 2589 NY 9H; (518) 758-9265. This rural farmhouse circa 1737 recreates Dutch farm life as it may have been when author Washington Irving used this house as the model for the Van Tassel home in *The Legend of Sleepy Hollow.* The house is a National Historic Landmark. The schoolhouse on this property was moved here in 1974 and has been restored to its 1930s appearance. Built in the 1800s, it served as a school until the 1940s. Both buildings are open June to Oct, Fri through Sun noon to 4 p.m. $7 adults, free to children under 12.

Martin Van Buren National Historic Site. 1013 Old Post Rd.; (518) 758-9689; nps.gov/mava. Our eighth president earned the nickname "Little Magician" early in his political career because of his ability to get others to talk about their views without revealing his own. Martin Van Buren's history as an elder statesman, former secretary of state, and vice president under Andrew Jackson helped secure his bid for the presidency, but his first and only term in that office suffered from financial woes inherited from his predecessor. Two months after Van Buren took office, the spectacular failure of 900 banks across the country caused the Panic of 1837, resulting in the worst depression of the 19th century and costing Van Buren a second presidential term. Nonetheless, Van Buren's flamboyant zest for life shows throughout Lindenwald, his 36-room estate, which he purchased during his presidency and expanded to a 226-acre working farm.

Learn about Van Buren's idiosyncrasies and his popularity as a target for media criticism—especially political cartoonists—by taking the ranger-guided tour of the mansion. (Van Buren's birth site is marked in town as well, though the house was demolished long ago. His gravesite is in the town cemetery.) Open daily mid-May to Oct 31 9 a.m. to 5:30 p.m.; closed Nov through Apr. $5 adults, $12 for a family with children; good for 7 days.

where to eat

Carolina House. 59 Broad St.; (518) 758-1669; carolinahouserestaurant.com. Signature dishes at this warm, friendly, traditional American restaurant include a Caribbean-spiced half-chicken with crispy, flash-fried skin, and a tortilla-crusted chicken breast stuffed with spinach, mushrooms, and goat cheese. Look for steaks, catfish, and other seafood dishes to round out the menu. Mon through Thurs 5 to 9:30 p.m., Fri and Sat 5 to 10 p.m., Sun 4 to 9:30 p.m. $$.

day trip 31

upper hudson valley

>>> a delightful corner of the berkshires
williamstown, north adams, ma

On the edge of the Berkshire Mountains at the farthest reaches of the Hudson River watershed, Williamstown and North Adams, Massachusetts, offer a pair of cultural oases in a predominantly rural area. Williamstown's position as the supporting town for the venerable Williams College and the Williamstown Theatre Festival make it a surprisingly upscale destination, with one of the nation's most respected personal art collections available for viewing by anyone with the admission fee in his pocket. Just a few miles up US 7, North Adams offers the remarkable Massachusetts Museum of Modern and Contemporary Art, the largest modern art museum in the United States, bringing a newly artistic sensibility to what was historically a technology and manufacturing town.

getting there

From the Albany area, take I-787 north to exit 9E, merging onto NY 7 east toward Troy/Bennington. Turn right onto NY 278 south. In 1.5 miles, turn left on NY 2 east, and continue into Massachusetts (NY 2 becomes MA 2). Continue 3.9 miles to the junction with US 7 north, and turn left. Continue to follow the combined MA 2/US 7 north about 3 miles to Williamstown.

williamstown, ma

A college town with panache, Williamstown takes its name from Colonel Ephraim Williams, an American officer who died in the French and Indian War. Col. Williams made a sizable bequest to his hometown of Hoosac, Massachusetts, on the condition that the town change its name to Williamstown. The bequest paid for the creation of Williams College, which has operated here since 1793 and is the top-ranking small liberal arts college in the United States, according to *U.S. News & World Report*. Among the college benefits this posh little town enjoys are the Williamstown Theatre Festival, one of the most prestigious summer festivals of plays in the United States, and the Williams College Museum of Art, a museum with a growing collection and changing exhibitions.

what to do

Sterling and Francine Clark Art Institute. 225 South St.; (413) 458-2303; clarkart.edu. Dedicated not only to presenting art to the public, but also to research and higher education, the Clark combines its stunning collection and its natural setting to provide a world-class museum experience to its guests. Here you'll find an in-depth collection of Flemish, Dutch, and Italian works, as well as the work of John Singer Sargent, Winslow Homer, Edgar Degas, Pierre-Auguste Renoir, and a variety of French Impressionists. In addition, the views of the Berkshire Mountains, the farms of Vermont, and forests that continue up to the top of Mount Greylock—the highest mountain in Massachusetts—make a visit to the Clark a particularly delightful experience. Open July 1 to mid-Oct, daily 10 a.m. to 5 p.m., with extended Fri hours to 7 p.m. in July and Aug. Mid-Oct to June 30, Tues through Sun 10 a.m. to 5 p.m. $20 adults, free for children under 18 and students with valid ID.

Williams College Museum of Art. 15 Lawrence Hall Dr. #2; (413) 597-2429; wcma .williams.edu. Look for the enormous stone dragon eyes watching you from the college's hilly grounds, and follow their gaze to this unusual museum. Here you'll find changing exhibitions that may feature anything from perspectives on abstract art to documentary photography, as well as selections from a permanent collection of more than 13,000 art objects. Most interesting is the WALLS project: Williams Art Loan for Living Spaces, lending pieces from a discreet collection to students to hang in their dorm rooms for an entire semester and develop a memorable relationship with their chosen art. Open daily 10 a.m. to 5 p.m.; closed Wed. Free admission.

Williamstown Theatre Festival. '62 Center for Theatre and Dance, 1000 Main St.; (413) 597-3400; wtfestival.org. Summer theater in the Berkshires—what could be better? Apparently hundreds of the finest actors of stage, screen, and television agree that the setting and the caliber of theatrical production at this perennial festival make a few weeks in a small New England town more than worthwhile—and you're sure to agree as well. Williamstown took the Tony Award for Outstanding Regional Theater in 2002, recognizing this festival's ability to produce both brilliant productions of classic plays and cutting-edge work by new playwrights. Check the website to see what's playing during your visit—or plan your visit around seeing a favorite star in a locally produced comedy, drama, or musical. July and Aug; show times and ticket prices vary by production.

where to eat

Hops & Vines. 16 Water St.; (413) 884-1372; hopsandvinesma.com. The beers are the stars at this casually eclectic eatery, with nearly 20 served by the glass; the extensive wine list is impressive, though it neglects the excellent vintages just over the state line in New York. You'll find a varied menu of small plates and entrees featuring the harvest of many local farms, from spring lamb to Camembert cheese. Don't miss the dressed-up beignets for dessert—it's not often you find these so far north of New Orleans. Lunch Tues through Sat from noon, dinner from 5 p.m. until closing; Sun noon to 10 p.m.; closed Mon.

Mezze Bistro + Bar. 777 Cold Spring Rd.; (413) 458-0123; mezzerestaurant.com. The menu changes daily at this long-trendy restaurant, depending on what's available from local farmers and artisan producers, but you always will find a tempting array of small plates that make the most of fresh seasonal fruits and vegetables and treats like local pâté and cheese. Entrees may include unusual preparations of local sausage, shellfish, beef, fish, and vegetarian dishes, each showcasing the bounty of farmers' fields. Look for something maple on the dessert menu for a truly local burst of flavor. Sun through Thurs 5 to 9 p.m., Fri and Sat 5 to 10 p.m. Closed Thanksgiving, Christmas Eve, Christmas Day, and New Year's Day. $$.

north adams, ma

Three decades ago, progress dealt North Adams a nearly fatal blow when the town's main industry, the high technology Sprague research and development center, closed its doors in 1985. North Adams rallied admirably and turned its focus to art and culture, constructing the largest museum of contemporary art in the United States and transforming abandoned factories into artists' lofts, restaurants, and smaller galleries. Today North Adams has become a destination, offering a fun and funky tourist experience in a setting surrounded by the Taconic Mountains, putting its architectural heritage, its scenic assets, and its commitment to the arts into the spotlight on a nationally significant scale.

what to do

Massachusetts Museum of Contemporary Art (MASS MoCA). 1040 Mass Moca Way; (413) 662-2111; massmoca.org. Are trees growing upside down art? They are at this internationally famous museum of modern and contemporary art, and they hold their own in a collection that also includes a room-size sculpture depicting the interaction of lightning, a stag, and a dramatic brass sculpture; two floors of disassembled engines now preserved for their inherent auditory resonance; and transparent, solid sculptures that reveal human beings from the inside. Startling, intriguing, sometimes moving and sometimes funny, the works of art selected by MASS MoCA will make you wish you could stop in every week to have your thoughts provoked one more time. Open Sun to Wed, 10 a.m. to 6 p.m.; Thurs through Sat 10 a.m. to 7 p.m. $18 adults, $16 seniors and veterans, $12 students with ID, $8 children 6 to 16, free to children 5 and under.

Mount Greylock/Appalachian Trail. 30 Rockwell Rd., Lanesborough; (413) 499-4262; mass.gov/eea/agencies/dcr/massparks/region-west/mt-greylock-state-reservation-generic .html. At 3,491 feet, Greylock is the highest point in Massachusetts and one of the highest stops on the Appalachian National Scenic Trail. Drive to the top and enjoy sweeping views of boreal forest, the Taconic Mountains, and the Berkshire Hills, as well as a view of the Massachusetts Veterans War Memorial Tower. Park road opens in mid-May, weather permitting, and is open through Oct barring any closures for snow. Free admission.

Natural Bridge State Park. 107 Natural Bridge Rd. (off MA 8); (413) 663-6392; mass.gov/ eea/agencies/dcr/massparks/region-west/natural-bridge-state-park-generic.html. This park is only 48 acres, but it contains the only naturally formed white marble arch in North America, now adjacent to a manmade white marble dam. Geologists say the marble is more than 550 million years old, carved just 13,000 years ago by glacial meltwater into this impressive shape. Enjoy the 0.25-mile walking trail through the chasm or the 0.5-mile trail through the woods. Open Memorial Day through Columbus Day, daily 9 a.m. to 5 p.m.; closed mid-Oct through end of May. $2 parking fee.

where to eat

The Hub. 55 Main St.; (413) 662-2500; facebook.com/pages/The-Hub/147066242007124. "Always good" is the most often heard comment about this mainstay of downtown North Adams. The firmly American menu features everything from barbecued pulled pork sandwiches to jambalaya, inspired by the chef's decade-long stay in Mississippi River bayou country. Homestyle meatloaf, vegetarian entrees, and a crowd-pleasing Cajun cod provide options on the something-for-everyone menu. Tues through Fri 11 a.m. to 9:30 p.m., Sat 8 a.m. to 9:30 p.m., Sun brunch 8 a.m. to 1:30 p.m. $$.

Firehouse Cafe. 47 Park St.; (413) 749-7104; firehouse-cafe.com. A converted firehouse is the right kind of setting for a casual restaurant serving a classic American menu. Try the Firehouse stuffed burger or one of the house special entrees, from seared apple bourbon pork tenderloin to mushroom and sausage lasagna.

Public Eat + Drink. 34 Holden St.; (413) 664-4444; publiceatanddrink.com. If you haven't encountered the culinary style that foodies call "New American," Public can introduce you to this amalgam of flavors, drawing from many different spice palates to create new twists on old favorite dishes. Check out the pan-roasted salmon with pears; the roasted pork loin with honey, chipotle-apple sauce, and smoked paprika jus; or the mussels paired with crumbled sausage and tomato butter. Public received a 2014 Certificate of Excellence from TripAdvisor, an honor given to restaurants with consistently high ratings and rave reviews. Lunch and dinner daily from 11:30 a.m.; bar is open until midnight. $$.

day trip 32

upper hudson valley

upper hudson valley wine trail
valley falls, schaghticoke, cambridge, galway, greenfield center, corinth, fort edward, ny

More than a dozen wineries dot this route through the hills and expansive country fields of the newest wine region in New York State—so you'll want to choose a few for your day trip and return to this area several times to enjoy them all. This guide to the wineries will help you decide which ones you will sample first. For Adirondack Winery in Lake George, see day trip 37; for two wineries in Saratoga Springs, turn to day trip 35.

getting there

This day trip begins at the southern end of the winery route in Valley Falls. **From the north,** take I-87 south to exit 14 in Saratoga Springs. At the end of the ramp, take NY 9P east for about 4 miles. Make a sharp left onto NY 423 east, and continue for 2.8 miles. Turn right onto CR 75. In 1.2 miles, turn left onto Lake Road. Continue 3.3 miles to Hudson Avenue, and turn left. Take the first right onto the Stillwater Bridge. Cross the bridge and continue 4.7 miles onto NY 67 east, and keep going straight to Geary Road. Turn left on Geary, and keep going straight as this turns into Cardis (Kardas) Road, and then into Beadle Hill Road. Once you're on Beadle Hill Road, watch for Colonel Burch Road on your right in about a mile. Turn right and continue 0.4 mile to Amorici Vineyard. **From the south:** Take I-787 north in Albany to exit 9E, and merge onto NY 7 toward Troy/Bennington. Turn left onto 10th Street, which will become NY 40. In 3.4 miles, turn right onto Plank Road, and take the first left onto Leversee Road (still NY 40). Continue about 9.5 miles to NY 67 east, and turn right. In half a mile, turn left onto Geary Road. Keep going straight as this turns into Cardis (Kardas) Road, and then into Beadle Hill Road. Once you're on Beadle Hill Road, watch for Colonel Burch Road on your right in about a mile. Turn right and continue 0.4 mile to Amorici Vineyard.

valley falls, ny

On the shores of the Hoosic River, the tiny village of Valley Falls has just under 500 residents and less than 0.5 square mile of land—a fraction of its former heyday when textile and powder mills made use of the falls for power and employed hundreds of people. The powder mills had a tendency to explode, however, and even the long-closed textile mill burned to the ground in 2009. Today a drive through the village reveals a number of 19th-century homes and municipal buildings, a nice lead-in to your winery experience.

what to do

Amorici Vineyard. 637 Colonel Burch Rd.; (518) 469-0680; amoricivineyard.com. Wines sourced entirely from New York State grapes include the varieties grown here at this sustainably managed farm: Aromella, Kay Gray, Frontenac, and Marquette. Amorici offers 9 wines including whites, reds, a rose, a blush, and 2 other fruit beverages: Apple Honey Wine and Apple Honey Port. Mar through Nov, 11:30 a.m. to 5:30 p.m.; closed Dec through Feb.

Northern Star Vineyard. 1106 Beadle Hill Rd.; (518) 290-4282; facebook.com/Northern StarVineyard. As of this writing, this brand-new winery was scheduled to open for tastings in fall 2014, with a promise to feature estate wines made from "bold new breeds of northern climate grapes"—specifically Marquette, La Crescent, Frontenac, and Prairie Star. Stop here to see how proprietors Andrew and Kathleen Weber are doing so far. Check the Facebook page for hours and tasting fees.

schaghticoke, ny

Named for a Native American tribe that came together in the 17th century, Schaghticoke became a center of tribal activity when European colonists began to arrive in the New World in earnest. Hoping to escape contact and conflict with the new residents, several New England tribes migrated westward and settled here, forming a new tribe. The State of Connecticut eventually gave the Schaghticokes some reservation land, but the tribe dissipated and its members live mostly in other parts of New England.

where to go

Victory View Vineyard. 11975 NY 40; (518) 461-7132; victoryviewvineyard.com. The bounty of cold-climate grapes has led Victory View, a new winery opened in 2013, to produce 4 fine wines—2 reds and 2 whites—from grapes grown here on the estate. You'll hear the names of these grapes again and again as you tour the upper Hudson: La Crescent, LaCrosse, Marechal Foch, and Marquette. Here you'll enjoy an intimate tasting room and a chat with the winemaker, who provides your tasting personally. Sat 11 a.m. to 5:30 p.m.

cambridge, ny

If you happen to visit the small town of Cambridge in April, you may have the opportunity to enjoy the Tour of the Battenkill, the largest one-day Pro/Am cycling race in the United States. Racers take on the challenge of riding 64 miles of rolling terrain in this massive tour of the Battenkill Valley on the edge of the Adirondacks. If you miss the race, you can still enjoy Cambridge's arts community atmosphere, with a number of interesting galleries and shops on Main Street, its food co-op and farmers' market, and an independent bookstore.

what to do

Natural Selection Farm Vineyard. 85 Darwin Rd.; (518) 677-5208; upperhudsonvalley winetrail.com/wineries/natural-selection-farm-vineyard2/. Cold-hardy Burgundy reds from estate grapes are the specialty at this winery, alongside dry, spicy New York State whites. If you can't make it to the winery, you'll find its wines on the menus of restaurants in Saratoga Springs and Glens Falls. Daily 2 to 6 p.m.

galway, ny

That's "Galloway," like the town in Scotland, not like the one in Ireland—the Scottish name and pronunciation were intended back when the town was settled in 1774, but during its incorporation a clerical error turned it into Galway. In defiance, the original name remained, and locals will be happy to correct you. This rural, residential town makes the most of its local farmers, as you will see when you visit the Cock 'n Bull.

where to go

Johnston's Winery. 5140 Bliss Rd.; (518) 882-6310; johnstonswinery.com. The wine grapes Johnston uses to make its pinot noir, chardonnay, and concord wines come from other vineyards in New York and from California, but local fruit pervades the strawberry, raspberry, cherry, and blueberry wines you'll find here. Seasonal meads round out a sizable tasting menu, and Johnston's also makes its own line of jams and jellies. Wed through Sat 11 a.m. to 5 p.m., Sun noon to 5 p.m., closed Mon and Tues. Call for this year's tasting price.

where to eat

The Cock 'n Bull. 5342 Parkis Mills Rd.; (518) 882-6962; thecocknbull.com. Dine in a post-and-beam barn built in the 1850s, where antique tools and several fireplaces create an old-timey ambiance. The menu relies heavily on the harvest by local farmers, a policy the restaurant has held since 1976 (long before farm-to-table was cool), and you'll taste the difference in the soups, entrees, salads, and sandwiches on the menu. Solidly American dishes range from a generous steak sandwich to Alaskan king crab; bring your appetite. Open Mon to Sat 5 p.m. until closing, Sun 3 p.m. until closing.

greenfield center, ny

About 5 miles north of Saratoga Springs, the town of Greenfield hosts 7,400 residents, making it the largest town in Saratoga County. It's a primarily rural, interior community on the way to Lake Luzerne to the north, Great Sacandaga Lake to the west, and Saratoga Spa State Park to the south.

what to do

The Fossil Stone Vineyards. 331 Grange Rd.; (518) 703-1784; facebook.com/TheFossil StoneVineyards. Scheduled to open for tastings in 2015, this brand-new winery resides on the lands of an 1802 farm. Cold-hardy grapes including La Crescent, Marquette, and Traminette now thrive in the vineyards. Check the Facebook page for opening information and updates about winemaking in progress.

corinth, ny

The small, residential village of Corinth enjoys a picturesque spot on the banks of the Hudson River and on the edge of the Adirondacks, making it a favorite place for water sports and a must stop during fall foliage season. Headquarters of the United States Snowshoe Association, the governing body for competitive snowshoeing, Corinth has dubbed itself the Snowshoe Capital of the World and looks forward to the sport someday becoming an Olympic-level competition.

where to go

Ledge Rock Hill Winery & Vineyard. 41 Stewart Dam Rd.; (518) 654-5467; lrhwinery .com. The first winery to produce an award-winning vintage using grapes grown within the boundaries of Adirondack Park, this "winery in the woods" enjoys a beautiful spot in the park's foothills between Saratoga Springs and Lake George. The cozy, wood-lined tasting room leaves no doubt that you're in the north country, and the celebrated wines include a specialty line of sweet wines with flavors like kiwi pear and a blackberry vintage called Sacandaga Sunset. Sat 1 to 5 p.m., Sun noon to 5 p.m. Call for this year's tasting price.

fort edward, ny

You'll find more about Fort Edward in day trip 38.

what to do

Oliva Vineyards. 2074 US 4; (518) 747-2156; olivavineyards.com. This fairly young winery shares its land with the owner's other passion: racehorses. The 150-acre property includes stables for Tony Oliva's horses, some of which have won races at Belmont, Aqueduct, Monmouth Park, and Philadelphia Park. The winery produces 6 varietals including its popular Sparkling Hannah, a red wine with bowl-of-fruit flavor. The tasting room offers a 6-wine flight of samples for each guest. Sat and Sun noon to 5 p.m.; tasting room is closed weekdays. $6 for 6 samples.

day trip 33

upper hudson valley

east of the capital
hoosick, brunswick, troy, ny

This day trip provides the perfect weekend drive at just about any time of year: a leisurely ramble through gentle, foliage-covered mountains and cheerful little towns. A dollop of Revolutionary War history and other bits of Americana emerge not far from the Vermont border, but for the most part, you'll enjoy farm stands, artisans' studios, country-themed shops, antiquing, and enchanting landscapes.

hoosick, ny

The town of Hoosick struggled to get started back in the 1750s, as raiders from the local Indian tribes—aided by the French—broke up the first settlement during the French and Indian War. The Battle of Bennington was fought here during the Revolutionary War, and after the war Hoosick settled into a long period of peace and modest growth.

getting there

From the west, take NY 7 east from Troy about 25 miles to Hoosick. **From the north,** take NY 22 south directly to Hoosick, or take I-87 south to US 9 in Latham, and turn east on US 9, continuing to Troy. Once in Troy, take NY 7 east to Hoosick. **From the south,** take NY 22 north to Hoosick, or take I-87 north to Albany and I-787 east to Troy; follow the directions above.

what to do

Bennington Battlefield State Historic Site. On NY 67 in Hoosick Falls; (518) 686-7109; nysparks.com/historic-sites/12/getting-there.aspx. Here General John Burgoyne and the British Regulars faced the patriot forces under Brigadier General John Stark in August 1777, when the British attempted to capture American storehouses in Bennington, Vermont. In what had already become a pattern of misjudging the strength of the American forces, however, Burgoyne's men found themselves overwhelmed, and most of them died in the attack. Two months later, after miserable losses in two battles at Saratoga, Burgoyne and his remaining troops surrendered to the Americans. Open May 1 through Labor Day, daily 10 a.m. to 7 p.m.; Labor Day to Columbus Day, Sat and Sun only, 10 a.m. to 7 p.m.; Veterans Day (Nov 11) 10 a.m. to 7 p.m. Closed Nov through Apr.

Louis Miller Museum. 166 Main St.; Hoosick Falls; (518) 686-4682; hoosickhistory .com. This museum uses furnishings and other items donated by local families to provide a glimpse of Victorian life in the late 1800s and early 1900s. Most interesting here is the dress that artist Grandma Moses wore to the White House in 1960 on her 100th birthday. Grandma Moses—whose name was Anna Mary Robertson—lived on her farm north of here in Eagle Bridge, turning to painting for the first time in her 70s. She rose to international fame when an amateur art collector discovered one of her paintings in a drugstore window in Hoosick Falls. The art collector convinced the Museum of Modern Art in New York City to include a Grandma Moses painting in a show, and soon the media took such an interest in this elderly, down-to-earth artist that her name became a household word. Open Mon and Tues 1 to 4 p.m.; other times by appointment.

where to eat

Man of Kent Tavern and Cafe. 4452 NY 7; (518) 686-9917; manofkenttavern.com. On a casual day in eastern New York, there's nothing like a half-pound burger or a grilled sandwich to fill your stomach and satisfy your craving. This gem in Hoosick provides these and more, with salads, wraps, and entrees including a meaty Yorkshire beef stew that harkens back to colonial days. Mon through Thurs and Sat 11 a.m. to 10 p.m.; Fri 11 a.m. to 11 p.m.; Sun noon to 10 p.m. $$.

Picasso's. 21277 NY 22; (518) 686-6088. A wide range of sandwich options, soups, fresh ingredients from the proprietors' own garden, and an extensive list of desserts including Gifford's Ice Cream (a Maine-based dairy) draw high marks for this eatery with locals. The country-store setting makes you want to relax and linger, while the opportunity to experiment with the make-your-own sandwich menu may make this your new favorite lunch spot. Mon and Tues 10 a.m. to 7 p.m.; Thurs through Sat 10 a.m. to 8 p.m.; Sun 10 a.m. to 6 p.m. Closed Wed. $.

where to shop

Big Moose Deli and Country Store. 4956 NY 7; (518) 686-5801; facebook.com/Big MooseDeli. This wacky souvenir and snack stop displays more merchandise than it can comfortably fit into a store this size, in a maze of shelves snaking throughout the building. Whatever Vermont-branded item you may want, from magnets and bumper stickers to jams and cheeses or an improbable assortment of maple-flavored food varieties, you will find it here—and some of it is actually made in Vermont. Oddly enough, you won't find much in here that features New York, but you will find bacon-flavored dental floss, if that's something you desperately need. A word of warning: Many signs point you to the "outhouse," but the only bathrooms are port-o-johns behind the building. Mon through Thurs 9 a.m. to 5:45 p.m.; Fri through Sun 8 a.m. to 6:45 p.m.

The Potter Hill Barn. 3864 NY 7; (800) 301-7776; (518) 686-7777; potterhillbarn.com. This well-merchandised country store warrants a stop long enough to browse with vigor. Here you'll find a wide and varied selection of country craft items for the home, including ceramics, holiday decorations for just about any season, tableware, textiles, furniture, embroidered pieces, candles, lamps, dolls, wooden signs, baskets, and a great deal more. Potter Hill is open daily year-round, so you won't miss the fun as long as you pass through during the business day. Open daily 10 a.m. to 5:30 p.m.

brunswick, ny

Settled by Europeans as far back as 1711, Brunswick thrived as an agricultural town well into the 20th century, hosting some manufacturing during the Industrial Revolution but returning to its roots—literally—until Troy's urban sprawl began to move in this direction. Today this former farming town hosts all the modern suburban amenities, making life in Brunswick desirable to more residents than ever before in its history. Even with the change in character that seems inevitable here, however, you will find a number of attractive places to see and shops unique to this area.

getting there

From Troy, take NY 7 east to Brunswick. Most of the attractions described below are on this route.

what to do

Grafton Lakes State Park. 61 N. Long Pond Rd., Grafton; (518) 279-1155; nysparks .state.ny.us/parks/53/details.aspx. Here on a ridge above the Hudson River Valley and the Taconic River, the 2,357-acre park provides swaths of rugged forests and 5 natural ponds. This multiuse recreational area offers its fields, streams, woods, and lakes for all manner of outdoor activities, from horseback riding to nature photography, as well as excellent fishing for a number of northeastern species. Twenty-five miles of trails pass through this park, with the Long Pond Trail rising to the top of my "favorites" list. If you take it on, wear boots that stabilize your ankles, as the trails are loaded with boulders and roots that make this level trail more challenging that you might expect. Open daily year-round 8 a.m. to dusk. A fee is charged from Memorial Day to Labor Day; the fee is higher when the beach is open.

Tomhannock Reservoir. On NY 7 between Pittstown and Brunswick; (607) 652-7366; www.dec.ny.gov/outdoor/84865.html. The water source for the city of Troy and much of Rensselaer County passes under NY 7 as you come out on the west side of Pittstown. This manmade lake holds 12.3 billion gallons of water at its peak level, and its 5.2-mile length hosts nearly 20 different species of fish, including smallmouth and largemouth bass, panfish, and walleye in abundance. To stop and enjoy the view of this shimmering reservoir, park on the west side of the causeway in the small parking area and walk out onto the bridge. Daylight hours daily; free admission, but if you want to do more than look at the reservoir (boat or fish, for example), you must obtain a permit from the City of Troy.

where to shop

Carpenter's Touch Wood Sculpture. 3205 NY 7, Johnsonville; (518) 423-3448; carpenters touch.net. It's worth a stop here to see the work of craftsman Charles Jennet, who creates more than chainsaw bears and totem poles (although these are very impressive); his work in handcrafted furniture makes use of the shape and grain of each individual section of wood, turning them into rustic pieces that bring the natural world into the home. Mon through Fri 9 a.m. to 7 p.m., Sun 10 a.m. to 7 p.m., closed Sat.

troy, ny

As you enter the city of Troy, you may not have any idea that this fairly small community—about 50,000 people, according to the 2010 census—served as one of the birthplaces of the Industrial Revolution in the mid-1800s. The first Bessemer converter in America, a device that permitted the mass production of steel from pig iron, was invented nearby and installed in Troy, allowing the city to become a leader in the steel industry. Using charcoal and iron ore mined in the Adirondacks, Troy became a key player in the production of gunpowder and weapons for the Civil War, supplying iron and steel to the federal arsenal at Watervliet across the Hudson River.

getting there

From I-87 north of Albany, take exit 7 to NY 7. At the end of the exit ramp, take NY 7 east. Continue on NY 7 east through Latham to Troy.

what to do

Rensselaer County Historical Society. In the Joseph B. Carr Building, 57 Second St.; (518) 272-7232; rchsonline.org. The museum features a collection of artifacts from Troy's business history, from shirt collars to cast-iron stoves and Troy-Bilt rototillers. You'll also find a collection of decorative arts, paintings, sculpture, textiles, military uniforms, and published materials from both the 19th and 20th centuries. Here you can get information about walking tours of Troy's older neighborhoods to see its steel facades and brownstones, some of them nearly two centuries old, as well as more than a dozen Tiffany windows in Beaux-Arts buildings in the city's downtown. Feb through Dec, Tues through Sat noon to 5 p.m.; closed late Dec and Jan; $4 donation.

Rensselaer Polytechnic Institute. 110 8th St.; (518) 276-6000; rpi.edu. A number of manufacturers of precision instruments sprang up around this proximity to steel, and they helped to support the creation of the nation's first engineering school and one of the top colleges for engineering and technology studies in the US. The campus, set in a hillside overlooking the city and the Hudson River, has been in its current location since 1905, with its first hall—the Carnegie Building—opening in 1907. The older, traditional buildings mix nicely with the modern facilities added over the ensuing decades, making a ride or walk around campus both pleasant and informative. You are welcome to stroll the campus during daylight hours; free admission.

where to eat

Daisy Baker's. 33 Second St.; (518) 266-9200; daisybakers.com. If you love the idea of dining in a 4-story 1892 brownstone commissioned by the Young Women's Association (what came before the YWCA), you will have a wonderful time at this downtown restaurant—one with its own colorful history and recent renaissance. The deliberately simple menu features a number of exciting surprises, like salmon "crowned with a cippolini/honey gastrique," or lamb dressed with fennel, sauvignon blanc, and great northern beans. Salads, a hefty appetizer menu, and a substantial burger complete a very appealing menu. Mon through Thurs 5 to 9 p.m.; Fri and Sat 5 to 10 p.m.; closed Sun. $$.

Lo Porto. 85 Fourth St.; (518) 273-8546; loportos.com. What would an upstate New York city be without a great Italian restaurant? Lo Porto fits the bill nicely, with an extensive menu of both traditional and imaginative dishes presented with grand style. Pasta purists can create their own spaghetti with the sauce of their choice, while guests with a sense of adventure might select one of the many treatments of veal or seafood to please their palate. You'll also find an exciting beverage menu here. Mon through Fri, lunch 11 a.m. to 3 p.m., dinner 5 to 10 p.m.; Sat dinner only, 5 to 10 p.m.; closed Sun. $$.

River Street Cafe. 429 River St.; (518) 273-2740; riverstreetcafetroy.com. Enjoy a leisurely meal from a menu that draws from many different nationalities, making the most of the natural flavors of each dish. Duck with pineapple salsa, lamb shoulder prepared with Greek overtones, or ravioli stuffed with asparagus and gruyère cheese will certainly get your attention, and the relaxed, intimate atmosphere will bring you back. Tues through Sat 5:30 p.m. to closing; closed Mon. $$.

Snowman Ice Cream. 531 5th Ave.; (518) 233-1714; thesnowmanicecream.com. While you're poking around Troy's neighborhood of numbered streets, be sure to stop at Snowman, where you can select from more than 30 flavors of ice cream made on the premises. Flavors like coffee Oreo, Kahlua fudge almond, and peanut butter cookie dough are among the selections available daily, but the pistachio nut flavor rose to the top of our list for its concentration of crunchy bits and its balance of sweet and savory. Expect long lines in summer, but the large portions more than make up for that. Open Mar through early fall, Mon through Fri 11 a.m. to 9 p.m.; Sat and Sun noon to 9 p.m.; closed in the winter months. $.

where to shop

Bennington Potters Factory Outlet. 2113 State Highway 7, Troy; (518) 663-9200; benningtonpotters.com. One of only two factory outlet stores for this regionally famous pottery company, this store features bakeware, mugs, bowls, pitchers, and serving pieces, all made in Potters Yard in Bennington, Vermont. Mon through Sat 9:30 a.m. to 6 p.m., Sun 10 a.m. to 5 p.m.

Gristmill Antique Center. 2250 NY 7, Troy; (518) 663-5115; gristmillantiquecenter.com. A 3,400-square-foot treasure hunter's paradise on the outskirts of Troy, Gristmill brings together more than 50 antiques vendors to show their late-19th- to mid-20th-century wares. China, jewelry, glassware, furniture, military collectibles, and much more come together in one of the largest multidealer antiques centers in this region—and Gristmill is open 7 days a week, giving you plenty of opportunities to stop. Daily 10 a.m. to 5 p.m.

River Street. Two blocks of antiques stores dominate this remarkably retro district, intermingled with home goods and other stores to provide you with a substantial afternoon's shopping experience. You'll find merchants with one-of-a-kind furniture, thrift shops with bargains on gently used items, artisans who turn wood and clay into treasures, and much more. Around the corner on Third and Fourth Streets, boutiques abound with unique jewelry designs, clothing styles you won't find in department stores, and even shops that carry stringed instruments. Open daily; hours vary by establishment.

Tarbox Farms Earth's Bounty. 1533 NY 7, Troy; (518) 279-9517. A family now in its fourth generation of dairy, beef, and vegetable farming, Tarbox prides itself on its sustainable practices and its antibiotic and hormone-free cattle. Depending on the season, you will find apples, berries, corn on the cob, pumpkins, and vegetables here, as well as eggs, cheese, meat, maple syrup, and jellies.

day trip 34

upper hudson valley

>>> **where the rivers meet**
waterford, cohoes, ny

When canals made New York State a central corridor for commerce back in the 1820s, the areas in and around Waterford and Cohoes figured prominently in New York's development. These pivot points became ports along a network of waterways including the Hudson and Mohawk Rivers, the Champlain Canal, and the Erie Canal. The transformation of New York State began with Elkanah Watson, a native of Massachusetts, who first proposed that the state's natural waterways could be connected by canals to create a continuous waterway to the Great Lakes. He brought his ideas to New York State Senator and General Philip Schuyler, and together they worked toward passage of an act to create a pair of canal corporations in 1792. With one military conflict after another absorbing time, resources, and manpower over the next 25 years, it must have seemed that Watson's vision would never come to pass—but the Champlain Canal finally opened in 1819 and the Erie Canal followed in 1825. The newly interconnected waterway made it possible to transport large loads of grains, minerals, and other goods between ocean ports in New York City, mines and timber companies in the Adirondacks and New England, and the agricultural fields and mills of central New York. The state became the nation's most prosperous commercial center almost overnight.

waterford, ny

All rivers and canals in this part of New York lead to Waterford, a fairly small village with a lively history. Mahican Indians held this land when Dutch settlers arrived in the late 1600s, but the Dutch renamed the area Half Moon Point and built a settlement that became the first incorporated village in the United States. Later the name of the village changed to Waterford to note its geographic location, at the ford between Peebles Island and the mainland. The fording point is long gone—turned into a canal lock when the Erie Canal opened in 1825—but the name remains, and the confluence of canals and rivers here has only made it a stronger reference point on the New York state map.

getting there

From I-87 north or south, take exit 7 and follow the exit ramp to NY 7 east. Drive east on NY 7 to the junction with NY 32 (if you reach I-787, you've gone too far). Turn left (north) on NY 32 and continue across the Mohawk River to Waterford.

what to do

Waterford Harbor Visitor Center. 1 Tugboat Alley; (518) 233-9123; town.waterford.ny .us/harbor-visitors-center.html. You'll find lots of information about the Erie Canal here and ways to make the most of your canal exploration. The Erie Canalway National Heritage Corridor, the Mohawk Towpath Scenic Byway, and Lakes to Locks Passage Scenic Byway share this visitor center, which offers lots of brochures, maps, and expert commentary about things you will see along the route. Open daily May through Nov 10 a.m. to 4 p.m. Free admission.

Champlain Canal locks. Continue up US 4 north and see the Champlain Canal—here in the form of the Hudson River—come into view on your right as you enter Saratoga County. You will see a total of 11 locks on this canal as you drive north toward Cohoes, though they are numbered 1–9 and 11–12, with no lock 10—the planned lock turned out to be unnecessary, so it was never constructed.

Erie Canal Lock 2. At the end of 5th Street; (518) 237-0812; canals.state.ny.us. This is the second lock in the currently functioning Erie Canal, giving you an opportunity to see how this simple but ingenious technology has evolved since the canal's first locks were completed in 1825. The process has become more automatic and the lock's parts move under power, but the result is the same: Water runs out of one side of the lock and into the other, raising or lowering the vessel as the water levels equalize. Lock 2 lifts boats 33.55 feet, from their starting level of 15.2 feet to their exit at 48.75 feet. When the lock is at rest, you can walk along its concrete walls within a fenced walkway to get a close look at the entire operation. Open daylight hours; free admission.

Erie Canalway Towpath Trail. Accessible from Lock 2, at the end of 5th Street; (518) 237-0812; canals.state.ny.us. This pedestrian and bicycle path runs the entire 363-mile length of the canal. You can pick up the path anywhere along the route and walk as far or as little as you like, enjoying the communities you will see along the way. The path has become one of the modern canal's most popular features. Here the Erie Canal also meets the Champlain Canal, a waterway once used for shipping goods south from Lake Champlain and its environs in northern New York State. Always open; free admission.

Flight of Five Locks. Flight Lock Road; (518) 237-0812; canals.state.ny.us. From the Lock 2 parking area, turn left onto Broad Street, drive 2 blocks on NY 32, and turn right at 4th Street. Turn left at Division Street and continue to Flight Lock Road. Turn left to see the famous Flight of Five Locks. This remarkable configuration of locks provides the necessary navigation around Cohoes Falls, raising barges and boats 165 feet in a little more than a mile. This flight achieved the greatest lift in the shortest distance on any canal in the world—a record that stands today. Open daylight hours for viewing; free admission.

Peebles Island State Park. 1 Delaware Ave.; (518) 237-8643, ext. 3295; nysparks.com/parks/111/details.aspx. Here at the confluence of the Mohawk and Hudson Rivers, this park provides an excellent 3-mile hiking trail around the island for views of both rivers and the swells and rapids that make this place particularly striking. You can see the confluence of the Hudson River flowing south, and the Mohawk River coming in from the west. Hiking trails all over this island bring you to wide vistas of the rivers and the communities above the shoreline. There's textile history here, too: Peebles Island played host to the **Cluett, Peabody & Company shirt factory,** home of Arrow shirts and collars. Arrow detachable shirt collars became a wardrobe staple for the common man of the 1910s and 1920s, and Cluett, Peabody turned out 4 million collars a week. Cluett invented a process for pre-shrinking the cloth with which men's shirts were made, and this "Sanfordizing" process made him a very wealthy man. Extensive interpretive displays inside the building will tell you all you need to know about men's shirt manufacturing. Open year-round; hours are subject to change, so call before visiting; $6 per vehicle.

Waterford Historical Museum. 2 Museum Lane; (518) 238-0809; waterfordmuseum .com Located in the 1830 Hugo White homestead at the first intersection of the Cohoes-Waterford Bridge (NY 32), this museum provides permanent exhibitions on a city and its relationship with its two rivers, as well as a Victorian period room and a model of Champlain Canal Lock 4. It's part of the Northside Historic District, a 60-acre area with buildings that date back to 1828, and some fine examples of Greek Revival and late Victorian architecture. Open in the summer months, Wed through Fri 10 a.m. to 2 p.m.; Sat 10 a.m. to 4 p.m.; Sun 2 to 4 p.m.; closed Mon and Tues.

where to eat

McGreivey's Restaurant. 91 Broad St.; (518) 238-2020; mcgreiveys.com. The chef here is a graduate of the Culinary Institute of America, and he certainly has a creative way with his menu: Try the filet Napoleon, a petite filet and shrimp on top of a crab cake, with a tomato demi-glaze awakened with a little brandy. For a real change of pace, the pork chops rubbed with coffee and brown sugar are decidedly unlike the ones you broil at home. This restaurant is a real find. Mon through Thurs 11:30 a.m. to 10 p.m.; Fri and Sat 11:30 a.m. to midnight; Sun 1 to 9 p.m. $$.

cohoes, ny

Imagine reaching this junction of the Mohawk and Hudson Rivers in the early 1600s, and seeing this massive series of waterfalls tumbling over a ridge. If your plan was to find the most advantageous site for a Dutch colony in the New World, you might have literally jumped for joy when you discovered Cohoes Falls, a source of virtually unlimited water-power for the mills you intended to build along the river.

Such a man was Killian Van Rensselaer, who purchased this land from the Indians in 1630 on behalf of the Dutch West India Company. Technology and manufacturing practices would not catch up with this abundant power source for another 200 years, but once the Cohoes Company began offering cheap waterpower to industrialists to come to eastern New York, the population soared. Among the many factories that opened here, Harmony Mills built a fantastic textile manufacturing operation that still stands today, repurposed as a condominium complex.

As electricity and labor became cheaper in the southern states, the companies that made Cohoes an industrial center relocated—but you can still see and enjoy the waterfall that made Cohoes great.

getting there

From Flight Lock Road, turn left onto Fonda Road and continue around the bed to the left. Turn left onto Halfmoon Road, going straight as it becomes Church Hill Road. There's a nice view of the bend in the Mohawk River as you turn left onto US 9, cross the Mohawk River, and enter the town of Colonie. Turn left quickly onto Crescent Cohoes Road. Follow the river on your left through a natural area and pass an old industrial dam with a manmade falls. In a moment, you'll arrive in the town of Cohoes.

what to do

Cohoes Falls Overlook Park. Corner of School and Cataract Streets; friendsofcohoesfalls .org. There's a viewing area for the falls just down the road on School Street, where Brook-field, the area's hydropower company, harnesses the falls to churn electricity that powers 26,000 homes annually. The powerhouse uses the same hydroelectric system built here in 1915—in fact, the dam, upper gatehouse, and power canal actually date back to the 1800s. Climb the stairs to the second-floor deck for an even more expansive view. Open during daylight hours; free admission.

Falls View Park. North Mohawk Street at the waterfall; friendsofcohoesfalls.org. This 4-acre park gives you the perfect place to view the magnificent Cohoes Falls. Named by the Iroquois long before Europeans arrived in the New World, written about in Dutch colonists' memoirs and poets' letters since the 1600s, and sketched and painted by explorers and artists for centuries, Cohoes Falls makes an unforgettable impression from its very first viewing. This gargantuan cataract stands nearly as tall as Niagara Falls and wider than Niagara's American Falls, topping out at roughly 1,000 feet across the mighty Mohawk River. The most interesting comparative statistic, however, involves the quantity of water flowing over Cohoes' ledges: While Niagara flows at 5,000 to 21,000 cubic feet per second, Cohoes Falls routinely moves nearly five times more water, at 90,000 cubic feet per second—reaching 100,000 cubic feet per second during major storms like 2011's Hurricane Irene. Open during daylight hours; free admission.

Harmony Mills. 100 N. Mohawk St.; (518) 237-6518; harmonymillslofts.com. Now a building of trendy loft apartments and a National Historic Landmark, Harmony Mills was once the largest cotton mill complex in the world. Built in 1866, Harmony Mills produced cotton muslin and printed calico fabric in a facility considered state-of-the-art in its day. Mill No. 3 sports a mansard roof and a finely crafted façade, unusual adornments for a manufacturing facility. It also received the nickname Mastodon Mill because of the discovery of a prehistoric mastodon skeleton under the construction site while workers dug the mill's foundation. The skeleton now resides in the State Museum in Albany. (You can see a blue-and-yellow New York State history marker at the northern corner of the building on N. Mohawk Street, where the mastodon was found.) The building is now a private residence and is not open to visitors.

day trip 35

upper hudson valley

>>> **battles & bubbles**
ballston spa, saratoga springs, ny

The story goes that back in 1771, surveyors calculating the boundaries of an area of land called the Kayaderosseras Patent stumbled across a bubbling spring near Kaydeross Creek. This little trickle turned out to be the first mineral spring found in America, and its mineral-rich smell and taste—a high content of magnesium, calcium, and salt—made people believe that the spring had healing powers. Despite the lack of mass communications, word spread quickly about the mysterious healing spring. Clever opportunists built hotels including the Sans Souci, the largest hotel in America, which opened in 1803 and offered luxurious spa accommodations. More construction led to the discovery of more springs in both Ballston Spa and nearby Saratoga Springs. It looked like permanent prosperity in this fairly remote corner of New York . . . until the springs began to fail in the 1830s, and one clever entrepreneur started bottling the remaining water and shipping it to merchants across the country. In no time, the tourism heyday of the two towns came to an end. Today you can enjoy the scenic setting of these two towns, explore their historic sites, feast on the bounty of local farmers' fields, and even take advantage of a spa experience.

ballston spa, ny

Today you can explore the history of Ballston Spa and gain a sense of what it must have been like to come here "for the waters." You also can see the energy that local residents have put into giving this town its 21st-century vitality, making it a center of tourist activity with shopping, restaurants, and up-to-date spa experiences. As you shop or eat in Ballston Spa, keep an eye out for the town's unusual concentration of fair trade businesses—establishments that sell or serve products that have been acquired from independent farmers and makers who do not use child labor, who respect gender equality, who are good stewards of the environment, and who practice cultural sustainability. These companies and individuals are paid a fair price for their goods, and they in turn pay fair wages to their workers.

getting there

From the north or south, take I-87 north to exit 12 for Ballston Spa. At the end of the exit ramp, head west on NY 67 and continue to the town of Ballston Spa. To reach Saratoga Springs, take NY 50 north from Ballston Spa for 5.5 miles to the town center.

what to do

Brookside Museum. 6 Charlton St.; (518) 885-4000; brooksidemuseum.org. Welcome to one of the former resort hotels at the mineral springs, constructed in 1792 and used as a school for boys, a boarding house, a sanitarium, a private residence, and an apartment building until the Saratoga County Historical Society bought it in 1970. Today the building preserves the county's unique history with 5 galleries, a hands-on history room, a research library, and a gift shop. You can see a replica of a resort guest room, learn about the building's history, and enjoy the current exhibits on the Saratoga region. Tues through Fri 10 a.m. to 4 p.m.; Sat 10 a.m. to 2 p.m.; closed Sun and Mon and on all major holidays. $2 adults, $1.50 seniors over 60 and students with ID, $1 children 5 and up, free to children under 5.

Dakota Ridge Farm. 189 E. High St.; (518) 885-0756; dakotaridgefarm.com. Here in 42 acres of woods, pastures, and ponds, owners Katrina and Gary Capasso breed llamas that can become pack animals, bearers of highly desirable wool, show animals, or companions. You can come and visit the 55 llamas, take a tour of the farm and pet and walk a llama, or take a trek (in spring or fall) on trails on the grounds and lead a llama on a group hike. Tours: $10 per person; hikes: $25 adults, $15 children 15 and under; 25 percent discount for veterans. To schedule a tour or hike, email llamawhisp@aol.com.

Living Well Day Spa and Healing Arts Center. 18 Low St.; (518) 885-9145; livingwell ballstonspa.com. In a restored Victorian home in downtown Ballston Spa, you can enjoy a massage, facial, eyelash extensions, microdermabrasion, waxing, manicure and pedicure, and other body treatments to rejuvenate in ways the visitors of the 18th century could not have imagined. Explore the benefits of naturopathic medicine, spirit medicine, Reiki, and the use of essential oils. Tues through Sat 11 a.m. to 7 p.m.; prices vary with the service provided. Call or visit the website to book an appointment.

National Bottle Museum. 76 Milton Ave.; (518) 885-7589; nationalbottlemuseum.org. Why a museum about bottles? Bottle-making was America's first major industry, and here at the mouth of the mineral springs, bottle-making became a critical part of the supply chain as resorts and visitors clamored for glass containers. Millions of glass bottles were manufactured here in the early 1800s in a glassworks in Greenfield. There's also a museum glassworks here, so you can see today's glass artists at work. Open Jan and Feb, Thurs through Sat 10 a.m. to 4 p.m., closed New Year's Day; Mar through Dec, Tues through Sat 10 a.m. to 4 p.m., closed Sun and Mon. Donations encouraged.

where to eat

Augie's Family Style Italian. 17 Low St.; (518) 884-8600; augiesrestaurant.com. If you love old-fashioned homestyle Italian cooking, you'll love this family-style dining experience. Augie Vitiello himself is the master chef, and he teaches his cooking techniques on Capital Region television. Each dish serves two or more people, so order two entrees for a family of four and you will be more than satisfied—especially if your entree is accompanied by salad, bread, and maybe Augie's famous broccoli rabe appetizer. No one leaves here hungry. Mon, Wed, Thurs, and Sun 4 to 9 p.m.; Fri and Sat 4 to 10 p.m.; closed Tues. $$.

D-Line Pub. 15 Prospect St.; (518) 885-6861; dlinepub.com. New owners took over this local gathering spot in January 2013, and the hearty meals and daily specials have drawn rave reviews from locals and visitors. Entrees include fresh fish every Friday and prime rib on Thursday, while Monday is macaroni and cheese night—with Buffalo-spiced chicken or bacon. Save room for the triple-chocolate brownies for dessert, voted the best dessert at the 2014 Ballston Chocolate Fest. Lunch and dinner daily, Mon through Thurs 11 a.m. to 9 p.m.; Fri and Sat 11 a.m. to 10 p.m.; Sun 11 a.m. to 9 p.m. $$.

Good Morning Cafe. 2100 Doubleday Ave.; (518) 309-3359; goodmorningbreakfast.com. Start your day at one of the town's fair trade establishments, where eggs from pasture-raised chickens, gluten-free pancakes and oatmeal, and fair trade coffee are prominently featured. The owners source their ingredients from more than 15 local farms. Tues through Sun 7 a.m. to 1 p.m.; closed Mon. $$.

saratoga springs, ny

In 1771, perhaps close to the time that surveyors found the spring in what would become Ballston Spa, Iroquois tribesmen took Sir William Johnson—head of North American Indian affairs for England—to show him the "great medicine spring" at High Rock. Settlement here became a priority, and the High Rock area became Saratoga Springs' Upper Village, while the Lower Village grew up about a mile south. By 1792, a second spring was found and tourism boomed. Saratoga Springs separated from the Town of Saratoga in 1819, and today it has a year-round population above 28,000 and more than 28 square miles of residences, businesses, and services. In summer, the population triples as vacationers and summer people arrive.

what to do

Children's Museum at Saratoga. 69 Caroline St.; (518) 584-5540; cmssny.org. Highly interactive exhibits give children the opportunity to learn new concepts about the world around them while playing. A child-size grocery store, schoolhouse, firehouse, construction zone, and bank are all part of the museum experience. Labor Day through June, Tues through Sat 9:30 a.m. to 4:30 p.m., Sun noon to 4:30 p.m.; closed Mon. July through Labor Day, Mon through Sat 9:30 a.m. to 4:30 p.m., Sun noon to 4:30 p.m. $6 per person, children under 1 are free.

Saratoga Casino and Raceway. 342 Jefferson St.; (518) 584-2110; saratogacasino .com. Saratoga's harness raceway may be even more famous than the mineral springs, immortalized in Broadway show tunes and movies and in full operation since 1941. Watch the races from the rail, the clubhouse, in the grandstand, or while enjoying a meal at one of the raceway's restaurants, and place your wagers on one of the mezzanine televisions. If the horses aren't running (or even if they are), you can enjoy more than 1,700 slot machines in the casino, or take in a show at the Vapor Night Club—local party bands play on Friday night, and video DJs create a multimedia show on Saturday with surprise guest appearances. Buffets and 3 full-service bars round out the action. Open daily 8 a.m. to 4 a.m.

The Saratoga Winery. 482 NY 29; (518) 584-9463; thesaratogawinery.com. There's more to do at this winery than sample the wine (although you definitely should sample some of the nearly 20 wines produced here): The Saratoga Winery features live music on Friday and Saturday evenings from 3 to 6 p.m., so you can buy a bottle of the wine you liked best, use a couple of the house's glasses, and relax (and savor a wood-fired pizza on Friday night). The wines made here incorporate grapes of New York's Finger Lakes region, using that area's famous Rieslings as well as chardonnay, pinot noir, merlot, cabernet franc, cabernet sauvignon, and some unusual blends. Mon through Thurs and Sat 11 a.m. to 7 p.m.; Fri 11 a.m. to 9 p.m.; Sun noon to 7 p.m.

Swedish Hill Winery. 379 Broadway; (518) 450-1200; swedishhill.com/our-locations/ swedish-hill-saratoga-springs. Swedish Hill received the Top Winery honor at the New York State Fair Commercial Wine Competition in 2013. The winery has produced its own wine since 1985, but its history of growing grapes in the Finger Lakes began back in 1969, when the farm raised grapes to sell to the area's earliest wineries. Swedish Hill grew under the leadership of its original owners, Dick and Cindy Peterson, and its popularity increased significantly when their son Dave received his PhD in viticulture and joined the winery. Today Swedish Hill has two spinoff wineries, Goose Watch and Penguin Bay (on Seneca Lake), and a tasting room in Lake Placid as well as this one in Saratoga Springs. Choose from 25 wines available for tasting, including Twenty to One Red, available exclusively at this tasting room. Mon through Thurs 11 a.m. to 6 p.m.; Fri and Sat 11 a.m. to 8 p.m.; Sun noon to 5 p.m.

where to eat

There are literally hundreds of restaurants in the Saratoga Springs area. Here are a few that are highly recommended by residents and tourists.

The Crown Grill at Circus Cafe. 390 Broadway; (518) 583-1105; crowngrillsaratoga.com. With so many restaurants on Broadway, you need to be good to compete, and the Crown Grill stands up to the competition. The inspired menu unites flavors in interesting ways, like the mussels bathed in a coconut curry sauce or the eggplant tossed in a fritti of fresh mozzarella, olives, tomatoes, and house-made basil pesto. On the lunch menu, you'll find burgers made of lamb, salmon, and black beans and lentils as well as the expected black Angus. The substantive beer list even includes 3 gluten-free varieties. Sun through Thurs 11:30 a.m. to 10 p.m.; Fri and Sat 11:30 a.m. to 10:30 p.m. Late night bar daily. $$.

Mio Posto. 68 Putnam St.; (518) 423-7022; miopostosaratoga.com. A tiny restaurant that provides a huge experience, this little American/Italian bistro has become legendary for its cuisine, its presentation, and its service. You'll find fresh rigatoni on the menu with the chef's special Bolognese sauce, but you'll also find braised pork cheeks with a bone marrow cider demi-glace, served with a cauliflower mash. There's grilled salmon, but also rabbit from local Wannabea Farms, and an intriguing dish called veal Danny (for the chef). It may be a little snug in the dining room, but it will be worth it. Reservation times daily: 5, 6, 6:30, 8, and 8:30 p.m. Reservations strongly recommended. $$.

Thirsty Owl Outlet and Wine Garden. 184 S. Broadway; (518) 587-9694; thirsty-owl -outlet-wine-garden.myshopify.com. Another Finger Lakes winemaker brings its world-class wines to the residents and guests of the Saratoga area, with a tasting room, gift shop, and bistro in the heart of town. The upscale bistro menu features tapas (small plates, Spain-style) and entrees, each with a suggested wine pairing, as well as a cheese board and meat board (charcuterie) for a special tasting experience. Open daily 11:30 a.m. to 10 p.m. $$.

Triangle Diner. 400 Maples Ave.; (518) 583-6368; facebook.com/pages/TRIANGLE -DINER/220202679335. For breakfast in Saratoga Springs, drive a little bit out of downtown to try this busy diner. The corned beef hash—made fresh on the premises—is one of the stars on this menu, but it's hard to top specials like the bacon and parmesan pancakes, the crab cakes Benedict, or the omelets loaded with fresh ingredients. If you see a line when you get there, rest assured the food will be worth the wait. Mon through Sat 6 a.m. to 2 p.m., Sun 7 a.m. to 1 p.m. $.

day trip 36

upper hudson valley

>>> **leatherstocking legends**
glens falls, ny

Visit the real-life location that inspired James Fenimore Cooper to write one of the most celebrated novels of the 19th century, and see what became of the massive falls he enjoyed when it became a critical source of industrial waterpower and transportation.

getting there

From the south, take I-87 north to exit 18. Take the exit ramp to CR 28 and turn east. Continue on CR 28 to Glens Falls. From the north, take I-87 south to exit 18 and follow the directions above.

glens falls, ny

If you're a fan of James Fenimore Cooper's most successful novel, *The Last of the Mohicans*, then you know all about Glens Falls. In fact, perhaps you've already visited Cooper's Cave, the author's inspiration for the "dark and silent caves" in which Hawkeye and his Mohican Indian traveling companions found shelter for the book's two heroines and their guide. Cooper describes this cave as being hidden behind the falls, and when he saw it for the first time in 1825, Glens Falls probably did mask its place—but today, a dam harnesses this falls and sends water through a millpond into turbines to generate electricity for Finch Paper LLC. On the south side of the dam, water flows into turbines for Boralex, Inc., which generates electricity for the New York State power grid.

The history of Glens Falls makes it a particularly interesting place: An explorer and colonist named Abraham Wing built the first dam here way back in 1765, and the feeder canal you see today began operation nearly 200 years ago in 1830. The falls itself, however, doesn't present much of a picture. If you want to see it in its full glory, visit during April or May when winter snowmelt and spring rains create a strong spillover. Otherwise, come to Glens Falls if subterranean geology interests you, as you'll have an excellent opportunity to view the rock wall that ordinarily would be invisible under the waterfall's flow. In summer, a trolley service travels around town in Glens Falls and on to Lake George, with stops including the nearby outlet shopping center.

what to do

Chapman Historical Museum. 348 Glen St.; (518) 793-2826; chapmanmuseum.org. This museum preserves the history of the city of Glens Falls and neighboring Queensbury, as well as memories of the southern Adirondacks at the turn of the 20th century. You'll find an evocative history of Lake George and the resort area tradition, images of steamboats and information about their use in the 19th century, and a well-preserved home in which the DeLongs, a prominent Glens Falls family, lived in the early 1900s. Tues through Sat 10 a.m. to 4 p.m.; Sun noon to 4 p.m.; closed Mon. $5 adults, $4 seniors 65 and older and students with ID, free for children under 12.

Cooper's Cave Overlook. 46 Saratoga Ave.; (518) 761-3864; sgfny.com/Coopers-Cave .htm. Visit a viewing platform where you can see into the cave that served to inspire *The Last of the Mohicans*. Before author Cooper cemented this cave's place in history, the falls and the Hudson River played an important role as a transportation route for Native Americans, colonial forces, and British soldiers, especially during the Revolutionary War. Later the timber industry floated literally millions of logs from the Adirondacks to parts south by sending them through this area. Memorial Day to Oct 31, daily 9 a.m. to 8 p.m. Free admission.

Glens Falls Feeder Canal. Access from Murray Street; (518) 792-5363; feedercanal.org. Built in 1822 and widened and deepened in 1832, this 7-mile canal transports water from above Glens Falls to the highest point on the Champlain Canal, keeping the canal filled with enough water to transport barges and other boats through the locks. While other forms of transportation eliminated the need for the Champlain Canal as a shipping lane in the early 1900s, the feeder canal still supplies the Finch Pruyn & Company Paper Mill with water and hydroelectric power for its operations. You can walk the 9-mile towpath along the canal, or bring your canoe or kayak to enjoy the canal's calm waters. Open dawn to dusk from Memorial Day to Columbus Day; free admission.

The Hyde Collection Art Museum. 161 Warren St.; (518) 792-1761; hydecollection.org. You may be surprised at the quality of the collection here, with works by American luminaries including Whistler and Homer, and masters including da Vinci, Picasso, van Gogh, and

Rembrandt. Special exhibitions highlight the work of contemporary artists like Larry Kagan, Ansel Adams, Edward Hopper, and Anne Diggory. Tues through Sat 10 a.m. to 5 p.m.; Sun noon to 5 p.m.; closed Mon. $8 adults, $6 seniors 60 and older, free to children 12 and under and to active US military and their families.

where to eat

Glens Falls is a sizable community with many fine dining and casual restaurants. Here are some standouts to help you narrow your decision-making.

132 Glen Bistro. 132 Glen St.; (518) 743-9138; 132glenbistro.com. Casual, unpretentious, and satisfying, this bistro near the Civic Center regularly features homemade soups and breads, fresh salads, and entrees based on the freshest ingredients available on any given day. This means that you may see a completely new menu on the day you visit, so be prepared for just about anything. Lunch Tues through Fri; dinner Wed through Sat; closed Sun and Mon. $$.

Aimie's Dinner and a Movie. 190–194 Glen St.; (518) 792-8181; aimiesdinnerandmovie .com. Enjoying a good meal as you watch a newly released movie—what could be better? At Aimie's, you're seated comfortably at a private table from which you will watch the movie as you dine on a fine meal, selected from an impressive menu of entrees or sandwiches. There's even a jazz bar to enjoy after your film. Reservations are recommended; check the website for show times and plan your mealtime accordingly. Dinner daily; matinees on Sat and Sun. $$, including a $7.50 charge per person for your movie ticket.

Bistro Tallulah. 26 Ridge St.; (518) 793-2004; bistrotallulah.com. Make a reservation and make a point of enjoying this restaurant and its distinctively creative menu. Nearly every entree provides a surprising combination of flavors, whether it's the shaved fennel slaw atop the coriander-grilled salmon or the Spanish chorizo under the scallops. If you want to try more than one, you can order small plates of nearly every entree. You'll want to come here more than once. Tues through Sat 5 p.m. to close; closed Mon. $$.

where to shop

The Shirt Factory. Cooper and Lawrence Streets. You'll find lots of interesting shops and galleries in this former industrial building, which has been cleverly converted to bring together the fun, the funky, and the highly talented. Handmade candles, aromatherapy supplies, quilts, art prints and note cards, artisan jewelry, teas and tea-making accessories, wooden ware, hand-crafted gifts, pottery, and more are here for your browsing enjoyment. Hours vary by establishment.

upper hudson: to the river's source

>>>

day trip 37

upper hudson: to the river's source

a trio of lakes
great sacandaga lake, lake luzerne, lake george, ny

Up north of the state capital region, the Hudson remains a wild and scenic river as it makes its way down from the Adirondacks, and it passes through an area on the outskirts of Adirondack Park where a plethora of lakes create some of New York's most pleasant places. Great Sacandaga Lake takes much of its waters from the Hudson River, reaching up the Sacandaga River and making the connection to the Hudson where the towns of Hadley and Lake Luzerne meet. Just a few miles northeast at the other end of NY 9N, Lake George serves as the playground of the Adirondack region, bursting with commercial attractions that will keep even curmudgeonly travelers amused for days. Together, these three lakes make for an enchanting scenic drive, and an especially diverting day trip.

getting there

From the New York State Thruway, take exit 28 (Fultonville/Fonda). At the end of the ramp, turn left onto Riverside Drive. Take the first right onto NY 30A north, and follow this for 14 miles to NY 29 east. Turn right onto NY 29 east. At the traffic circle, take the third exit onto NY 30 north. In 0.4 mile, continue straight onto CR 155, which becomes N. Main Street. Take a slight right onto North Street, which becomes CR 110. Stay on CR 110 for 4 miles. The lake will come into view on your left. From the Adirondack Northway, take exit 14 (Saratoga Springs), keep right at the fork, and merge onto Union Avenue. Continue for 1.9 miles into Saratoga Springs. Turn right on Circular Street, and left onto Spring Street. In 0.2 mile, turn right onto Broadway and take the first left onto NY 29 west. Follow NY 29 west for about 18 miles, and turn right onto CR 138. In 4.3 miles, turn left onto Eagle Mills Road. Take the third left onto CR 110 as Great Sacandaga Lake comes into view.

great sacandaga lake, ny

Residents of the area around Great Sacandaga Lake call it "the best kept secret in the Adirondacks," and they may be right—when I wrote *Scenic Routes & Byways New York*, I didn't even encounter this lake until the book had gone to press. How we could miss a 29-mile-long lake with 125 miles of shoreline remains a mystery, even here in the less populated area of Adirondack Park. Granted, there is no concentration of attractions that bring people to resort areas, but if you prefer seclusion and solitude during your holiday in the wilderness, this lake can provide just the break you need.

It turns out that Great Sacandaga is not a natural lake; it's a reservoir formed in 1930 when the Conklingville Dam diverted the Sacandaga and Hudson Rivers. The project flooded the valley with 283 billion gallons of water, the best solution to the annual spring flood damage residents had experienced since the area was settled hundreds of years ago. The peaceful lake now attracts boaters, anglers, and water sport enthusiasts of all kinds in summer, and snowmobilers and skiers in winter. If you're not likely to pull out your water skis during your visit, get ready to enjoy some wonderful views of the lake and the surrounding wilderness.

what to do

Copeland Covered Bridge. CR 4, Edinburg; (518) 863-2034; edinburg-hist-soc.org. This carefully restored 1879 covered bridge provides a sheltered viewing platform over Beecher Creek, from which you can enjoy the burbling waters of Beecher Creek Falls. Constructed by farmer Arad Copeland to give his livestock an easy route to pastures beyond the creek, the 35-foot-long bridge is the only queenpost truss structure in New York State—a construction technique that uses two supporting truss posts instead of just one to hold up the roof. The Edinburg Historical Society acquired the bridge from Copeland's great-great-grandson in 1997 and undertook the restoration and landscaping project that you can enjoy here today. Always open, free admission.

Scenic drive. Take CR 110 all the way north on the lake to its junction with CR 7, where you can follow the eastern "arm" of the lake all along the lakeshore to Lake Luzerne. There are no towns along this route (though you will see many summer cottages), but you can enjoy miles of uninterrupted scenery with spectacular views of lake and forest. Once you reach the north end, you can continue your scenic drive down the west side of the lake by crossing the bridge to CR 4, and following CR 4 west and south to return to the main body of the lake. Always open, no admission fee.

lake luzerne, ny

The Hudson River's northern waters and banks see far fewer residents and tourists than you find between the capital region and New York City, making a trip to the adjoining towns of Hadley and Lake Luzerne particularly enlightening. To get a sense of the history of this area and the changes it has seen since its first settlement in the 1700s, stop at the bridge over the Hudson that connects the two towns and look north to see Rockwell Falls. Not only do these falls present a stunning sight to those who stop long enough on the bridge to take a look, but the surrounding landscape of deep green hills, dense forest turned golden and crimson in fall, and rust-colored gneiss cliffs makes this a painting-worthy view.

With plenty of waterpower available here, industrious citizens built Rockwell Falls Fiber Company in 1878, harvesting the seemingly endless forests and turning Hadley into a center of paper production. The company built a dam below Rockwell Falls and became Union Bag and Paper in 1892, and owner Charles Rockwell formed a partnership with a company in Ballston Spa, just down the road, to manufacture manila paper for envelopes and other uses. Historians say that the company became the largest manila paper mill in the country, with more than 75 employees. Rockwell sold Union Paper to Nu Era Paper Company before the business closed its doors in the 1920s. The dam washed out of its own accord in the 1930s.

what to do

Beaches. Lake Luzerne has 3 beaches: Hudson Grove Beach, Luzerne Heights Public Beach, and Wayside Beach. If you don't have your bathing suit with you, you can still enjoy the views of the lake, the pleasures of sunshine, and a barefoot walk in the sand on summer days. The beaches are open from noon to 5 p.m. daily from June 1 to Labor Day. Admission to the beaches is free.

Mill Park. At the intersection of NY 9N and Mill Street; (518) 696-2711; townoflakeluzerne .com. A natural waterfall flows just below a dam, and it would be easy to miss if the town had not had the good sense to build a lovely park around it. Your stroll here takes you past the dam and over a sturdy pedestrian bridge to view the falls from the comfort of some shady woods beyond the stream. Beyond the attraction of the falls, the park spoons us up just enough history to make this little place memorable. In 1866, Albrecht Pagenstecher saw the natural waterpower at the outlet of Lake Luzerne and established the Manufacturers Paper Company, creating jobs for about 10 men. The brown building at the end of the foot-path housed the first wood pulp grinder made in the United States that was put to practical use (you can see a replica here in the small museum on the site of the old mill). "Here for the first time," a plaque tells us, "wood pulp was produced and sold in large quantities and the success of the industry was assured." Pulping led to widespread logging in this area, a practice largely cut short by the creation of the vast Adirondack Park and the protection of wild forests throughout the surrounding mountains. The mill moved to Corinth after a few years because of the greater waterpower at Palmer Falls, and its success drew the attention of International Paper, which bought it in 1898. The mill continued to operate there until 2000. The park is always open; free admission.

where to eat

UpRiver Cafe. 29 Main St.; (518) 696-3667; lakegeorge.com/business/upriver-cafe-16085. Enjoy casual dining in a cafe that overlooks the Hudson River, with patio seating for summer days and an old-fashioned parlor when it's chilly. The menu features down-home favorites like meatloaf, and more elegant fare (lamb shanks in fennel sauce as a special, for example) for the more discerning palate. Wed through Mon 11 a.m. to 9 p.m., closed Tues (open Tues in summer).

lake george, ny

Let's start by taking it as a given that Lake George is loaded with every vacation attraction you can name—indoor and outdoor adventure mini-golf, an amusement park and arcade, go-karts, zip-line courses, water slides, motion simulator rides, and a Six Flags Theme Park. Instead of taking up your reading time with these well-understood attractions, I'd like to point out a few other things that may not have high-resolution digital billboards or flashing lights to get your attention.

Adirondack Winery. 285 Canada St.; (518) 668-9463; adirondackwinery.com. With a newly opened tasting room designed to accommodate the large influx of guests this winery receives year-round, this winery creates both traditional and fruit-infused wines, each sporting an Adirondack scene on its label. The Jewel Collection offers 3 semi-sweet wines with easy drinkability and glimmering labels, while the traditional reds and whites feature just about every grape that grows here in New York State. Open daily 10 a.m. to 10 p.m. $5 tasting fee (7 wines and a souvenir glass).

Fort William Henry Museum. 48 Canada St.; (518) 668-5471; fwhmuseum.com. Constructed in 1755, this British outpost played a significant role in the outcome of the French and Indian War. A costumed tour guide will accompany you into the fort to explain the ongoing conflict and the battles that took place here, and how the real story differs from James Fenimore Cooper's account in *The Last of the Mohicans.* Don't miss the Sutler Shop, the largest gift store in Lake George. Open May 8 through June 30, 9 a.m. to 5 p.m. daily, open until 7 p.m. Fri and Sat; July 1 through Aug 31, 9 a.m. to 7 p.m. daily; Sept 1 through Oct 31, 9 a.m. to 5 p.m., Fri and Sat until 7 p.m. $16.95 adults, $13.95 seniors, $7.95 children 5 to 15, children under 5 are free. Military and veterans free with ID.

Lake George Battleground. 2224 NY 9; (518) 623-1200; www.dec.ny.gov/outdoor/24453 .html. On September 8, 1755, British officer Sir William Johnson led an army of 1,500 men—British troops and Iroquois Indians—against the French in a battle to force France to leave North America. The French troops, however, knew Johnson was coming and deployed their forces in a hook shape along the dirt road, blindsiding Johnson's men with a successful ambush. The ensuing series of skirmishes and engagements lasted the entire day, but in the end the British were victorious, even though they lost as many as 300 men in the process. You can visit the ambush site, follow the military road, and see the monument on the site where Colonel Ephraim Williams of the British militia was shot and killed. Open daily dawn to dusk, free admission to view the battlefield (fees for camping).

Lake George Historical Association Museum. 290 Canada St.; (518) 668-5044; lake georgehistorical.org. If you love poking through local history museums, this one will delight you. Your tour begins in the original courtroom where cases were heard since 1845, and continues through exhibits and into the well-preserved jail in the basement of the museum. Artifacts include a 1756 powder horn, tramp art (art made by prisoners from materials on hand), and statuary by artist John Rogers. Open Memorial Day weekend to Columbus Day weekend. Memorial Day weekend through June and Oct 1 through Columbus Day, Sat and Sun 11 a.m. to 4 p.m.; July and Aug, Tues, Fri, Sat 11 a.m. to 4 p.m., Wed and Thurs 3 p.m. to 8 p.m.; Sept, Fri through Sun 11 a.m. to 4 p.m. Always closed Mon. Donations encouraged.

where to eat

You'll find more than 100 restaurants in the Lake George area. Here are some standouts to help you narrow the field.

Bistro LeRoux. 668 NY 149; (518) 798-2982; bistroleroux.com. Taking Adirondack cuisine up a notch, this acclaimed restaurant turns the North Country's basic dishes into truly special experiences. It's not that the entrees are so unusual—short ribs, surf and turf, and seared swordfish show up on many menus—but it's the addition of a cabernet braising sauce, cheddar and bacon hominy, whipped cream cheese and chives in the mashed potato side dish, or a cipollini and Andouille sausage couscous that makes you sit up and take notice. Guests can even order half-plates for lighter meals. These are the things that get a restaurant a "Best of Lake George" first place award. Open daily 5 p.m. to closing. $$.

The Boathouse Restaurant at the Lodges at Cresthaven. 3210 Lake Shore Dr.; (518) 668-3332; cresthavenlodges.com/boathouse.asp. Dine right on the shores of Lake George and enjoy an unobstructed view of the lake from an 1876 boathouse built for former *New York Times* publisher Adolph Ochs. Casual dining here goes well beyond the bar food you'll find on the Lake George strip: You'll find traditional entrees like filet of sole and steak bordelaise, as well as up-to-date specialties including lobster macaroni and cheese and shrimp picatta. Lighter and lunch fare includes salads, burgers, and sandwiches. Dinner daily 5 to 9 p.m., lunch in summer months only. $$.

Sammy D's Cafe. 1444 NY 9; (518) 793-3978; facebook.com/SammyDCafe. In an odd spot inside the Adirondack Outlet Mall, this little sandwich shop has visitors and locals raving about its sandwiches and wraps. All of the breads and pizza dough are baked here from scratch, and the meats are roasted by Sammy D's using Chef Dan's personal recipes. It's worth going a little out of your way to try out this unusual mall fare. Open during all mall hours. $.

Smokey Joe's Saloon & Grill. 20 Canada St.; (518) 668-2660; smokeyjoessaloonandgrill .com. You can get wraps, burgers, and salads here, but it's really all about the ribs, and not to try them would be like going to the North Pole and not seeing Santa. These baby backs are brushed with the house's barbecue sauce, and they fall off the bone just the way great ribs should. If you're not into ribs, there's a full menu of sandwiches, salads, wraps, and Italian fare as well. Equally important, this place is one of the cleanest in Lake George—and you'll see why that matters if you try some of the bars on the strip. Open daily for lunch and dinner; call for hours. $$.

day trip 38

upper hudson: to the river's source

>>> **from locks to lakes**
the champlain canal, stillwater,
schuylerville, fort edward, whitehall, ny

Follow the path of one of the canals that made New York State a central corridor for commerce—the Champlain Canal, the one on the northeastern state border. Here a handful of settlements became the lines of defense in the French and Indian Wars, the Revolutionary War, and the War of 1812. Once these conflicts were resolved, these pivot points became ports along a waterway that connected Lake Champlain to the north with the Hudson River, the Mohawk River, and the Erie Canal, making it possible to ship raw materials out of the north country and into the American West, as well as to other countries through the Port of New York.

getting there

From the Adirondack Northway (I-87), take exit 12 toward Malta. Merge onto NY 67 east, and continue straight onto CR 108. Continue about 2 miles to the junction with CR 76, and turn right. Follow CR 76 into Stillwater.

the champlain canal, ny

The Champlain Canal will be visible in all the towns on this day trip, so let's take a moment to understand the magnitude of its impact. The transformation of New York State began with Elkanah Watson, a native of Massachusetts, who first proposed that the state's natural waterways could be connected by canals to create a continuous waterway to the Great

Lakes. He brought his ideas to New York State Senator and General Philip Schuyler, and together they worked toward passage of an act to create a pair of canal corporations in 1792. A series of wars and other issues pushed the project back nearly 30 years, but the Champlain Canal finally opened in 1819, and the Erie Canal followed in 1825, making it possible to transport large loads of grains, minerals, and other goods to and from ocean ports in New York City, mines and timber companies in the Adirondacks and New England, and the agricultural fields and mills of central New York. The state became the nation's most prosperous commercial center almost overnight.

You will see a total of 11 locks on this canal as you drive north. They are numbered 1–9 and 11–12, but there is no lock 10—the planned lock turned out to be unnecessary, so it was never constructed. From south of Stillwater to Fort Edward, eight locks raise boats a total of 126 feet, making it possible to move up the river around the 130-foot drop at Hudson Falls. Locks 9–12 then lower boats 43 feet to meet the level of Lake Champlain. The first six of these locks work as part of a system of features including dams, spillways, and hydroelectric plants, making them distinctly different from the five locks that follow them.

stillwater, ny

If you're a history buff, the name of Stillwater, New York, should be familiar: This is where the Battle of Saratoga took place, turning the tide of the Revolutionary War in the Americans' favor. Here you can visit Saratoga National Historical Park to help you understand how the Continental Army swung the war away from the British, or you can go there simply to enjoy the stunning views of the Hudson River from the park's hilltops, or walk the pathways through the area's carefully preserved natural lands and see dozens of species of native wildflowers. Whatever you choose, this is a particularly pleasant place to spend the day.

what to do

Saratoga National Historical Park. 648 NY 32; (518) 664-9821; nps.gov/sara. Here American artillery on Bemis Heights blocked the advance of General John Burgoyne and the British army. Brilliant engineering of the fortifications at Bemis Heights by Colonel Tadeusz Kosciuszko, a Polish military engineer, made the heights virtually impenetrable. In the battles that ensued on September 19 and October 7, 1777, Burgoyne would lose more than 1,200 men, while the Americans lost fewer than 500. Burgoyne and his 6,000 men retreated on October 8 and finally surrendered on October 17—and with this victory, Americans knew they had begun to win the war.

At this National Park Service site, you can drive through the battlefield and listen to the narration of the battle on your mobile phone (call 518-665-8185, and enter the number of the tour stop you've reached), or you can choose to walk the fields on one of several meticulously maintained trails. Whichever way you select to enjoy the park, make a point of pausing at Stop 9 on the battlefield trail for one of the best views of the Hudson River you will see anywhere along the river's length. Visitor Center: 9 a.m. to 5 p.m. daily. The tour road is open daily dawn to dusk, Apr 1 to the end of the first weekend in Dec, weather permitting. $5 per vehicle, valid for 7 days, May 1 through Oct 31; free admission Nov 1 through Apr 30.

Schuyler House. US 4 about 8 miles north of the battlefield; (518) 664-9821; nps.gov/sara. This is the country estate of General Philip Schuyler, who served his country admirably by assisting in the transport of supplies to the troops, though he began the war as the third in command under General George Washington. After the Americans lost Fort Ticonderoga (more on that shortly), Congress relieved Schuyler of command, and he faced further hardship when his home and farm were destroyed in the British retreat from Saratoga. Schuyler rebuilt this much plainer home that fall. Memorial Day weekend through Labor Day: Fri through Sun and holidays, 9 a.m. to 4:15 p.m. by guided tours only. After Labor Day through third weekend in Oct: Fri through Sun 9 a.m. to 5 p.m. Closed end of Oct through end of May. Free admission.

Stillwater Blockhouse Museum. US 4; (518) 664-1847, ext. 39; albany.org/listings/ Stillwater-Blockhouse-Museum/1006. Learn about 1770s lifestyles at a re-created blockhouse—a single building in which townspeople gathered to shield themselves against the enemy—in which you'll find a small museum. In addition to displays about Stillwater in the time of the Revolution, the blockhouse offers peaceful views of the Hudson River, a walking path, and benches and picnic tables if you've brought your lunch. You may find costumed interpreters demonstrating daily colonial activities on special days throughout the summer, or soldiers in period dress completing military drills. Don't forget to stop at the gift shop, the proceeds from which support the National Park Service. Memorial Day weekend through Columbus Day: Wed through Sun noon to 4 p.m. Free admission.

schuylerville, ny

The sleepy town of Schuylerville is actually part of the Saratoga battlefield, though not in the national park—but the battle officially ended here when General Burgoyne surrendered to the Americans on October 17, 1777. Its walkable commercial district offers a number of restaurants and shops, so stop here when it's time for lunch, dinner, or a coffee break.

what to do

Saratoga Monument. At the Prospect Hill Cemetery, Burgoyne and Cemetery Roads; (518) 695-6917; villageofschuylerville.org. The 154-foot-tall monument stands on the spot where General Burgoyne actually surrendered to US General Horatio Gates. The monument was erected in stages from 1877 through 1912, and finally dedicated on the 135th anniversary of the British surrender. If you visit when the monument is open, you can climb 188 steps to the top and enjoy several levels of bas-relief plaques, brass moldings, stained glass, and other tributes to the American victory. Memorial Day weekends through Labor Day: Fri through Sun and holidays, 9:30 a.m. to 4:45 p.m. Labor Day through third weekend in Oct: Fri through Sun 9:30 a.m. to 4:45 p.m. Free admission.

where to eat

Eli's Broad Street Breakfast. 70 Broad St.; (518) 695-5253; facebook.com/pages/Elis-Broad-Street-Breakfast. The room is small, but no one beats Eli's for breakfast in Schuylerville. Real maple syrup with the pancakes, homemade hash, freshly baked bread, and a harvest omelet that includes apples—it's all good here. Tues through Sat 6:30 a.m. to noon; Sun 7 a.m. to noon; closed Mon. $.

Espressohuis. 31 Ferry St.; (518) 507-6315; facebook.com/espressohuis. For fresh salads and sandwiches using organic greens, daily soup specials, sweets and smoothies, and fair trade coffee, this coffeehouse provides exactly what you need. There are even gluten-free cookies and green smoothies if you've got to watch your intake. Mon through Fri 7 a.m. to 7 p.m., Sat 8 a.m. to 5 p.m. $.

Kitchen at the Dovegate Inn. 184 Broad St.; (518) 695-6095; dovegateinn.com/restaurant. This casual fine-dining restaurant borrows some of its charm from the bed-and-breakfast in which it lives, making the most of the traditional furnishings and wainscoting to create a sense of history. Its menu offers upscale dishes without the over-the-top pricing you might expect from a country inn—this is the kind of place where filet of sole and Cornish game hen are on the menu, but you can afford dessert at the end of the evening. Wed through Sun 4 p.m. to 9 p.m.; Tues 5 p.m. to 9 p.m. during Saratoga racing season. $$.

fort edward, ny

US 4 takes you right through Fort Edward, where a marker at the Anvil Inn, a former 1840 blacksmith's shop, denotes the site of the northeast bastion of the original fort that stood here from 1755 to 1780. To get a sense of the fort's perimeter, turn right onto Old Fort Street and watch for another marker in a resident's yard, noting the location of the old moat. Continue to the dead end on this street to see the site of the fort itself, noted by a plaque on a boulder past a white rail fence. (The adjacent land is privately owned.) A blue and yellow historical marker on US 4 at Duer Road also notes the location of Duer House, the headquarters of the British army for 3 weeks in August and September 1777 during the Revolutionary War. Like the fort that once stood here, Duer House did not withstand the test of time, but stories of the war pervade this area and pop up on signs or in street names, barely hinting at the drama and intrigue behind them.

what to do

Old Fort House Museum. 29 Broadway; (518) 747-9600; oldforthousemuseum.com. A resident named Patrick Smyth and his family lived here as they settled into life in the colonies in the 1770s. Built using timbers taken from the ruins of Fort Edward, the house's strategic location made it ripe for takeover, so it became a headquarters for generals from both sides of the Revolutionary War. General George Washington had dinner here twice in 1783. Today 5 buildings on the property include an 1840s tollhouse from the Plank Road, including the toll collector's living quarters, a one-room schoolhouse, and the Cronkhite Pavilion from the Washington County Fairgrounds, which houses displays on the history of the Fort Edward area. Open June through Aug, daily 1 to 5 p.m.; Sept through mid-Oct, Tues through Sun 1 to 5 p.m. $5 adults, free to children under 18. Gift shop is open year-round.

Oliva Vineyards. 2074 US 4; (518) 747-2156; olivavineyards.com. This fairly young winery shares its land with the owner's other passion: racehorses. The 150-acre property includes stables for Tony Oliva's horses, some of which have won races at Belmont, Aqueduct, Monmouth Park, and Philadelphia Park. The winery produces 6 varietals including its popular Sparkling Hannah, a red wine with bowl-of-fruit flavor. The tasting room offers a 6-wine flight of samples for each guest. Sat and Sun noon to 5 p.m.; tasting room is closed weekdays. $6 for 6 samples.

where to eat

Anvil Inn. 67 Broadway; (518) 747-0556; fortedwardchamber.org/anvil.inn. Named "anvil" because the building used to be a blacksmith's shop back in the mid-1800s, this rustic dining room sports lots of wooden coffers and reclaimed barn wood, as well as a massive stone fireplace and lanterns for lighting. With this kind of decor, you can only assume that the menu will be solidly American fare, and it lives up to exactly this expectation. Clam chowder, scallops casino, chicken liver pâté, Welsh rarebit, and a number of beef selections lead the menu, while scrod, salmon, and other seafood round out the selections. Relax in your captain's chair and enjoy. Open daily, lunch noon to 3 p.m., dinner 6 to 11 p.m. $$.

whitehall, ny

Cropland, pastures, and views of the distant Adirondack Mountains guide you along US 4 to Whitehall, where you will bear right to get to the historic waterfront. Don't miss the castle-like Whitehall Armory, built in 1899, which now houses the Whitehall Athletic Club. At the Whitehall Urban Cultural Park, a 19th-century main street and a canal-side park give you the opportunity to take in the northern terminus of the Champlain Canal at Lock 12.

what to do

Skenesborough Museum and Heritage Area Visitor Center. 1 Saunders St.; (518) 499-0716; skenesborough.com/skenesborough-museum. The museum building is a 1917 reinforced concrete canal terminal, rescued from demolition by the Historical Society of Whitehall in 1959 and pressed into service as a visitor center. Whitehall was the official birthplace of the US Navy, where shipbuilders designed and constructed the Valcour Fleet of ships that became the first American vessels to be used in military combat. Racing against time for control of Lake Champlain, the new Americans constructed enough ships to confront the British fleet in the Battle of Valcour in October 1776, off the shore of Valcour Island. Here you can view artifacts, see a diorama of the shipyard that built the first US Navy fleet, and pick up information about the 20-minute walking tour past historic buildings and monuments. The original hull of the USS *Ticonderoga*, a ship built for the War of 1812, is here outside of the museum. Mon through Sat 10 a.m. to 4 p.m., Sun 12 noon to 4 p.m. Free admission.

where to eat

Skene Manor. 8 Potter Terrace; (518) 499-1906; skenemanor.org. This striking stone castle sits atop a crest along the east shoreline of the Hudson River, where it was built in the late 1800s for New York State Supreme Court Judge Joseph H. Potter. Now a restaurant open for lunches and tours, the house was constructed using gray sandstone quarried from Skene Mountain. Its colorful past includes a long string of owners, a bogus legend about a body interred in a basement coffin, an on-again/off-again restaurant business, and a preservation project that landed the building on the National Register of Historic Places. You are welcome to visit to enjoy the Victorian gothic style of the place. Mid-Apr through Dec, Fri through Sun noon to 4 p.m. Free admission for tours; lunch is served during these hours. $$.

day trip 39

upper hudson: to the river's source

>>> **heart of the adirondacks**
indian lake, blue mountain lake, ny

With its more than 300 miles of hiking trails, three lakes, and the Hudson and Cedar Rivers all passing through the same concentrated area, Indian Lake and Blue Mountain Lake mark the Adirondack midpoint for all manner of treks and sports. Peaceful canoeing, kayaking, or riding the Hudson's whitewater can all begin here, while the river, creek, lakes, and adjacent wetlands draw anglers of many different stripes. If you're passing through in winter, these two small towns offer many cross-country ski adventures or wilderness snowshoe hikes, and the lakes provide smooth, hard surfaces for ice skaters.

getting there

From the south, take the Adirondack Northway (I-87) to exit 23 in Warrensburg/Diamond Point. At the end of the exit ramp, turn right on US 9 north and drive about 4 miles to the junction with NY 28. Turn left onto NY 28 south and continue 33 miles to Indian Lake. **From the north and east,** take I-87 south to exit 26 at Minerva/Pottersville. At the end of the ramp, turn right onto US 9 south, and continue about 11 miles to NY 28. Turn right onto NY 28 and drive about 23 miles to Indian Lake. From the west: Take the New York Thruway (I-90) to exit 33 (Verona/Rome). Merge onto NY 365 east. Stay on NY 365 east for about 30 miles to the junction with NY 8 north. Turn left on NY 8 and continue about 35 miles to the junction with NY 30. Turn left on NY 30 north and continue 24 miles to Indian Lake.

indian lake, ny

Welcome to the Moose Capital of the Northeast, a place where you may find large, charismatic animals crossing the road in front of you and birds filling the air with their song. A town built to take best advantage of the bountiful scenery in and around it, Indian Lake sits at the north end of the lake that provides its name, and close to the middle of Adirondack Park, the protected area of northern New York that prevents developers and resource harvesters from plundering this magnificent landscape.

what to do

Adirondack Park. Supervised by the New York State Adirondack Park Agency, PO Box 99, Ray Brook, NY 12977; (518) 891-4050; apa.ny.gov. Adirondack Park became a model for states across the country when New York created it in 1892, a move precipitated by 19th-century timber and mining companies' clear-cutting of forests and dumping of waste into waterways. The innovative approach the state took to restoring and preserving this land created the largest publicly protected area in the contiguous 48 states, a mass larger than Yellowstone, Everglades, Glacier, and Grand Canyon National Parks combined. Today Adirondack Park's boundaries contain 6 million acres of land, more than 3 million of which are privately owned by individuals, families, and businesses who develop towns and industrial sites in concentrated areas to maintain massive tracts of wild land. The rest of the land—nearly 3 million acres—virtually bursts with natural beauty, offering views of forest-covered mountains, crystal lakes, towering waterfalls, secretive gorges, and seemingly endless rivers. Explore to your heart's content. Always open; no admission fee.

OK Slip Falls and Blue Ledges. New York State Department of Environmental Conservation; (518) 473-9518; www.dec.ny.gov/lands/91888.html. As of this writing, a road to a new trailhead is expected to begin about 8 miles east of Indian Lake. This new trail will provide the first-ever public access to OK Slip Falls, the tallest waterfall in the Adirondacks, raining straight down for 250 feet from the top of the gorge that bears its name. The falls thunders in spring and early summer and maintains a steady pace through the late summer months, refueling during fall rains for another impressive season. Previously, this falls could be seen only from a distant point in public lands across the gorge, and only after a rigorous 4-mile round-trip hike, so the opportunity to walk to the edge of the gorge and view it at close range has Adirondack hikers buzzing with anticipation. Add to this spectacle another natural phenomenon in the same area: the Blue Ledges, outcroppings of Grenville marble that mark their age in the billions of years. Top it all off with one of the finest views of the Hudson River Gorge to be found anywhere along the length of the river's northern transit, and you have a very fine North Country wilderness experience. Watch for this road and trailhead on your drive between North River and Indian Lake. The planned hike will be about a mile in each direction over mostly level land, so it's worth the extra effort to see this falls. Open daily dawn to dusk; no admission fee.

Scenic driving. Even if you prefer to view the outdoors from the comfort of your car, you'll find plenty of vivid sights to enjoy here—sparkling mountainsides in winter, brilliant fall colors, wildflowers blanketing hillsides and crowding along roadsides in spring and summer, and lakes shimmering under expansive blue skies. Stop here for lunch and sit outside on one of several restaurant or deli patios and give yourself time to take in all of this wild, wide scenery.

where to eat

Chrissy's Cafe. 6461 NY 30; (518) 648-9905; facebook.com/pages/Chrissys-Cafe. Open for breakfast and lunch, this fairly new restaurant is a crowd pleaser. Don't miss the "waffled" sandwiches, panini pressed with a waffle iron. Watch for lunch specials posted on Facebook. Mon and Thurs through Sun 7 a.m. to 3 p.m.; Tues and Wed 7 a.m. to 4 p.m. $.

Indian Lake Restaurant and Tavern. 6296 NY 30; (518) 648-5115; facebook.com/ ILRestTavern. The wide-ranging menu at this favorite hangout presents choices in American, Indian, Cajun, and Asian fare—and all of them are delicious. You'll find this place crowded with locals around the historic bar (imported from Princeton University) and first in line for tables, so reservations on weekends are strongly recommended. Mon and Thurs 11 a.m. to 8 p.m.; Tues and Wed 11 a.m. to 6 p.m.; Fri and Sat 11 a.m. to 9 p.m.; Sun noon to 8 p.m. $$.

blue mountain lake, ny

When you visit the tiny hamlet of Blue Mountain Lake, you may be surprised to discover that it serves as a center of culture and natural history for the entire Adirondack Park. Here the Adirondack Museum explains the science behind the restoration of this mountain landscape, and the effects of climate change and other forces on the area. The Adirondack Lakes Center for the Arts is here as well, bringing entertainment and artistic expression to local residents and visitors.

You may want to stay overnight in this remote but well-appointed area, so here are a couple of things to keep in mind: If having cable television, Wi-Fi connectivity, or radio reception in your room is a priority, ask about these things when you make your hotel room reservation. Many guests come to this area to get away from the constant prattle of these modern conveniences, and some of the inns and rental cottages pride themselves on excluding TV, radio, and even telephone service from their rooms. Mobile phone service can be entirely absent as well. You may want to head south for Old Forge if you need to stay connected during your time in the 'Dacks.

what to do

Adirondack Lakes Center for the Arts. 3446 NY 28; (877) 752-7715 or (518) 352-7715; adirondackarts.org. The home of the Adirondack Summer Playhouse Theatre and the Arts Center Gallery, this performing arts center hosts concerts, plays, and special events involving local and visiting artists. Gallery open Thurs through Sat 10 a.m. to 4 p.m.; see website for scheduled performances. Ticket prices vary with the events.

Adirondack Museum. 9097 NY 30; (518) 352-7311; adkmuseum.org. Here in the shadow of Blue Mountain and just outside the hamlet of Blue Mountain Lake, this largely open-air museum features 22 exhibition galleries, as well as historic buildings including a 1907 schoolhouse and camp cottages built from the 1870s to the 1960s. Top off your visit with the view of Blue Mountain. Memorial Day weekend through Columbus Day weekend: open daily 10 a.m. to 5 p.m. Closed mid-Oct to end of May. $18 adults, $16 seniors 62+, $12 students with ID and teens 13 to 17, $6 children 6 to 12, free to children 5 and under and active-duty military.

Blue Mountain and Tupper Lakes. Just as you turn south, you will see a parking area with a viewing platform that provides a panoramic view of Tupper Lake. Here you may see great blue herons fishing, hawks flying, otters or muskrats swimming, or loons crossing the water with their young close behind (or riding astride). Interpretive signs here supply information about the Tupper Lake/Raquette Pond/Simon Pond ecosystem, the intricately interdependent wetland that thrives here because of careful protection. Across the water, northern hardwood forest covers the mountains with a strikingly uniform blanket of green, changing to yellows and oranges in fall. Always open, no admission fee.

day trip 40

upper hudson: to the river's source

high peaks scenic byway
keene, lake placid, ny

If you want to show off New York State at its most glorious to visitors who believe the Rocky Mountains are the only peaks worth admiring, this route will prove that New York contains spectacular country that includes some of the oldest mountains in America.

getting there

From the Adirondack Northway (I-87), take exit 30 for US 9/NY 73 and Keene Valley. Turn left onto US 9 and continue for about 2 miles to NY 73 west. Turn left onto NY 73 west. Continue about 30 miles to Keene Valley, where the High Peaks Scenic Byway begins.

keene, ny

The Hudson River begins its trek southward from this part of the Adirondack Mountains, high on Mt. Marcy, the state's tallest peak at 5,343 feet. Fifteen of the famed 46 high peaks are visible from Keene and along this first section of the High Peaks Scenic Byway on NY 73. As if this imposing scenery were not enough, the town of Keene also provides access to the Ausable Lakes, the cluster of water bodies from which the Ausable River emerges and flows through the park.

Mountains stand high on either side of the road in Keene. The only community of any size in the midst of the Adirondacks' 46 high peaks, Keene caters to lovers of the outdoors, supplying everything from rustic furniture for residents to energy-producing provisions for backpackers. Its hamlets of Keene Valley and St. Hubert's exist almost entirely to accommodate people planning or returning from long wilderness hikes up mountains that rise above 5,000 feet, so if you stop here for a meal, no one expects you to dress for dinner.

As you drive north from here on NY 73, watch for impromptu waterfalls pouring down the rock faces along the roadside, especially in spring snowmelt season or after a heavy rain.

what to do

High Peaks Scenic Byway. NY 73 between Keene and Lake Placid; (518) 457-6277; www.dot.ny.gov/display/programs/scenic-byways/high-peaks-byway-rte-73. Sit back and enjoy the view as you drive this 30-mile highway through the most spectacular part of New York State. The road weaves through the valleys between high peaks, with plenty of pull-off areas for viewing and taking photos. Watch for some of the area's most easily accessible natural sights, like Chapel Pond—a short, easy walk down from the road to this glasslike water feature. You will glimpse a number of waterfalls along the route as you follow the course of the Ausable River, which you will cross repeatedly on your drive. When you see Cascade Lakes on your left, watch for a place to pull off on a narrow strip of land between the two lakes. Stop here and look up high on the mountainside to see Cascade Mountain Falls, a ribbon of shimmering water that pours down through the slot its flow has created in the rock face. As you approach Lake Placid, another parking area is labeled Giant Mountain/ Roaring Brook; if there's room to stop on the roadside or in the parking area, pause here to look up at the rock face to see Roaring Brook Falls. Even in fall, water pours down from the mountaintop here, especially if it's been a particularly wet season.

where to eat

ADK Cafe. 2837 NY 73; (518) 576-9111; facebook.com/TheADKCafe. Arguably the most popular restaurant in the area, the ADK serves breakfast, lunch, and dinner and demonstrates its commitment to using eco-farmed, free-range products from local farmers. Whatever your dietary restriction—vegan, gluten-free, all natural—this cafe can meet your needs and still provide a hearty meal. Best of all, your breakfast can come with 100 percent real maple syrup. Open daily 6:30 a.m. to 9 p.m. $$.

Cedar Run Bakery & Cafe. Grist Mill Road; (518) 576-9929; cedarrunbakery.com. For freshly made baked goods, fancy picnic supplies, and other items you may need as you explore the scenic wonders of Adirondack Park, this little bakery will fill your basket—and the adjoining Cedar Run Wine & Spirits provides the libations you'll want once you're done driving. Come early to secure one of the delicious pies, as they disappear fast. Open daily 7 a.m. to 7 p.m., wine and spirits open Mon through Sat 8 a.m. to 7 p.m., Sun 12 noon to 7 p.m. $.

where to shop

Bald Mountain Rustics. 3 Market St.; (518) 576-9916; baldmountainrustics.com. Bald Mountain features Adirondack-style furnishings built in the shop behind the store, and many of these finely crafted pieces will fit into even the most formal living room as well as your lakeside cottage. May 15 through Oct 31, daily 10 a.m. to 6 p.m.; Nov 1 through May 14, Thurs through Mon 10 a.m. to 5 p.m.

The Birch Store. 1778 NY 73; (518) 576-4561; facebook.com/pages/THE-BIRCH -STORE. Once you arrive in the Adirondacks, you may suddenly be seized with a need to own one of the famous Adirondack chairs or rustic furnishings made of logs and local wood. You'll find plenty of this at the Birch Store, along with gifts and clothing and the work of local artists. Open daily 10 a.m. to 5:30 p.m.

Black Rooster Maple. 10819 NY 9N; (518) 576-9792; blackroostermaple.com. This family-owned maple sugaring business taps 600 trees every spring to collect sap and make its own maple syrup, candy, and cream.

Dartbrook Rustic Goods. NY 73 at NY 9N; (518) 576-4360; dartbrookrustic.com. Furniture and accessories in the Great Camp style set this maker apart from others in the area, and its blue-ribbon design and building team are nationally famous for their skill. You'll find one-of-a-kind pieces here made from local wood, antique barn wood, tree roots, and even antlers. If you like, you can order a custom piece for your home. Daily 10 a.m. to 5 p.m.

lake placid, ny

Traffic will pick up as you approach Lake Placid, home of the 1932 and 1980 Winter Olympics—and the Herb Brooks Arena, in which the "Miracle on Ice," the victory of the United States hockey team over the Soviet Union's team, took place on February 22, 1980. The arena now bears the name of the coach who trained his team of American college students for a year and led them to this startling victory over the USSR's team, who had led the international hockey world for two straight decades. (Remarkably, this game was not the gold-medal match: The United States went on to beat Finland for the gold on February 24.)

In the town of Lake Placid, you'll find plenty of shops and restaurants, both unusual and well known (such as Izod, Eastern Mountain Sports, and Van Heusen), and a number of hotels—including some with brand names. The streets of Lake Placid become crowded by late morning as sightseers and morning hikers return for lunch, so plan your day accordingly if you want to stop here and browse the galleries and gift shops.

what to do

John Brown Farm State Historic Site. 115 John Brown Rd.; (518) 523-3900; nysparks .com/historic-sites/29/details.aspx. Just outside of town and in the shadow of the ski jumps, John Brown Farm provides a startling contrast to the ski resort atmosphere in Lake Placid. Solitary and contemplative, this little farm once belonged to the fierce abolitionist who organized a raid on the US military arsenal at Harpers Ferry, West Virginia, on October 16, 1859, before the Civil War began. Brown had the noblest of goals: He intended to arm the African-American slaves in the South so that they could battle their way to freedom. The US government did not see his point of view, however, and sent the US Marines (led by Colonel Robert E. Lee) to defeat Brown and his raiding party of 20 men. Brown was wounded in the Marines' attack, captured, tried, and convicted of treason in the courthouse in Charles Town, Virginia, and hanged on December 2, 1859. His body lies in a grave on his own land, beneath a tombstone he himself moved from his grandfather's grave several years earlier. Twelve of his fellow raiders are buried here as well. Grounds open year-round sunrise to dusk; house open May through Oct, Wed through Mon 10 a.m. to 5 p.m.; closed Tues. $2 adults, $1 seniors and students, free to children 12 and under.

Olympic Center and Lake Placid Olympic Museum. 2634 Main St.; (518) 523-1655; whitefacelakeplacid.com. Three ice rinks, a museum that documents the legacy of the Olympic games, and a conference center are open to the public year-round, giving you the opportunity to relive your favorite highlights of the 1980 Olympics through videos, exhibits with athletes' uniforms and equipment, torches, and medals. If you ice skate, some of the rinks are open during specific hours (and you can rent skates here as well). Major international competitions continue here in a facility that Lake Placid maintains to world-class standards. Open daily 10 a.m. to 5 p.m.; closed on Ironman Sunday, Thanksgiving, and Christmas. $7 adults; $5 students, children 7 to 12, and seniors 65 and older; free to children 6 and under.

Olympic Jumping Complex. 52 Ski Jump Lane; (518) 523-2202; whiteface.com/activities/ olympic-jumping-complex-tour. The most striking landmarks of Lake Placid's Olympic heritage tower over the town and the surrounding landscape at 90 and 120 meters (roughly 295 and 394 feet). In snowless seasons, you can buy a ticket and take an elevator to the top of the taller jump to see through the eyes of Olympic athletes before they race down this slope at breakneck speed. Take a behind-the-scenes tour and receive a complimentary gift—and meet some of the athletes who spend the summer soaring hundreds of feet in the air at this complex. Tours July 2 through Aug 30, Wed through Sun 11 a.m.; second tour Thurs, Fri, and Sun at 1 p.m. $11 adults, $8 juniors and seniors, higher ticket prices on event days.

where to eat

You'll find more than 90 restaurants in Lake Placid, from locally owned diners to brand-name chains. Here are some of the standouts to help you narrow your selection.

Big Mountain Deli and Creperie. 2475 Main St.; (518) 523-3222; facebook.com/pages/Big-Mountain-Deli-and-Creperie. Homemade soups, salads, sandwiches on just-baked bread, panini, sweet and savory crepes, and specialty dishes make this an easy and fun place to find a great lunch. Be prepared for the blackboard menu—it may take you some time to make a choice, but there are no wrong choices here. You can also enjoy a beer, a glass of wine, a mimosa, or a Bloody Mary with your meal. Daily 8 a.m. to 4 p.m.; in summer open until 7 p.m. Tues through Sat. $.

Brown Dog Cafe and Wine Bar. 2431 Main St.; (518) 523-3036; thebrowndogcafeandwinebar.com. A one-of-a-kind view of Mirror Lake, an intimate atmosphere with candlelight and walls lined with wood, and an air of sophistication and elegance all make the Brown Dog a favorite romantic night spot. You'll find a menu that brims with ingenuity, pairing smoked duck with cranberries, cheese, and tortillas for unusual quesadillas, macaroni and cheese made with brie, gruyère, and white truffle oil, and a charcuterie that combines pistachios and Grand Marnier with pâté alongside wafer-thin slices of Italian meats. The extensive wine list includes more than 60 by the glass. Open daily 11:30 a.m. to closing. $$.

The Cowboy. 2226 Saranac Ave.; (518) 837-5069; placidcowboy.com. Don't be fooled by the name—this is more than a beef-and-bottle restaurant. The menu changes daily, but you can expect to find artfully prepared fish, chicken, and seafood as well as steaks, and burgers and sandwiches for lunch. You'll see plenty of locals here—a clue that you want to be here as well. Mon, Wed, Thurs, and Fri 5 to 9 p.m.; Sat and Sun 11 a.m. to 3 p.m. and 5 to 9 p.m.; closed Tues; also closed Wed in late fall and winter. $$.

The Good Bite Kitchen. 2501 Main St.; (518) 637-2860; thegoodbitekitchen.com. The menu changes daily at this fresh vegetarian restaurant, but its many followers check the Facebook page every day to see what's on the brown paper sign. Soups, salads, fruit and yogurt parfaits, sandwiches, and smoothies round out each day's substantial menu. Tues through Sat 11 a.m. to 5 p.m., Sun 9 a.m. to 3 p.m., closed Mon. $.

Paradox Lodge Restaurant. 2169 Saranac Ave.; (518) 523-9078; paradoxlodge.com. If you want a sense of what dining in an Adirondack great camp may have been like, make a reservation at this restaurant in the lodge at Paradox Lake. Cozy, homelike dining rooms, polished wood and area rugs on shining floors, warmly subdued lighting, and relaxed service make this an uncommonly pleasant experience. The continental menu features specialties like a smoked trout appetizer and wild boar sausage, as well as filet mignon, grilled duck breast, and a pasta dish featuring lobster, shrimp, and Andouille sausage. The management recommends that children who attend be age 13 and up. Thurs through Sun 6 to 9 p.m. $$$.

The View at the Mirror Lake Inn. 77 Mirror Lake Dr.; (518) 302-3000; mirrorlakeinn.com/dining/the-view. The only AAA Four Diamond restaurant in Lake Placid (and perhaps in the Adirondacks), this remarkable dining experience also has received the *Wine Spectator's Dining Guide* Award for Excellence for the last 14 years. It's open for breakfast and dinner with a menu that changes with the seasons, and it goes without saying that the chef chooses the freshest local ingredients to inspire his cuisine. The menu itself is solidly continental with the elements of fine dining applied to your night-out favorites. Stay for dessert and the impressive after-dinner liqueurs menu. Reservations recommended. Breakfast daily, Mon through Fri 7:30 to 10 a.m., Sat and Sun 7:30 to 11 a.m.; dinner daily 5:30 to 9 p.m. Closed for lunch. $$$.

where to shop

Main Street and beyond. Lake Placid's delightfully walkable main drag offers dozens of clothing shops, galleries, gift shops with handcrafted items by local artisans, skiwear and equipment, outdoor outfitters, toys, jewelry, and much more. It's easy to get caught up in the stores that got the most prominent real estate, but don't forget to venture down the side streets for highly original shops run by proprietors with excellent taste. A day trip may not allow enough time to cover it all, so consider planning a summer or winter weekend to fully appreciate all of the bounty here.

day trip 41

upper hudson: to the river's source

>>> **whiteface veterans memorial highway**
wilmington, ny

Travel through the heart of the Adirondacks to Wilmington in summer and early fall, and take a 5-mile meander up the fifth highest mountain in the region.

wilmington, ny

The town of Wilmington in the heart of the Adirondacks High Peaks Region exists to accommodate anglers, hikers, and skiing enthusiasts, so you'll find plenty of hotels, inns, bed-and-breakfasts, restaurants, and other amenities in this concentrated area. More important, however, are the extraordinary sights to see within a 10-mile radius: some of the region's most impressive waterfalls, gorges, rock formations, and rushing rivers.

what to do

Adirondack Wildlife Refuge and Rehabilitation Center. 977 Springfield Rd.; (855) 965-3626, (518) 946-2428; adirondackwildlife.org. Mammals and birds are brought here for rehabilitation after injuries in the wild, or because they have been orphaned and cannot survive on their own. The result is an extraordinary collection of animals that you can see up close, from baby bears to gray wolves, as well as birds of prey including several species of owls. Best of all, you can come along on the Wolf Walk, when refuge staff members take the wolves out on an easy 1-mile hike, and learn more about wolves in an hour and a half than you will in a documentary. Thurs through Mon 10 a.m. to 4 p.m., closed Tues and Wed. No admission charge, but donations are encouraged.

The Flume. NY 86 just outside of Wilmington; no phone. Here you can see the river rushing through a narrow channel with great force, creating a flume effect that fascinates visitors. A number of fairly easy hiking trails begin here if you fancy a walk; check the map at the information kiosk in the parking area. Always open; free admission.

High Falls Gorge. 4761 NY 86; (518) 946-2278; highfallsgorge.com. We were dubious about stopping at an "attraction" in the middle of a natural area, but Roanka Attractions Corp. has done a real public service in making this place extraordinarily accessible to viewers. The gorge contains 700 feet of waterfalls—3 major falls in all—with a network of brilliantly engineered bridges, stairs, and walkways that seem to defy gravity. Visitors have the pleasure of standing directly opposite one of the most spectacular natural wonders in the Adirondacks and watching the river plummet downward through the gorge. End of Nov through Mar, and mid-Apr through beginning of May: Sat through Tues 9 a.m. to 5 p.m.; closed Wed and Thurs. Closed Nov 1 through Thanksgiving, Christmas Day, and first 2 weeks of April. May through Oct: Open daily 9 a.m. to 5 p.m., open until 6 p.m. in July and Aug. Winter: $13.95 adults, $9.95 children 4 to 12, free to children 3 and under. Summer: $11 adults, $8 children 4 to 12, free to children 3 and under. Check website for holiday hours and special package rates.

Santa's Workshop at the North Pole. 324 Whiteface Memorial Hwy; (518) 946-2211; northpoleny.com. Yes, you can enchant your children and grandchildren with a trip to Santa's Workshop at the North Pole, a fairly convincing theme park (if you're 5 years old) just outside of Wilmington. Visit Santa Claus in his home, see his toy and candy makers at work, meet some reindeer, ride in Santa's sleigh (actually a roller coaster), enjoy a meal at Mother Hubbard's restaurant, and see a children's show in one of the park's theaters. There's even a nativity pageant, if you want to remind your young ones of the other meaning of Christmas. The hamlet of North Pole, New York, has a real US Post Office at the park, so you can send holiday letters and cards from here and have them postmarked from the North Pole. At the gift shop, you can purchase a letter from Santa and have it sent to the child of your choice at Christmastime. July and Aug: Tues through Sat 10 a.m. to 4:30 p.m. Sept and Oct: Sat and Sun 10 a.m. to 4 p.m. Nov 22 to Dec 23: Sat and Sun 10 a.m. to 3:30 p.m. Closed Dec 24 through June 30. $22.99 adults and children 2 and up, $20.99 seniors 65 and older, free to children under 2.

University at Albany Atmospheric Science Research Center (ASRC). Whiteface Veterans Memorial Highway; (518) 437-8705; asrc.albany.edu. You'll see the ASRC at the top of Whiteface Mountain when you reach it at the end of the road. Here researchers measure chemicals including carbon monoxide, nitrogen oxide, hydrogen peroxide, and formaldehyde in cloud, fog, and rainwater, while maintaining measurements of one of the longest continuous records of surface ozone in the world—a critical factor in air quality studies. You are welcome to visit the extensive laboratory and observatory; if you have an interest in climate change, you may pick up some useful facts here. Open during the highway's season; free admission.

Whiteface Mountain Memorial Highway. At the north end of Wilmington, you'll find a turn to the west that leads to Whiteface Veterans Memorial Highway, the only route in the Adirondacks that takes you to the top of one of the high peaks. Climbing 2,500 feet in 5 miles, this winding mountain road ends at a corridor to an elevator in the heart of the mountain, where you can ride easily to the summit at 4,867 feet, the fifth-highest peak in New York. From here, you can enjoy a 360-degree view of the entire mountain range—one of the northeastern US's most astonishing vantage points. If you're here on a weekend during peak fall foliage season, you may wait in line for an hour or more at the tollhouse until parking spaces open up at the top of the mountain.

Once you're on the highway, you will find plenty of places to pull off for a bit, including a prime viewpoint for Lake Placid—the only place you can reach by car to see the entire horseshoe-shaped lake at once. At the top, follow the instructions of the parking area attendants and circle through the stone castle. Built with the mountain's own granite excavated during the road construction project, Whiteface Castle stands at an elevation of 4,610 feet and contains a restaurant with a surprisingly healthy, casual menu as well as a gift shop, clothing store, and restrooms. The road winds through the castle to provide a turnaround point for cars, making it easy to park along the road once you've completed the loop. From here, you have the option of climbing stone stairs to the summit (another 276 feet up) or walking down a 426-foot-long corridor through the mountain itself to an elevator that will take you to the top.

On a clear day, your view from the summit extends all the way to Lake Champlain and the Green Mountains of Vermont to the east, and includes all 45 of the other high peaks, including Mount Marcy, the tallest point in the state. Maps on interpretive signs at the top help you find major landmarks. Mid-May to end of June: The road is open Sat and Sun 9 a.m. to 5:30 p.m. July 4 through Sept 1: Fri through Sun 9 a.m. to 5:30 p.m. Labor Day through first weekend in Oct: Sat and Sun 9 a.m. to 4 p.m. Closed weekdays and early Oct through end of May. $10 for car and driver, $7 each additional passenger.

Whiteface Mountain Ski Center. 5021 NY 86; (518) 946-2223; whiteface.com. If it's summer and there's no snow, or if skiing one of the best mountains in the Adirondacks doesn't appeal to you, you'll find plenty of other activities here at Whiteface. In particular, the Cloudsplitter Gondola Ride takes 8 people to the top of the mountain in a completely enclosed gondola in just 15 minutes, showing you the entire Adirondack High Peaks Region and all of its lakes and valleys. At the top, you can enjoy a picnic area and a viewing platform for as long as you like before you catch the return leg of the trip. The ski center offers gondola rides up the mountainside in summer and fall, and some of the area's best skiing in winter. Gondola ride: Daily from opening day until the end of the season, 8:30 a.m. to 3 p.m.; June 20 through July 2, 9 a.m. to 4 p.m.; July 3 to Sept 1, 9 a.m. to 5:30 p.m.; Sept 5 to Oct 13, 9 a.m. to 4 p.m. $20 adults, $14 seniors and children, free for children 6 and under.

where to eat

The Hungry Trout. 5239 NY 86; (518) 946-2217; hungrytrout.com. In a dining room overlooking the Flume Falls in the West Branch of the Ausable River, you can almost see where your trout dinner last swam—and if trout isn't your favorite, there's venison (in a Madeira wine sauce) or quail prepared in grand Adirondack style, or some seriously sizable steaks. You won't leave here hungry. Call for this season's hours. $$.

Rosalia's Italian Kitchen. 5675 NY 86; (518) 946-8271. There's no menu in this extraordinary restaurant, but you won't need one—the server will tell you about the day's selections, and they will be just what you wanted when you arrived. Rosie bases her offerings on what's fresh and local that day, cooking everything to order and accommodating special requests. You are welcome to linger to fully enjoy your meal, bread, wine, dessert, and the cozy ambiance. Open for dinner only; call on the day you plan to visit to check the hours. $$.

Wilderness Inn II. 5481 NY 86; (518) 946-2391; wildernessinnadk.com. The prime rib is the menu item that brings people back to this restaurant again and again—tasty, ample portions, and served with a generous salad bar. Indeed, the Wilderness is a meat-eater's paradise with a menu of reasonably priced steaks and chops, as well as a broiled half-chicken and a number of seafood choices. For standard continental fare in a rustic setting at a good price, you'll be glad you came here. Check out the lounge and deck menu if you're more in the mood for a sandwich or a burger. Hours vary, but open nightly in season. $$.

festivals & celebrations

february

Catskill Ice Festival. New Paltz; alpineendeavors.com. Ice climbing clinics at all skill levels will help you get your climbing legs under you to take on the most popular Catskill ravines. This festival takes place during the second weekend in February.

Chili Bowl Fiesta, Women's Studio Workshop. Rosendale; wsworkshop.org/studios/wsw-events. Every year on the last Saturday in February, the Women's Studio Workshop offers more than 800 handmade bowls and tumblers for purchase, and fills them with chili donated by area restaurants. The bowls are made throughout the year and at a family bowl-making event in January.

Hudson River Eaglefest. Teatown Lake Reservation, Croton-on-Hudson; teatown.org/teatown-events/eaglefest.html. Eagle experts with spotting scopes are stationed at locations along the Hudson River to guide visitors in viewing the river's resident eagles. Shelters with hot cocoa are available at each of the viewing stations, and raptor shows, bird walks, and bus tours round out the activities.

Hudson Valley Rail Trail Winterfest. Highland. Area food establishments compete for the Best of Fest Award for the best chili. A children's tent, wagon rides, wood carving, and roasting chestnuts and marshmallows over a fire are all part of the event. Winterfest takes place at the Rail Trail Depot at 101 New Paltz Rd. in Highland.

march

St. Patrick's Day Parade. West Orange; westorangeparade.com. Every year on the Sunday before St. Patrick's Day, West Orange turns out in force to celebrate its proud Irish heritage, beginning with mass at Our Lady of Lourdes Church at 9:30 a.m. The parade begins at the corner of Main Street and Mt. Pleasant Avenue at 12:15 p.m., and features thousands of marchers.

april

Sheep to Shawl at Philipsburg Manor. Sleepy Hollow; hudsonvalley.org/events/sheep-shawl. April is shearing season, and this spring festival explores each step in the process of turning wool into cloth, 18th-century style. Dyeing wool and weaving, demonstrations of sheep herding using Scottish border collies, and a fashion show of clothing from the 1700s are all part of the festivities.

Tour of the Battenkill. Cambridge; tourofthebattenkill.com. The largest one-day Pro/Am cycling race in the US takes place in Cambridge on a Saturday in April. The race covers 65 miles of hills, covered bridges, family farms, rural villages, and backcountry roads. Nearly 3,000 cyclists race every year.

may

Annual commemoration of Tadeusz Kosciuszko's life and works. West Point; kosciuszkoatwestpoint.org. Held each spring at the site of the Kosciuszko Monument on the West Point Military Academy campus, the Friends of Kosciuszko at West Point commemorate the work of this military engineer who design of the fortifications at Saratoga and led the American forces to defeat the British and, eventually, win the Revolutionary War.

Antiques Fair. Rhinebeck-Dutchess Country Fairgrounds; rhinebeckantiquesfair.com. This Memorial Day weekend event features exceptional antiques dealers in a pristine, all-indoor venue, with the addition of vintage and decorative arts in 2015.

Crafts at Lyndhurst. Tarrytown; artrider.com/lynds2014.html. One of the best-known outdoor craft festivals in the country, this semi-annual event takes place on the grounds of Lyndhurst historic site and features more than 275 artists and craftspeople exhibiting, selling, and discussing their work. Jewelry, fashion, furniture and home decor, functional and sculpture ceramic work, glass, metal painting, photography, wood, and more are featured, as well as a wide variety of foods and children's activities.

Hudson-Berkshire Wine and Food Festival. Columbia County Fairgrounds; hudson berkshirewinefestival.com. The 5 beverage-trail members and other regional wineries, distilleries, cideries, and craft breweries come together to showcase the area's specialties. Cheeses, baked goods, and grass-fed meats are featured, and celebrity appearances, wine and food pairing seminars, and home-brewing and cheese-making demonstrations round out the weekend.

Pinkster. Philipsburg Manor, Sleepy Hollow; hudsonvalley.org/events/pinkster. Pinkster, a Dutch celebration of Pentecost and an African-American celebration of spring, was held in the Hudson Valley as early as the 17th century. This cross-cultural festival brings together music, dance, food, and fun in a rousing colonial-style celebration. Festivities include drumming and traditional dance, African folktales, and demonstrations of the use of traditional African wares.

Stone Barns Sheep Shearing Festival. Pocantico Hills; stonebarnscenter.org. Watch farmers shear Finn-Dorset sheep, learn about wool and sheep at education booths, see professional weavers and spinners, and try carding, combing, and felting wool at this annual event.

Village of Waterford and RiverSpark Canal Festival. Waterford; waterfordcanalfest .com. Held on Mother's Day weekend, this festival coincides with the spring opening of the Erie Canal Heritage Corridor. The festival features live music, free children's activities, vendors offering quality items, performances and exhibits by area schools and businesses, and concession stands hosted by local community groups.

june

Annual Hoboken Baby Parade. Hoboken; hobokenmuseum.org/events/calendar-of-events/ june/baby-parade. It's an annual tradition in Hoboken to invite every baby in the area—and their parents—to walk in this parade and demonstrate their local spirit and creativity. Parents dress up their babies in their best outfits or costumes, decorate wagons and strollers, and walk the parade route.

Clearwater's Great Hudson River Revival. Croton Point Park, Croton-on-Hudson; clearwaterfestival.org. Music, dance, storytelling, and family programming on 7 sustainably powered stages, a juried Handcrafters' Village, a green living expo, boat exhibits and rides on the working waterfront, an Artisanal Food and Farm Market, and a Circle of Song are all part of this festival inspired by Pete Seeger back in the 1970s.

Hoboken Secret Garden Tour. Hoboken; hobokenmuseum.org/events/calendar-of-events/ june/secret-garden-tour. Tour the gardens hidden behind Hoboken's row houses and repurposed factories. You may see gardens with Japanese, English, and distinctly American styles, small getaways from city life.

Hudson Valley Craft Brew Festival. Rhinebeck-Dutchess Country Fairgrounds; beer bourbonbacon.com. Enjoy craft beer and distilled beverages with more than 70 vendors from across the country, food, live music, and merchandise during this 1-day event.

Path Through History Weekends. New York; paththroughhistory.ny.gov. More than 370 special events are planned throughout the state on 2 weekends in June, to help visitors and residents experience the state's rich heritage and history. Check the website for special events in the Hudson River Valley.

july

Falcon Ridge Folk Festival. Hillsdale; falconridgefolk.com. More than 40 folk bands and performers gather for this 2-day event, and many more appear in the Falcon Ridge/Grassy Hill Emerging Artist Showcase. Food and crafts round out the event.

Hurley Stone House Day. Hurley; stonehouseday.org. The 10 stone houses in Hurley were built between 1685 and 1786, and you can reach them all on a 0.25-mile walking tour. A number of these houses played important roles in history and continue to stand to tell the tale. While these houses are all private residences and are not open to the public for 364 days of each year, on the second Saturday in July the homeowners open their doors to tourists for a town-wide event with house tours, costumed re-enactors, a Revolutionary War military encampment, demonstrations of 18th-century skills and crafts, and other festivities.

Mountain Jam. Hunter; mountainjam.com. A 4-day, multistage event features 40 or more bands in a pristine natural amphitheater on Hunter Mountain. This is considered one of the top music festivals in the country.

Mount Tremper Arts Summer Festival. Mount Tremper; mounttremperarts.org/summer -festival. Beginning in early July and continuing through August, this festival brings music, dance, theater, and films to the Catskills.

Old Austerlitz Blueberry Festival. Austerlitz; oldausterlitz.org/events. On the last Sunday in July, the Blueberry Festival features 19th-century craft demonstrations and wares, antiques, live music, children's entertainment, vendors, and foods, as well as a blueberry pancake breakfast and lots of blueberry items.

Williamstown Theatre Festival. Williamstown; wtfestival.org. Every summer in July and August since 1954, this Tony Award–winning festival has brought audiences classic theater and new plays starring actors who are known for their films, television, and Broadway roles. Performances take place on 2 stages on the campus of Williams College.

august

Columbia County Fair. Chatham; columbiafair.com/index.php. Livestock, food, music, art, vendors, a demolition derby, and much more make this one of the classic county fairs in the Hudson Valley, held the last week in August.

Dutchess Fair. Rhinebeck-Dutchess County Fairgrounds; dutchessfair.com. Nearly half a million people attend this fair over 6 days in August to see farm animals, agricultural exhibits, and horticultural displays. Free music acts and food and merchandise from more than 100 vendors make this a major event.

Heirloom Tomato-Tasting Festival. Hoboken; hobokenmuseum.org/events/calendar-of -events/august. Traditional tomatoes in many colors come to this site from Wantage, New York, for tasting and sale.

september

Arlington Street Fair. Poughkeepsie; arlingtonhasit.org/event/arlington-street-fair-save -the-date. On the third Saturday in September, the Arlington neighborhood comes alive with musical guests, live entertainment, more than 100 vendors, and inflatable rides for children. The fair takes place on Fulton and Collegeview Avenues in Poughkeepsie.

Dobbs Ferry Fiesta. Dobbs Ferry; ferryfesta.com. Main and Cedar Streets in Dobbs Ferry close for the day to provide the stage for a massive block party. Food, music, vendors, and activities make this a day that draws more than 15,000 people each year.

Green Corn Festival at Philipsburg Manor. Sleepy Hollow; hudsonvalley.org/events/green-corn-festival. Celebrate the history and culture of the Native Americans who were the first to settle in this area. Folk tales, songs, storytelling, dance, and open-hearth cooking demonstrations are part of the festivities.

Ferragosto (Italian) Festival. Arthur Avenue between Crescent Avenue and 187th Street, Bronx; ferragosto.com. Celebrate Little Italy and all of its old-world charm at this one-day festival, with food, crafts, and other items from family-owned businesses steeped in Italian culture.

Hooley on the Hudson. Kingston; ulsteraoh.com. This free, Irish-themed festival features cultural exhibits, live music, food and craft vendors, and activities for children on the Sunday of Labor Day weekend.

Hudson River Valley Ramble. Hudson Valley area; hudsonrivervalleyramble.com. This annual event celebrates the history, culture, and natural resources of the Hudson River Valley National Heritage Area and the communities throughout the region. Hikes, local festivals, field trips, historic site tours, paddling outings, and educational events round out the Ramble.

Hudson Valley Garlic Festival. Saugerties; hvgf.org. Celebrate the garlic harvest with celebrity chef lecturers, local and regional musicians, a garlic marketplace, food and craft vendors, and children's activities.

Hudson Valley Wine and Food Festival. Rhinebeck-Dutchess Country Fairgrounds; hudsonvalleywinefest.com. Wine and beer tastings, cooking demonstrations, and other activities to enhance the gourmet lifestyle are offered at this popular festival.

Mum Festival. Saugerties; village.saugerties.ny.us. The annual Mum Festival begins with the Mum Bowl football game at Saugerties High School, and features the Mum Queen and her court presenting flowers, live music, arts and crafts, martial arts demonstrations, face painting, and food among the blooming mums in Seamon Park.

Waterford Tugboat Roundup. Waterford; tugboatroundup.com. Walk through a tugboat, ride one on the river or through the Erie Canal locks, and enjoy music, vendors, and food for the 3 days of Labor Day weekend. Tugboats will compete on Saturday and Sunday to see which can pull the heaviest load.

Woodstock Museum Free Film Festival. Woodstock; woodstockmuseum.com/2014_film_festival.htm. Screenings of new films based on a specific theme are free and open to the public.

october

Antiques Fair. Rhinebeck-Dutchess County Fairgrounds; rhinebeckantiquesfair.com. This Columbus Day weekend event features exceptional antiques dealers in a pristine, all-indoor venue, with the addition of vintage and decorative arts in 2014.

Applefest. Warwick; warwickapplefest.com. Since 1989, this harvest celebration show-cases the variety of Warwick's apples while offering entertainment, more than 200 craft vendors, dozens of food vendors, local nonprofit exhibitors, a children's carnival, a farmers' market, and plenty of apples and apple pie.

Apple Festival and Craft Show at Goold Orchards. Castleton; (518) 732-7317. On the second weekend in October (call for this year's dates), food and wine vendors, crafters and artisans, and local and regional musicians come together to eat, drink, and celebrate the harvest.

Burning of Kingston Reenactment. Kingston; revolutionaryday.com/usroute9w/kingston. On October 16, 1777, the British marched into Kingston—then the capital of New York State—and torched more than 300 homes, barns, and businesses. Kingston re-enactors recreate the event on one day in October every year.

Crafts at Lyndhurst. Tarrytown; artrider.com/lynds2014.html. One of the best-known outdoor craft festivals in the country, this semi-annual event takes place on the grounds of Lyndhurst historic site and features more than 275 artists and craftspeople exhibiting, sell-ing, and discussing their work. Jewelry, fashion, furniture and home decor, functional and sculptural ceramic work, glass, metal painting, photography, wood, and more are featured, as well as a wide variety of foods and children's activities.

Horseman's Hollow at Philipsburg Manor. Sleepy Hollow; hudsonvalley.org/events/horsemans-hollow. For 13 evenings in October, Philipsburg Manor becomes a terrifying landscape in which the undead, the insane, and the evil dwell. Walk a haunted trail and navigate a maze of horrors to the Horseman's lair for a party in his honor. This profession-ally staged haunted house experience is one of the most critically acclaimed in the country.

New York State Sheep and Wool Festival. Rhinebeck-Dutchess County Fairgrounds; sheepandwool.com. Sheep, livestock shows and sales, wool items for sale, workshops, book signings, cooking demonstrations, a fleece sale, and much more make this statewide event a real showcase for the fiber industry in New York.

O+ Festival. Kingston; opositivefestival.org. Chapters of O+ across America host this weekend-long annual art and music festival, at which artists and musicians exhibit their talents in exchange for access to health and wellness services provided by caring professionals.

Sunnyside Legend Celebration. Tarrytown; hudsonvalley.org/events/legend-celebration-3. On the grounds of Washington Irving's estate, spend a fun and scary weekend with colorful characters at this daytime festival. In the evening, extend the fun at the Horseman's Hollow haunted house, the Great Jack-o-Lantern Blaze, or a dramatic reading of *The Legend of Sleepy Hollow*.

november

Hudson River Valley Restaurant Week. Hudson Valley area; hudsonvalleyrestaurant week.com. For 2 weeks in November, top restaurants in the mid- and lower Hudson Valley offer special 3-course dinner menus at a reasonable price. No tickets are required; just choose from the list of participating restaurants and call to make a reservation.

december

WinterWalk and Winter Parade and Festival. Valatie; veravalatie.com/Winter_Walk.html. On one evening every December, the Kinderhook, Valatie, and Niverville communities come for the annual holiday parade. Fire trucks, marching bands, Scout troops, community organizations, and others march in the parade, and Santa Claus brings up the rear in a sleigh. After the parade, Santa stops at the Valatie Community Theatre to listen to what the village children want for Christmas, while merchants open their doors and offer samples and special features for customers.

Christkindlmarkt. Port Jervis. On the first Sunday after Thanksgiving, Port Jervis hosts an old-fashioned German Christmas market with lights, music, food, crafts, and entertainment.

index